ECONOMIC HISTORY AND THE

SOCIAL SCIENCES

# ECONOMIC HISTORY AND THE SOCIAL SCIENCES

## Problems of Methodology

ELIAS H. TUMA

UNIVERSITY OF CALIFORNIA PRESS

BERKELEY AND LOS ANGELES 1971

University of California Press
Berkeley and Los Angeles, California
University of California Press, Ltd.
London, England
Copyright © 1971, by
The Regents of the University of California
International Standard Book Number 0-520-01771-4
Library of Congress Catalog Card Number: 79-123619
Printed in the United States of America
Designed by W. H. Snyder

*There is no waste more criminal*
*than that of erudition running, as it were,*
*in neutral gear,*
*nor any pride more vainly misplaced*
*than that in a tool valued*
*as an end in itself.*
—MARC BLOCH


*To John, Mary, and Rabiya*
*who never stop asking*
*"why?"*

# PREFACE

It is often said that debates on methodology are futile because they rarely solve a problem or promote agreement. Carried to an extreme this attitude would mean that graduates in the social sciences are little exposed to the methodological difficulties of their disciplines. At best they are indoctrinated with the ideas of their professors, and thus the schism between the various schools of thought is perpetuated.

Whether agreement is possible should not be the issue. It is more important that communication and understanding of the different points of view be facilitated to reduce the problems and overcome the difficulties. This study is the result of a long search for better understanding of the role of the economic historian and the social scientist in explaining human behavior. The apparent conflict between the "traditional" and the "new" economic historians has been accompanied by few attempts to explore the reasons for that conflict. This study is in part an attempt to focus attention on the basic issues and problems of research in social science and to explore the degree to which such research can be more "scientific" than it has been. Therefore, the problems treated in this study belong to social scientists in general and to economic historians in particular.

Many people have helped me in this endeavor. Different chapters in earlier versions were read by Andrzej Brzeski, Rondo Cameron, Gordon King, and David Olmstead. Several readers and commentators gave me extensive critical and helpful advice through the University of California Press. Most of the credit, however, goes to the four successive groups of graduate students who attended my seminars on "theory and method of economic history" at the University of California at Davis. These students provided me with the stage for trying out my thoughts; they wrote papers in which they tested the usefulness of the evaluation scheme proposed in this study; they also graciously put up with all the uncertainties and possible errors of the study in its different versions. I am very grateful to all these people. Mrs. Shirley Kelly helped me by taking charge of the typing, for which I thank her. A summer appointment to the Institute of Humanities of the University of California allowed me to revise the manuscript and take advantage of the constructive criticisms I had received. Finally, I wish to thank Raymond

Ford for copyediting the manuscript and Grant Barnes, Social Science Editor of the University of California Press, for his patience and guidance in bringing this study to completion. I bear the responsibility for errors of omission or commission.

EHT

*Davis, May 1970*

# CONTENTS

## Part Three
## The Conflict and Its Resolution

# INTRODUCTION

## A Look into the Past

In 1853 Inama-Sternegg delivered one of the first academic lectures on the subject of economic history.[1] Within half a century from that date a great transformation took place. Not only was an extensive literature produced, but economic history began to occupy a place in academic circles. As L. L. Price observed in 1906, "not merely do modern writers of textbooks on principles admit without reserve that economic history presents a wide field of inquiry . . . not only do they readily allow that the advantages which attend a division of labor wisely planned are likely to follow the consecration of the main efforts of one set of workers to historical study . . . but some manuals which have been recently published, especially in the United States, have also intentionally prefaced their exposition of principles with an introductory sketch of the economic history of Great Britain and America, and into other standard treatises on economics issued lately in this country . . . historical chapters have been purposely introduced." [2] By the end of the next half-century economic history had come to stay, both as a field of research and as an academic discipline.

Economic history has passed through different phases, during which it was characterized by changing methods and by new emphases in subject matter. The changes and the difficulties were, in a way, reflections of the times when they occurred, of advances in the methods of research, of the widening division of labor, and of the broadening intellectual perspective. These difficulties and adjustments were integral features of the development of the field and have therefore actually strengthened and immunized the field against serious future handicaps.

Economic history has been written for as long as history books have existed. The Greeks and the Romans, the Chinese and the Arabs, and the medieval Europeans all wrote economic history. Though they did

---

[1] N. S. B. Gras, "The Present Condition of Economic History," *Quarterly Journal of Economics* 34 (February 1920): 223.

[2] L. L. Price, "The Study of Economic History," *Economic Journal* 16 (March 1906): 17–18.

not classify their works as economic history, these books were replete with material such as the history of trade, agriculture, government finance, and reforms and regulations. These writings did not distinguish between economic, political, and social history. Such distinctions became apparent only when separate treatises dealing with trade, commerce, tariffs, or agriculture began to appear early in the seventeenth century.[3] From that time on, writing in economic history has been little interrupted and has become gradually more diversified in both method and substance. An examination of the major writings of the seventeenth through eighteenth centuries suggests that trade and commerce and related fields were the main topics treated. National debt, coinage, and production were slowly attracting attention, particularly as manufacturing and industry gained ground. During the first half of the nineteenth century a new trend appeared. Studies of specific industries such as cotton, wool, iron, and railways were being undertaken. However, no general economic history was written until about the middle of the nineteenth century. In fact, some modern writers have denied that any economic history was written even at a later period. According to Gras, "the decade from 1879 to 1888 . . . saw economic history reach its majority, its full manhood." [4] Brodnitz, however, had observed that as late as 1910 "no economic history had been written." Ironically, at the time Gras agreed with him, asserting that "at the close of the decade [1920s] this is still true." Apparently both writers understood economic history to be "historical work of a general character." [5]

The second half of the nineteenth and early part of the twentieth centuries saw a new dawn in the history of the field. The period produced a rich crop of monographs and specialized studies, such as those of the German historical school. These studies were diversified and in many cases comprehensive enough to cover national economy. However, with a few exceptions, general economic histories, as understood by Brodnitz and Gras, had to wait until later in the twentieth century, partly because of the lack of data, but also because of the previously shaky position of economic history. In the meantime a debate over the

[3] N. S. B. Gras, "The Rise and Development of Economic History," *Economic History Review* 1, no. 1 (January 1927): 12–34.

[4] *Ibid.*, p. 20.

[5] Gras, "Present Condition of Economic History," p. 223.

meaning, methods, and objectives of economic history continued, in Europe as well as in America.

The tendency of the field to develop from the narrow and specialized to the general and comprehensive may also be explained by the changing trend of economic activity in Europe and America. The diffusion of economic activity from trade and agriculture into manufacturing and industry and from limited and regional into national and international markets has made it imperative that history books should become more comprehensive and general. The evolvement of what may be called an international economy may also have been influential in modifying the methods and the substance of economic history research. Partial explanations of data became inadequate for the understanding of economic change in a much larger and more integrated society.

To discuss the development of research in economic history as a progression from one phase to another would be misleading. The different phases usually overlapped, both in chronology and in content. Yet, each phase had unique features such as a new emphasis or objective, and therefore, a slightly different approach. These phases can be roughly classified as descriptive-quantitative, descriptive-qualitative, institutional-analytical, and synthetic-comparative. Now we are on the threshold, of a new phase that has been called econometric history, or cliometrics.[6]

The first two of these phases had in common an emphasis on recording and describing economic phenomena on the assumption that economic history consists of unique incidents and facts. The contributors to these approaches were anxious to record details to the greatest extent possible, and to explain individual facts or events without tying them together in search of deeper or indirect relations. However, the accumulation of data relating to national economic histories aroused interest in explanations of a broader scale, which characterized the third phase. Economic history or change was now conceived as closely related to institutions. In a sense the "institutionalists" regarded economic change, as in fact all societal change, to be related to institutions and therefore to be studied within such a framework.

Although the institutionalists differed from each other in method and economic philosophy, they had in common certain significant ideas. Almost invariably they rebelled against the contemporary school of eco-

6 L. E. Davis, J. R. T. Hughes, and S. Reiter, "Aspects of Quantitative Research in Economic History," *Journal of Economic History* 20 (1960): 539–547.

nomic thought. They were critical of the abstractions of economic
theory, its presumptuous claim to universality, and its lack of realism.
They emphasized instead a historical (empirical) approach that in many
ways can be regarded as evolutionary. Their writings were quantitative
and specific to a large extent. The institutionalists emphasized comparison and tended to approach economic history with an eye on the significance of institutions—labor organizations, banks, or private property.
They tried to explain change, not just record it. This approach also
allowed the formulation of at least partial generalizations. However,
the major contributions to interpretation and generalization came
through the synthetic-comparative approach, which was applied only
sporadically and overlapped with all other approaches.

A deeper insight into the history of the field suggests that the theories
that have stimulated controversy and further research and scientific
investigation were the result of daring studies such as those of Marx,
Weber, Nef, Bloch, Schumpeter, and Pirenne. These men were not
economic historians *per se*; they were students of society and of social
philosophy. They studied national economies, compared them, and paid
great attention to the interdependence of economic and noneconomic
factors in the causation of change. To them, history appeared as a
process in which the economy constituted a system of interdependent
components. They observed trends that represented or explained change
and provided grounds for generalization and in some ways for prediction
of economic change. These scholars had in common the tendency to use
both induction and deduction; some of them went as far as building
models of economic change, as did Marx and Weber, whereas others
depended mostly on induction, as did Nef and Bloch.

However, the contributors to the synthetic-comparative approach
differed from each other in a number of ways. Some of them, including
Nef and Bloch, accumulated original data; others like Marx and
Schumpeter depended mostly on secondary sources. Some sought the
answers to their questions primarily in economics, whereas others like
Pirenne looked outside economics and outside the societies they were
studying. The differences in approach and in emphasis resulted from
their individual training and philosophical inclinations, and from the
fact that they were observing different environments for different objectives. In a sense, these differences were related to the assumptions
each of them started with and to whether or not they had hypotheses
to start with. Therefore, they were bound to arrive at different answers,

even when they dealt with the same questions, as was the case with Marx, Weber, and Schumpeter in trying to explain the development of capitalism.[7]

The periodic crises that characterized the development of the field still recur. The drama is currently being reenacted in the debate on the role of the most recent phase, econometric, or new history. The new economic history, though not uniformly defined by its proponents, calls for a renewed and vigorous interest in economic theory, more precise measurement, and a more "scientific" treatment of the data. Some emphasis has been placed on the hypothetico-deductive approach as a means of making economic history more scientific. Although the objectives of research have not been redefined, there is a tendency to put more emphasis on methods and less on objectives than has been the case in more traditional approaches.

The debate regarding the various approaches of economic history results from differences of opinion as to what economic history means, what problems it should deal with, and what methods can be applied. The difficulty arises mainly from the fact that economic history is a social science and therefore shares the strengths and weaknesses of all the other social sciences in addition to the problems unique to historical analysis. The present study has two main objectives. The first is to explore the nature of research problems in economic history and the social sciences and to propose a theme by which some of these problems may be reduced if not eliminated. The usefulness of this theme will be explored by using it to critically analyze various approaches to economic history. In the process of this comparative critique we shall explore the degree to which the new economic history has resolved the problems that seem to have characterized earlier approaches. The second objective is to explore how related social sciences have tried to overcome problems also common to economic history and the extent to which their attempted solutions can be applicable to economic history.

[7] For a brief survey of the recent past, see Shepard B. Clough, "A Half-Century in Economic History: Autobiographical Reflections," *Journal of Economic History* 30 (1970): 4–17.

# PART ONE

## Themes for the
## Study of Economic History and an
## Evaluation Framework

# I

# Economic History and
# Economic Change

Economic history has been defined in various ways. Tawney, who looked at the concept broadly, saw the role of the general historian as "observing social behaviour in different conditions and varying environments, to determine the characteristics of different types of civilization, to discover the forces in which change has found its dynamic, and to criticise the doctrines accepted in each epoch as self evident truths in the light of an experience ampler than, without his assistance, any one of them can command." Tawney described the role of the economic historian as similar, but "with special reference to the interests . . . concerned with the acquisition of a livelihood in a world of limited resources, the social groupings which arise from them, and the problems which they produce. It is ultimately to widen the range of observation from the experience of a single generation or society to that of mankind." In that pursuit the economic historian begins "with the particular," but "his business is to systematise the turbulent world of concrete facts," which he would use to test the applicability of given hypotheses.[1]

After a fairly comprehensive survey of the development of the field, Gras suggested a variety of definitions of economic history. (1) "It is the time sequence or chronology of economic happenings." (2) It is "an evolutionary sequence." (3) "In the conception of economic history as a causal sequence . . . we try to explain why things have happened." According to Gras, however, "the scholar who is worth his salt is commonly bigger than the narrowest aspect of his special interest. The broader the treatment, the more significant the result. Economic history is the study of economic phenomena in their time, genetic and causal sequences."[2] A more recent, but functional defini-

[1] R. H. Tawney, "The Study of Economic History," *Economica*, o.s. 13 (February 1933): 11, 18.
[2] N. S. B. Gras, "The Rise and Development of Economic History," *Economic History Review* 1, no. 1 (January 1927): 29–30.

tion described economic history as the "basic research field for all analyses of the process of development. Not only does it provide us with a mass of empirical evidence far more varied and enlightening than contemporary field-work; it can also be the source of our concepts and the testing ground for our hypotheses." [3] Another recent approach suggested as more fruitful "to the study of economic history is that used by the physical sciences—to test hypotheses rather than strive to develop a new conceptual framework." [4]

One may contrast these recent approaches with an earlier and more conventional one held by Ashley, to whom economic history meant "primarily and unless expressly extended, the history of actual human practice with respect to the material basis of life. The visible happenings with regard—to use the old formula—to 'the production, distribution, and consumption of wealth' from our wide enough field; and, unless otherwise specified, we shall not include in it the views, right or wrong, which men have entertained, or the doctrines they have put forth, with respect to them." [5]

The list of definitions can be extended, but few need be added here. Certain observations, however, are in order. First, there is no accepted definition. Each scholar or generation of scholars defines the field in the most convenient way so as to make his contribution possible. Therefore, with each new generation or definition there is bound to be, explicitly or implicitly, a claim to novelty. Often the novelty is a reflection of the times, of the tools available, or of the expectations motivating the research. Second, there seems to be a tendency toward a more operational or workable and measurable conception of economic history, in contrast with the more absolute conception that predominated in earlier writings, which valued history for its own sake. This tendency has been reflected in the increased emphasis on the relation between history and economic development and growth.

These various conceptions may be acceptable and adequate, given specific points of emphasis, but they fall short of a comprehensive definition of what constitutes economic history. For example, "development is any change which has a continuous *direction* and which

[3] H. G. J. Aitken, "On the Present State of Economic History," *Canadian Journal of Economics and Political Science* 26 (February 1960): 92.
[4] W. C. Scoville, "Summary of Discussion," *Journal of Economic History* 17 (1957): 599.
[5] Sir William Ashley, "The Place of Economic History in University Studies," *Economic History Review* 1, no. 1 (January 1927): 1–2.

culminates in a phase that is qualitatively *new*." [6] The study of development and growth, therefore, does not take into consideration conditions of decline or stagnation, unless these phenomena happen to be treated incidentally. Yet, world economic history embodies as many cases of stagnation and decline as of development and growth. Development and growth are themselves recent features and occupy only a relatively short period of recorded history. Therefore, it may be as significant to study decline or stagnation as to study development, if not more so, since these are the problems that need to be solved. This is especially true if the study of historical tendencies is to be used for shedding light on policy problems. The study of decline and stagnation is important because it allows one to compare cases of success and failure, or development and lack of it, before reaching conclusions regarding the process of development. Why, for example, did Europe develop and Asia fail to do so? Why did the U.S. grow and become much more prosperous and densely populated than its next door neighbors Canada and Mexico? Why does population increase seem an asset in the Western world and a burden in India and China? The answers to these questions are far from obvious. Theoretical explanations do not suffice because many of them are based on assumptions that are neither empirical laws nor universal premises. Therefore, to reach meaningful conclusions, comparison of the economic histories of these contrasting cases becomes imperative.

A more pertinent conception of economic history must be general, comprehensive, and operational or relevant to the problems studied. Such an approach may be developed around a central theme. A conception of history that meets these qualifications might be based on economic change so that "the central problem of history is the analysis of change." [7] This conception would also encompass Gras's view that economic history is the study of time, genetic, and causal sequences. According to this conception, the study of economic history would be a qualitative and/or quantitative analysis of change in the economic situation under consideration. It would involve the observation and identification of economic change, the specification

[6] Sydney Hook, "The Problem of Terminology in Historical Writing: Illustrations," in *Theory and Practice in Historical Study: A Report of the Committee on Historiography*, Social Science Research Council Bulletin no. 54 (1946), p. 117.
[7] For a general statement on the significance of change in historical study see Hugh G. J. Aitken, ed., *The Social Sciences in Historical Study*, Social Science Research Council Bulletin no. 64 (1954), chap. 5.

of indicators, the selection, classification, and analysis of the data, and
the ability to reach conclusions regarding the origins and effects of
the change. However, to be able to explain change, it is necessary to
consider the process by which change has taken place and by which its
effects have been transmitted. Finally, the study of economic history, as
a search for knowledge of human behavior, involves the synthesis of the
various results obtained for the purpose of formulating generalizations
or discovering laws that may be helpful in predicting and controlling
future behavior.

The study of economic stagnation requires special attention. If
research seems to indicate that change should have occurred, then the
main problem would be to explain why the expectations were not
realized. Using an analogy as an example, it has been observed that
rigidity in the social system, or the difficulty of change may be due,
among other things, to *"the extent to which a proposed change affects
favorably or unfavorably the status of those segments of society that
possess influence, authority, and power, and the position of leaders;*
. . . the extent to which there is a latent *fear of change* in the society
in question. . . . Rigidity is increased if a society has little *surplus
energy and resources* for experimentation. . . . Rigidities in society
depend in part on *physical environment* and in part on the biological
composition of the population."⁸

Many more questions with more detail can be formulated, but all
of them would be built around the concept of economic change in the
environment under study. These prescriptions for economic history,
many of which are still controversial and debatable, will be treated
in three parts. The problems of the data will be treated in the re-
mainder of this chapter; chapter 2 will discuss the methods of analysis
and the results that can be expected; chapter 3 will present a scheme
for the critical evaluation of research in economic history and the
social sciences.


## THE CONCEPT OF ECONOMIC CHANGE

The concept of economic change is not new to economic historians.
In fact, Keirstead has suggested that the theories advanced by the
founders of economic science were theories of economic change.⁹

⁸ *Ibid.*, pp. 113–115.
⁹ B. S. Keirstead (*The Theory of Economic Change*, chap. 4) elaborates on this.

However, the concept has not been adhered to systematically as a theme of investigation in economic history, even though sporadic studies have been based on it. To focus on economic change as a theme of study implies a research methodology in which the unit of study is a system of interdependent components. It also implies an integrative approach that requires the cooperation of various disciplines. According to Keirstead, the study of economic change can be "the meeting-place of the theoretic and historical methods," since to make any sense of the factual data on economic change the researcher "must have formed explicitly or implicitly a *theory* of change." [10] This point will be treated more fully below.

Economic change implies direction, a certain degree of permanence or nonreversal, a certain degree of generality, and a process or rate of change. The concept of economic change applies regardless of the direction of change, whether progress or decline; it also applies to stagnation as the absence of change. Because the concept of change is neutral as far as the direction is concerned, it is the responsibility of the investigator to identify the direction according to specified criteria. Only then can he begin to investigate the economic history of the unit under consideration. [11]

In the context of economic history, change implies a certain degree of permanence or a secular trend reflected in the economy as a whole, in contrast to short-run fluctuations. Fluctuations are changes in direction such that a decline or a rise can be reversed. A relatively permanent change means that the forces that might inhibit change have been submerged, and the resulting tendency cannot be reversed nor the former condition restored. For example, a recession can be overcome and the level of employment restored with little or no impact left to be observed. However, a recession can be a reason for change by causing to be institutionalized certain policies that tend to change the character of the whole system. A recession is a tem-

[10] *Ibid.*, p. 11.

[11] Simon Kuznets used the concept of economic change to tie together a collection of essays relating to business fluctuations and trends of economic behavior. As he defines it, economic change means "the movement of economic processes over time, and their differences across space viewed largely as the cumulated product of different past rates of change starting from different initial levels" (*Economic Change*, p. vii). Another approach has been followed by A. Gerschenkron, who prefers to use the concepts of continuity and discontinuity in the study of economic history (*Continuity in History and Other Essays*, pp. 11–39).

porary fluctuation that might soon be forgotten, but its effects can represent a permanent change and be a focus of study. Therefore, permanence in economic change means that the conflict between the forces instigating and those inhibiting change has left an impact. Whether positive or negative, the impact on the economy will be observable either as progress or decline. If the impact cannot be observed, the case is one of stagnation, although an outgrowth of the conflict may still be perceptible.

In any of these cases, the impact must be felt by the total unit under study, even if the change originated in and directly affected only a certain component of the system. In other words, economic change differs from economic fluctuation in that the latter may or may not cause any alteration in the structure of the unit of study, while the former always does. An enterprise can suffer losses in its business for a short while without undergoing any structural changes. However, if the losses continue, the enterprise might not only have to change its structure, but even go out of business. An economy can suffer temporarily from unemployment without having any of its basic features change; however, a continuation of unemployment can lead to a new economic system altogether.

It is important to note that change relates to certain components of the unit of study, or to the unit as a whole. Strictly speaking, change in any of the components must affect the total unit. However, some components can develop or improve in certain aspects while others decline so that the unit continues to have the same general characteristics. The study of economic change must therefore concentrate on the general rather than the partial effects, without ignoring internal changes within the system. This is a general equilibrium approach focusing on the total rather than the components.

Economic change is the dynamic movement of a unit through time, and its study involves the observation of direction and rate. Yet, an observable change can be detected only when it has reached a certain magnitude. Furthermore, change can be observed only at specific instants in time or at distinct points in the life span of the unit. Therefore, to study the process of change, it must be possible to observe the features of the system at two distinct points of time at least; at the beginning and at the end of the process. In other words, economic change can be studied only as a problem in comparative statics and only by comparing the conditions of the economic unit at different points in time. However, underlying such comparison is the assumption that the process of change during the period between these specified points has been going on gradually, for even though change may seem to have been brought about abruptly, as in the case of a revolution, a sudden change can be regarded as merely the consummation of a process that has been going on for some time. Change implies a modification of the patterns of economic behavior and of the consequences or impact of such behavior on the economic agents in the system, both of which require time for adjustment and for the new behavior patterns to impart any effects.

The economic historian, however, cannot be satisfied with the study of change in only a few periods. He is interested in the history of change as well. That is, he considers it imperative to compare as many periods as possible in order to understand the trend as well as the distinct changes that have taken place. In studying the process of change it is useful to shorten the intervals between points of observation, to shorten the length of the periods during which change is supposed to have happened. This would make it possible to observe as many of the details of the process of change as are needed, rather than to concentrate only on the results of the change. And because the historian deals with historical data, by definition he can observe consequences only after the event, and can understand these consequences or detect them only by comparing them with the initial condition. Therefore, the historian cannot transform his investigation into a study of the dynamics of change, because these phenomena are neither repeatable nor observable until they have happened, and in fact are not identifiable without comparison. All he can do is make the intervals between the points of observation as short as is technically feasible, while accepting the fact that comparative study is the most useful approach available to him for the identification and explanation of economic change.

## THE UNIT OF STUDY AND
## INDICATORS OF ECONOMIC CHANGE

Economic change relates to the conditions of an economic unit at a given time as compared with those at another time. The unit of study in this case can be the total economy of a country, of a region, or of any smaller unit such as a specific industry or firm. The economic history of a specified unit, then, is the study of economic change relative to that unit, whose initial dimensions and features at the beginning of the period must be known. These initial conditions can be regarded as the background against which all future changes are measured and evaluated.[12] The unit of study can be specified only by the investigator on the basis of his interests and the questions he is trying to answer. Therefore, a definition of the problem is basic to the identification and definition of a unit of study. Although these remarks may seem obvious, one of the basic problems of historical analysis often derives from the lack of a clear definition of the unit of study.[13] The definition could be an accepted view of the unit, or it could be an operational definition imposed by the investigator. In either case, a relatively precise definition would permit communication and help to identify the relevant components and variables of the unit to be studied. The study of feudalism provides one of the best examples of the complications resulting from the lack of a precise definition. Not only has feudalism varied from one place to another, but its character has varied over time within the same environmental context.[14] It has been said that Leibniz "laid down exact definitions which deprived him of the agreeable liberty to misuse his terms upon occasion." [15] Precision and clarity may be inconvenient, but they are essential.

It is true that a precise definition is not always possible, especially if by definition is meant description in terms of the "known essences" of a thing. In many cases the narrower approach of specifying the relevant properties may be undertaken. What is important is clarity and precision.[16] Precision, however, is a matter of degree, and careful approximation is frequently adequate. Furthermore, the investigator has the choice of criteria to be used in the definition. For example, the unit could be defined in terms of national boundaries, chronology,

[12] For a concise and illuminating discussion of systems analysis see E. E. Hagen, *On the Theory of Social Change* (Homewood, Ill.: Dorsey Press, 1962), pp. 505–513.

[13] On the importance of definitions see L. E. Davis, "Professor Fogel and the New Economic History," *Economic History Review* 19, no. 3 (December 1966): 657–658.

[14] Joseph R. Strayer and Rushton Coulborn, "The Idea of Feudalism," in *Feudalism in History*, ed. Rushton Coulborn (Princeton Univ. Press, 1956), chap. 1.

[15] Quoted in Marc Bloch, *The Historian's Craft*, p. 175.

[16] On the difference between definition and specification see John Dewey and Arthur F. Bentley, *Knowing and the Known* (Boston: Beacon Press, 1949), chaps. 6, 7.

or organizational components. The components could also be specified in terms of their structural or functional relations. The definition could in fact be a combination of these criteria. Finally, the definition of the unit of study is closely related to the identification of the indicators of economic change and is therefore indispensable in establishing the relevance of the data. For example, data on per capita income would be relevant in a study of development, but would be of little help if income distribution were the problem of study. Thus, the definition of a problem and the identification of the indicators of change determine the choice and adequacy of the data.

Two groups of indicators can be distinguished, primary and secondary indicators. Primary indicators represent change directly, or describe realized change. In contrast, secondary indicators represent change indirectly, or, more correctly, they indicate potential change. The significance and relevance of each group of indicators depend on the objectives of the investigation and the questions asked. Questions concerned with the results of economic behavior require the study of primary indicators. However, questions relating to changes in the basic structure of a unit of study, or to the apparent absence of change, require emphasis on secondary indicators. A few examples will clarify this distinction. An increase in credit facilities may or may not lead to an increase in loans actually contracted, but the latter phenomenon can be studied only by reference to the actual number of loans advanced. The distribution of income might be changed by government programs; such programs have the potential to change the distribution, but whether a change has taken place can be determined only by studying the distribution patterns in the relevant periods. In other words, secondary indicators suggest what could be obtained or the changes that might have happened but failed to materialize. It might be of interest to find out why, for example, banks were established but credit did not increase; or why credit increased but investment failed to increase proportionally.

The distinction between primary and secondary indicators has an important implication for the interpretation and explanation of economic change or its absence. Primary indicators are mainly descriptive, whereas secondary indicators are analytic in the sense of anticipating potential change. Therefore, identification of the secondary indicators implies a knowledge of the relation between the modification of these indicators and the possible results in economic or material terms;

understanding secondary indicators implies a theory of the behavior of the relevant sector of the economy. To expect changes in the investment sector because of changes in the rate of interest implies knowledge of the functioning of the financial and credit sectors or of interest rates and investment. In other words, secondary indicators of change are indispensable when explaining change. Primary indicators, in contrast, are indispensable for measuring, identifying, and describing change.

The relation between expected and realized change is an area in which the economic theorist and economic historian can find a meeting place. The economic theorist can contribute greatly by exploring the nature of expected change and by guiding the historical study into those avenues where the realized change may be detected. Thus, the economic theorist can formulate theories or propose hypotheses regarding economic behavior and the economic historian can evaluate his historical findings against these theories or hypotheses to make sure they are logical consequences of the prevalent economic relations. The theory would also provide a checklist (as represented by table 1) so that the historian could be sure he has not left out anything that needs to be investigated.

TABLE 1
Processes of Economic Change

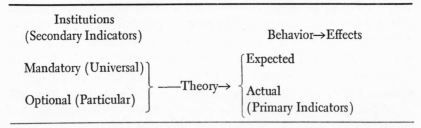

Thus, treating the institutions as secondary indicators, theory would suggest the behavior and effects to be expected. However, the expectations might not be realized, so the actual behavior and results would have to be observed as primary indicators. Inconsistency between actual and expected results would suggest that the observations were inaccurate or incomplete, or that the theory requires modification. History, as an empirical discipline, provides the basis for theorizing. Accumulated theory facilitates the work of the historian by suggesting the relation between observed behavior and the underlying institutions. The correlation between various effects suggests *what* to expect; analysis of the relation between the effects and the behavior or process suggests *how* the effects happened; taking both the institutions and the theory into consideration would explain *why* they happened. As can be seen from table 1, the institutional framework would also help the historian to determine the degree of free choice and determinism in the given behavior. Studying the institutional framework would suggest that free will exists only within a given range of behavior, which is determined by the encompassing institutions over which the individual has little control.

To the extent that the economic historian studies actual change, his first concern must be with primary indicators. To focus attention on secondary indicators might give the wrong answers or modify the original questions so that the secondary indicators would *de facto* become primary. For example, the primary indicator of increased productivity is an improved output/input ratio, for which an advance in mechanical engineering or in business organization may be a secondary factor. However, to concentrate on changes in mechanical engineering or business organization as indicators does not tell whether productivity has actually risen or not. The answers obtained would tell about changes in mechanical engineering and business organization, and what seemed to be secondary would now appear as primary indicators. This point is quite significant in defining the objectives of economic history. Concluding from primary indicators is history. Concluding from secondary indicators need not be.

The study of economic change can be tackled in another way by treating economic institutions as secondary indicators. Change in general, and economic change in particular, relates to phenomena that might not be perceptible. Perceptible phenomena such as income distribution or per capita income can be studied directly by measuring them on a given yardstick, but these phenomena might be consequences of deeper and more permanent changes that cannot be measured directly. For example, a change in the system of property or ownership might have little perceptible significance unless related to effects such as income distribution or a change in the level of input. These imperceptible but significant phenomena include the economic institutions that hold the economy together as a functioning unit. In that sense, economic institutions can be regarded as benchmarks around which perceptible changes can be centered and studied. Accordingly, a change in economic institutions would suggest changes in the effects of economic activity. Therefore, the study of change in economic institutions would be a contribution to the study of economic change but would not substitute for it. The continued existence or change of an institution, however, is a necessary, but not a sufficient indicator of the functioning of the economy and of other institutions. For example, the laws of property can be deceptive as to whether the economy is competitive, cooperative, or centrally coordinated. The degree to which given institutions of property are upheld could be more indicative of the behavior of the economy than are the institutions themselves.[17]

The role of secondary indicators in the study of change can be explored further by using institutions as an illustration. The term *institution* has been defined as "a verbal symbol which for want of a better describes a cluster of social usages. It connotes a way of thought or action of some prevalence, which is embedded in the habit of a group or the customs of a people. In ordinary speech it is another word for procedure, convention or arrangement. . . . Institutions fix the confines of and impose form upon the activities of human beings." [18] An institution, then, is a mode of individual behavior prescribed by the group, either by agreement or through formal legislation. When applied to economic behavior, an economic institution prescribes or defines the pattern of the relevant economic behavior.

At least in part this was the conceptual basis of the institutionalist school of economics.[19] According to Mitchell, an institution is "merely a convenient term for the more important among the widely prevalent,

[17] For a similar view see Walter Eucken, *The Foundations of Economics*, pp. 85–86.

[18] W. E. Hamilton, "Institutions," in *Encyclopedia of the Social Sciences* (1957) 8: 84.

[19] The confines of that school are not well defined. A. P. Usher suggests that "the term 'institutionalism' may be applied to the wide range of interpretations of economic history represented by the German historical schools, older and younger; the entire group of socialists; and the writers using some or all of the basic socialist concepts" ("The Application of the Quantitative Method to Economic History," *Journal of Political Economy* 30 [1932]: 187). This view is too broad to be of use in this context.

highly standardized social habits." [20] J. R. Commons defined an institution as "collective action in control, liberation and expansion of
individual behavior." [21] The institutionalists, assuming they can be
grouped together, used these definitions as the bases of their research.
They emphasized the historical or empirical, the quantitative or statistical, and focused attention on change. They also insisted on the interdependence of the different aspects of behavior, both individual and
collective, and insisted on the need for comprehensiveness in research
in order to understand economic behavior.[22]

Institutional economics, however, embodied a certain philosophy
that conflicted with the contemporary economic thinking. The methods
used were based on a certain conception of human and economic
behavior. As described by Commons, institutional economics is an
approach that regards the conflict rather than the harmony of interests
as basic to economic behavior. It "avows scarcity, instead of taking it
for granted," and holds that out of scarcity "derives not only conflict
but also the collective action that sets up order on account of mutual
dependence." Institutional economics regards efficiency "a universal
principle, because it overcomes scarcity by cooperation . . . [which]
does not arise from a presupposed harmony of interests. . . . It arises
from the necessity of *creating a new harmony* of interests." [23] Some
interpretations of institutional economics are more extreme. Frank
Knight, for example, sees in institutionalism a "fatalistic" method
based on determinism and inevitability.[24] Another sweeping interpretation of institutionalism as applied to economic history is that "the
essence of the doctrine lies in the conviction that certain institutions

---

[20] Quoted in Joseph Dorfman et al., eds., *Institutional Economics* (Berkeley &
Los Angeles: Univ. California Press, 1963), p. 97.

[21] *Ibid.*, p. 72.

[22] For a brief look at institutional economics see W. Mitchell, "The Prospects of
Economics," in *The Trends of Economics*, ed. R. G. Tugwell (New York: A. A.
Knopf, 1924), pp. 3–34; J. R. Commons, "Institutional Economics," *American Eco-
nomic Review Supplement* (March 1936): 237–249; Paul T. Homan, "Institutional
Economics," in *Encyclopedia of the Social Sciences* (1957), 5: 388ff; Dorfman et
al., *Institutional Economics*.

[23] J. R. Commons, *Institutional Economics: Its Place in Political Economy*, 2
vols. (Madison: Univ. Wisconsin Press, 1959), 1:6. Also R. A. Gordon, "Institutional Elements in Contemporary Economics," in *Institutional Economics*, ed. Dorfman et al., pp. 124–125.

[24] Frank H. Knight, "Confusion on Morals and Economics," *International Journal of Ethics* 45 (1934/1935): 217.

are an 'end' or purpose, of the historical process. The nationalistic state and the socialistic state are thus presented as ultimate ends of historical process." [25]

However, using institutions as secondary indicators of economic change does not mean one should adopt the philosophy of the institutionalists or any particular philosophy of human and economic behavior. Nor is it necessary to adopt any of the above critical interpretations or to refute them. It is sufficient to recognize the potential of institutions in regulating economic behavior. Once that role has been recognized, it should be possible to use economic institutions as benchmarks. For example, a change in credit institutions might suggest a change in economic behavior or in the level of production or prosperity. It is true that a change in credit institutions can be closely related to a change in attitudes, but it can merely suggest such a change in attitudes or in perceptible economic phenomena. Similarly, a change in the institution of competition might suggest a change in efficiency, productivity, or distribution without indicating whether competitiveness is a universal phenomenon or an instinctive characteristic of man. In other words, the economic historian can begin the study of economic change by regarding economic institutions as given and then observe the changes that have occurred and the economic effects associated with them.

The role of institutions in the study of social and economic phenomena is complicated by several factors.

First, to use institutions as benchmarks, it is essential to understand the society one studies. In writing economic history it is hardly adequate simply to collect data on exports and imports, saving and investment, or on the pattern of growth. The economic historian may have to specialize to a high degree before he can be confident his research on a given economy is meaningful. His research may have to turn into a comprehensive study in depth, rather than be partial and restrictive to a study of consequences, for a thorough understanding of change.

Second, institutions can have different roles in different situations, and there can be many institutions relevant to a given situation to

[25] Usher, "Application of the Quantitative Methods," p. 193. Needless to say, there is hardly any school of thought that fits Usher's interpretation, least of all socialist theory that regards the state as a means to more significant ends after the attainment of which it should wither away.

permit adequate treatment. In the absence of exhaustive study, it might be difficult to differentiate between relevant and irrelevant institutions for serious consideration. Yet, the researcher must choose what he considers the most relevant institutions for study. Veblen, for example, paid special attention to the corporation and to technology. J. R. Commons considered collective action in all possible forms, although he reduced it to one common denominator which he called transaction. Tawney paid attention to spiritual institutions, or religion, as did Weber. Marx regarded the mode of production and class organization as the most important institutions. Schumpeter related change, to a large extent, to innovation and the creative response. Each of these scholars emphasized one or the other of the many possible institutions, but they did not ignore the other relevant ones.

The range of institutions "is as wide as the interests of mankind." [26] The researcher need not emphasize a single institution, although a certain number of institutions can be proposed as the most relevant benchmarks in studying economic change—the institutions of ownership and property, credit, exchange, profit, occupational organization, taxation, and government. The list could be expanded or set out in more detail according to the demands of the study and the ambitions of the researcher.

Third, some institutions may be related to economic behavior only indirectly. War, for example, may not be considered an economic institution, but certainly it affects the economic institutions and must therefore be taken into consideration. To clarify their economic significance, institutions can be classified into directly and indirectly related institutions, the former being mainly economic.

In dealing with directly related institutions, a set of questions must be raised in the process of tracing the changes that have taken place between one point of time and another. For example, what kind of property tenure prevailed in each period and how did it influence the distribution of ownership and income? Was ownership individual or collective, private or public, active or absentee? Or, what was the source of and attitude toward profit? What alternative rewards were substituted for or competed with material profit as a source of incentive?

The significance of the indirectly related institutions is difficult to assess, because these may or may not have any permanent influence

[26] Hamilton, "Institutions," p. 84.

on the directly related institutions, even when they have an impact on the perceptible results of economic behavior. The researcher might have to simplify greatly before he can reach any conclusions. Even then, his conclusions may still be highly tentative. The extent to which war affects labor organization can be assessed only tentatively, particularly since many other factors are usually operating in war time. Yet it can hardly be overlooked that war affects wages and the distribution of income. The multiplicity and interdependence of factors is a common problem in all social research, regardless of the approach, and should, therefore, he handled according to the situation.

Fourth, change in institutions can precede as well as follow economic change. Any possible causal relationship becomes very hard to identify. For example, labor organization can be a consequence of industrialization and mechanization or of higher labor remuneration. But it can also be a cause of the rise of wages and therefore of mechanization. Or—the more common case—these changes may be so interdependent and simultaneous that they interact both as cause and effect. It is also possible that a lag exists between the need for change in institutions, as dictated by the economic structure, and the consummation of the change. However, the lag can also appear in the opposite direction, namely a change in institutions can precede change in economic behavior. These problems lead to another complicating feature of economic institutions. Change can be due to either internal or external factors. It can also be an abrupt or an evolutionary change. An abrupt change can be introduced by imposition or legislation, whereas evolutionary change is established gradually by adoption or internalization. In most cases these various influences function simultaneously and the rate of change varies enough to show both abruptness and gradualism. An excellent example of the simultaneous functioning of these factors is the change of the tenure system in postwar Japan. The Japanese people had been debating reforming their tenure system for many years, and the country might even have been ready for it, but the change did not come until induced by the external influence of the United States occupation army. The internal factors were aided by external forces, and gradualism was abruptly turned into revolutionary change. Yet, while legislation changed the tenure institutions, the behavior of many groups in the subsequent framework remained uncooperative for many years after reform.

Finally, institutional change can lead in the opposite direction and hinder economic change. For example, legislation can act as a pacifier by arousing sufficient hope that change is forthcoming, thereby reducing the pressure for change. Or legislation can lead to changes small enough not to affect a given economic order but big enough to pacify the forces for change. It has been a common practice in developing countries to introduce just enough change to create the minimum amount of harmony necessary to sustain the system. Therefore, a warning must be raised against conceiving a straightforward causal relationship between institutional and economic change. Even if the relationship is apparent, the conclusion can at best be only intelligent speculation. A case in point is the problematic question of whether labor unions caused wages to rise or whether wages would have risen anyway and only happened to have taken place at a time when unions were gaining acceptability and power. Although the bargaining power of unions may be a causal factor in wage rise, economic theory suggests that wages depend on productivity and therefore should rise when productivity rises, with or without union bargaining. The student of economic change may never be able to provide conclusive answers to these questions. Nevertheless, the establishment of a correlation can be highly significant, especially if similar correlations are discovered in a number of relevant situations.

## THE MEASUREMENT OF ECONOMIC CHANGE

Measurement in general can be on one of three levels, ordinal, interval, or ratio scale, which is also known as cardinal measurement. The assignment of a number as the measure of an object or state is restricted, according to two operations.

*Operation* (1). A comparison between every two objects or states, $x_i$ and $x_j$, which imposes an *order* restriction on assignment of numbers:
$$m(x_i) > m(x_j) \text{ or } m(x_i) = m(x_j).$$
This first criterion merely establishes an ordinal scale, and must be supplemented by another for cardinality. . . .

*Operation* (2). A method of *combination* of objects $x_i$ and $x_j$ must exist, such that it imposes a restriction upon assignment of numbers $m(x_i)$, $m(x_j)$ and $m(x_i \text{ comb. } x_j)$ to objects $x_i$ and $x_j$, and $(x_i \text{ comb. } x_j)$ as follows:
$$m(x_i \text{ comb. } x_j) = m(x_i) + m(x_j).$$

This second criterion permits the assignment of a metric, or a quantity measure.[27]

To measure change it is more appropriate to use the *interval* scale. "Interval measurement is cardinal measurement of the *intervals* separating two states of an object or two objects. Assignment of numbers to these intervals may be made via comparison and combination operations upon the intervals (or changes) between the states or objects, rather than upon the states or objects themselves. Formally, this implies that all alternative measures of the intervals $m_j(\triangle x)$ must be related to one another by a scale constant. This implies further that the measures of the concept of property itself, $m_j(x)$, must be related to one another by a linear transformation. Then the zero point is arbitrary." [28]

The operations of comparison and combination are fundamental criteria that can be validated in certain cases, as in the measurement of mass and weight. In many other cases, however, validation is not possible, as in rolling dice, in which case measurement is mere counting, based on the implicit assumption that each trial is equal to the other. In the absence of comparison or combination, validation is carried out by prediction. If the prediction on the basis of given measurements is true, the measures are considered validated, even though they may be invalidated in other instances, and thus the strict criteria of valid measurement is avoided.[29]

The economic historian depends mostly on interval scales for measuring change. Like other social scientists, he faces obstacles inherent in the nature of the material he works with whenever he tries to measure his variables with any degree of precision. However, the historian meets with extra complications, because of his interest in phenomena through time and over periods during which change might have taken place, which render consistency and uniformity in handling the data rather difficult.

These complexities can be summarized as inaccessibility, variability, and nonquantifiability of the data. Because the historian deals with events of the past, he is totally dependent on the records of the periods he is interested in. The records might be official documents, commer-

[27] James S. Coleman, *Introduction to Mathematical Sociology.*

[28] *Ibid.*, p. 65; see also Ernest W. Adams, "On the Nature and Purpose of Measurement," *Synthese* 16 (1966): 125–153.

[29] Coleman, *Mathematical Sociology*, pp. 70ff.

cial papers, personal correspondence and diaries, or artifacts that express the level of economic activity or change. Depending on the time and place under consideration, such records might or might not exist. They may have been lost, thus rendering a study of the period next to impossible. This, however, is an extreme case. More probably, the investigator will be dealing with a period on which at least some records exist. The problem of inaccessibility is then reduced to filling gaps in order to measure the intervals of change.

Inaccessibility has usually been tackled by estimating the missing data, at least for purposes of filling gaps. Given the slow rate of economic change, and the possibility of observing certain patterns of change, it is often possible to estimate what probably happened over a relatively short period of time. For example, data on income distribution might be available for fifteen out of twenty five-year intervals during a whole century. The pattern established from the available data can be assumed to apply to the missing intervals and a graph fitted to represent the changes over the whole century. The same, however, may not be true if for fifteen out of the twenty intervals there are no data. In some cases, historical data do not exist and hypothetical data are derived by inference from other available information. For example, the investigator might be interested in the degree to which change should have happened or the extent to which it could have happened. An alternative condition could be posited and its results compared with the historical conditions on which data are available, as has been done by a few economic historians and other social scientists. This approach will be treated in detail later. It is sufficient to note here that dealing with hypothetical data, except for filling minor gaps, cannot be regarded as history. History deals with facts, with what happened, not with what might have happened. Hypothetical data can be useful for certain theoretical purposes, but not for the study of history.

The problem of variability results from the fact that historical data represent values and conceptions of earlier periods which might be quite different from those of the current period. The data usually represent past human behavior that might not be fully or correctly understood either by the recorder or by the interpreter of the data. For example, the income concept of one period might mean something different in another period; the income records of the two periods would be dissimilar. Another example is the concept of property, which has certainly varied in meaning over time. In both cases, it is necessary for the investigator to become acquainted not only with the general meaning of the concept in the given environment, but also with the recorder's understanding and motive in recording. It might be that the recorder kept two sets of records, each of them for a different purpose. This is not a question of validity of the data since both records may be valid representations of what they were set up to record.[30] Standardization of the data removes or at least reduces the potential inconsistencies.

The measurement of change requires uniform data for the period under consideration. Where the data are not uniform, the investigator will have to devise a standardization formula or index by which these data become comparable. If the relevant concept expresses material values, it may be possible to identify its components and reduce all the data to a given standard. However, where motives are involved and where material components are hard to identify, the investigator may have to depend on his own judgment. The main safeguard against the misinterpretation of historical change would be a deep understanding of the environment, with the help, if necessary, of experts in other disciplines.

Finally, measuring requires a yardstick. A yardstick would be easy to apply if the data were quantitative or at least quantifiable. In actuality most of the information on earlier periods is not quantitative or quantifiable. Although the trend in the social sciences, including economic history, has been toward quantification, quantified data need not be held *a priori* superior to qualitative data for all cases of historical analysis. The subject matter and the objectives of the research must determine the appropriate data.

Quantitative data have many advantages. They reduce ambiguity of communication; they permit precision; and they render statistical inference possible, as will be shown below. However, it is also true that figures or statistics are blind facts that require interpretation, especially where they relate to past periods and to human behavior. As Clapham expressed it, "Figures are invaluable; but the statistician's world is not the historian's. Nor is the general historian's world that of the monograph writer. As a balance to the unreality of the gen-

[30] Separate sets of records for tax purposes are common today. Records of agrarian policies that were politically motivated in different historical periods provide another example.

eralized statistical statement and the undue influence of monographs and particularly important trades and topics . . . it has seemed wise to quote many scattered individual facts from all up and down the country and all over the economic field." [31]

Another handicap in depending primarily on quantitative data is that such data often exist only for limited periods or specific issues. Such limitations, if taken seriously, would reduce the results to limited value in understanding trends of change, which is the objective of historical analysis. Three approaches have been applied to reduce the problem of quantification. Some investigators have converted the qualitative into quantitative data by applying shadow values to the accessible information. For example, by noting what was consumed in a peasant's home, it may be possible to estimate the income of a peasant in a given period in standard units of measurement and to construct an index of consumption or income with an appearance of cardinality. Another approach has been to forget about cardinal values and apply ordinal measures only. Thus, on the basis of qualitative information, conditions can be described so that a rank order is assigned to each condition. Economists have utilized this approach for a long time fairly successfully. The advantage of this approach is that some statistical analysis may be applicable to such data and the ambiguity reduced. Trends can then be observed, even if arbitrariness and imprecision are not eliminated. The third approach has been to avoid the problem completely by selecting research topics for which quantitative data are accessible. The results of this alternative have tended to restrict research to certain periods and limited questions.

The economic historian has to decide whether to stick to quantitative data and forego the advantages of comprehensiveness, and whether to use hypothetical data or stick to history. He has to decide also whether the advantages of quantification through the use of shadow values and ordinal measures would offset the costs of quantification and outweigh the value of the impressions gained in qualitative analysis. The choice must depend on the problem and on the objectives of the research. If the objectives are to observe trends, formulate hypotheses, or understand in general terms a given economic period, qualitative data are sufficient. If, however, accuracy and precision are necessary, as in the case of statistically refuting or supporting a hypothesis, even crude

[31] J. H. Clapham, *An Economic History of Modern Britain*, 3 vols. (Cambridge Univ. Press, 1926), 1: viii.

quantification may be worth trying. A careful scholar might combine the two and make use of both quantitative and qualitative data to the extent to which historical records contain them.

The conflict between quantification and comprehensiveness can be approached from another aspect, namely the relevance of noneconomic data, both primary and secondary. If the economic historian is to go beyond recording and verifying facts, that is, if he is to attempt the interpretation and explanation of economic change, he cannot afford to ignore the noneconomic forces that have a bearing on economic behavior. It has been true throughout history that economic decisions are influenced by noneconomic factors—political, social, religious, and cultural. Population changes, wars, the church, and nonrational traditions have always redirected economic change or modified its pace. Similarly, ideologies implied in concepts such as capitalism, socialism or communism have greatly colored the economic conditions of nations.[32] The economic historian cannot ignore these influences, nor can the economic theorist ignore them as long as he is concerned with economic behavior. Long ago Comte emphasized the "solidarity of social phenomena." Mill approved of such emphasis, adding, "A person is not likely to be a good economist who is nothing else. Social phenomena acting and reacting on one another, they cannot rightly be understood apart." [33] More recently Keirstead has emphasized "that a general theory of economic change must relate the various major causes of change and explore their inter-relationships. . . . It should include the institutional channels through which the process operates, its effects on these institutions and the possibility and method of social direction and development." [34]

Cairns elaborated on this interdependence of the major causes of change.

Harrod's "Gn" and Domar's "a" and "s," just as also Keynes' "marginal efficiency of capital," all depend partly upon social and political factors and human motives, and once we are concerned with changes over time we cannot properly make use of them, without serious risk of error unless social, political and psychological factors are taken into account. It is not

[32] Recognizing these influences is nothing more than recognizing the real questions or economics of the everyday experiences. Eucken, *Foundations of Economics*, pp. 28–33.

[33] Quoted by Alfred Marshall, *Principles*, 8th ed. (London: Macmillan & Co., 1922), p. 82.

[34] Keirstead, *Theory of Economic Change*, p. 99.

a matter that these factors are influenced in the social or political sphere and that if inquiry is carried on there it is social or political science, *it is merely a matter of following an inquiry into the effect of scarcity on human behavior* as far as it properly leads. . . . It seems that the decision on what we should examine, or how far we should go, should not be made on *a priori* philosophical or methodological grounds, but alone on the ground of what scope and content is necessary if we are to answer the questions that a scientific study of the effects of scarcity . . . will raise.[35]

In a more recent discussion of the problem Leibenstein states that "the system that the economist is interested in is really part of a larger system of relations that is unknown in its totality. Thus he is interested in part of a total system. Can we know the part without knowing the system as a whole?" [36]

Finally, looking at the relation between economic and noneconomic factors, Adelman and Morris find an "intimate interrelationship" between social and political conditions and per capita income. Basing their study on seventy-four countries from different regions, classified on the basis of twenty-two social and political characteristics, as well as per capita GNP, the authors find that sixty-six percent of inter-country variations in per capita GNP are associated with these socio-political features. The authors warn against a hasty interpretation of the results as causal relations. These results suggest "the existence of a systematic pattern of interaction among mutually interdependent economic, social and political forces." In a cautious but highly suggestive concluding statement, the authors observe that "the splitting off of *homo economicus* into a separate analytic entity, a common procedure since Adam Smith in theorizing about growth in advanced economies, is much less suited to countries which have not yet made the transition to self-sustained economic growth." [37] How much less suited is such splitting-off to economic history!

[35] J. F. Cairns, "Some Problems in the Use of Theory in History," *Economic Record* 26 (December 1950): 251; italics in original.

[36] Harvey Liebenstein, "What Can We Expect from a Theory of Development?" *Kyklos* 19, no. 1 (1966): 6.

[37] Irma Adelman and Cynthia Taft Morris, "A Factor Analysis of the Interrelationship Between Social and Political Variables and Per Capita Gross National Product," *Quarterly Journal of Economics* 4 (1964): 6. See also E. A. J. Johnson, "New Tools for the Economic Historian," Supplement to *Journal of Economic History* 1 (1941), reproduced in part in *Readings in United States Economic and Business History*, ed. R. M. Robertson and J. L. Pate (Boston: Houghton Mifflin Co., 1966).

There is no doubt it would be beneficial to isolate these influences, but not to ignore them or hold them constant. To ignore them would be just as harmful as to handle them in a careless or dilettante manner. Many years ago Professor Tawney expressed the view that the "future of economic history lies in its becoming more consciously sociological." Professor Nef concurred and added his conviction that the future lay in its also becoming "more consciously philosophical." [38] More recently, attempts have been made to isolate economic phenomena in order to increase specialization and precision. In defending this tendency, Conrad and Meyer suggest that "as a social scientist with a strong orientation toward public policy problems, the economist seeks to establish theories with at least some generality and timelessness. He is interested therefore in the systematic, repetitive aspects of economic behavior. Consequently, the economic historian should not be surprised if the economist shows little interest in the social competence and family relationships of some nineteenth-century merchants—*unless it is previously or concomitantly established* that social competence and family relationships help to explain the successes or failures of individuals in general. The economic historian, in sum, should seek the limited generalization that is the objective of all science: only if that course is adopted can economic history expect to influence the development of economics." [39]

This attitude, however, imposes on the economic historian objectives that may conflict with his interests and the available data. It also ignores the contributions of economic history resulting from the interdisciplinary and broader scope proposed above.[40] It appears as relevant as ever that the economic historian can hardly ignore noneconomic data. More positively, his contribution may be enhanced by taking into consideration the interdisciplinary implications of his subject of analysis. Therefore, it is essential to strike a balance between measuring quantitatively and precisely, and using nonquantifiable and imprecise data.

[38] On limitations of the scope of quantitative analysis see R. A. Gordon, "Economic History: Its Contributions to Economic Education, Research, and Policy," *American Economic Review* 60, no. 2 (May 1965): 117–118.

[39] A. H. Conrad and J. R. Meyer, *The Economics of Slavery* (Chicago: Aldine Publishing Co., 1964), p. 17.

[40] L. L. Price, "The Study of Economic History," *Economic Journal* 16 (March 1906): 16–18; Marshall, *Principles*, pp. 756–783.

## 2

# The Method of Analysis
# and the Expected Results

The method of analysis depends on the data, the research objectives and expectations, the state of knowledge and availability of the tools, and the personal interests of the investigator. These factors overlap and influence each other. The research objectives determine the method, but the method often determines the objectives, and both can be influenced by the tools at the disposal of the researcher.

Before discussing the choice of method and the approach proposed in this study, two basic questions need to be answered. First, to what extent does the economic historian seek causal explanation? Second, is there a place for generalization in historical analysis? The answers to these questions determine the nature of the problems and the objectives of historical analysis. Each will be treated separately.

## BASIC PROBLEMS OF HISTORICAL ANALYSIS

### CAUSAL INTERPRETATION IN HISTORY

Causal interpretation is basic to economics in general and to economic history in particular. The historian asks not only what happened and how it happened, but also why it happened.[1] As Carr has asserted, "the study of history is a study of causes. The historian . . . continuously asks the question: Why? . . . We no longer speak of historical 'laws'; and even the word 'cause' has gone out of fashion, partly owing to certain philosophical ambiguities . . . and partly owing to its supposed association with determinism. . . . Some people therefore

---

[1] Trevelyan quotes Alfred Marshall as saying, "The economist needs imagination above all to put him on the track of those causes of events which are remote or lie below the surface." He adds, "how much more it is necessary for the historian if he wishes to discover the causes of man's actions" ("Clio Rediscovered," in *The Varieties of History*, ed. Fritz Stern [New York: Meridian Books, 1958], p. 232). For a more recent discussion see A. H. Conrad and J. R. Meyer, *The Economics of Slavery* (Chicago: Aldine Publishing Co., 1964), chap. 1.

33

speak not of 'cause' in history, but of 'explanation' or 'interpretation' or of 'the logic of the situation' or of 'the inner logic of events' . . . or reject the causal approach (why it happened) in favour of the functional approach (how it happened), though this seems inevitably to involve the question of how it came to happen; and so leads us straight back to question why." [2]

The assumption underlying the why question is that each event must be caused by some other event or sequence of events. The effect is the dependent variable and the causal factor the independent variable. The recurrence of similar events from similar conditions presupposes the existence of what might be called a causal law. According to Bertrand Russell, a causal law is "any general proposition in virtue of which it is possible to infer the existence of one thing or event from the existence of another or of a number of others." Whereas both the causal factor and the factor affected may be variables, "the *relation*" between them is constant.[3]

The definition of a causal law has varied greatly. According to Nagel a causal law satisfies four conditions. (1) "The relation is an invariable or uniform one, in the sense that whenever the alleged cause occurs so does the alleged effect." (2) "The relation holds between events that are spatially contiguous, in the sense that the spark and the formation of water occur in approximately the same spatial region." (3) "The relation has a temporal character, in the sense that the event said to be the cause precedes the effect and is also 'continuous' with the latter." (4) "The relation is asymmetrical, in the sense that the passage of the spark through the mixture of gases is the cause of their transformation into water, but the formation of the water is not the cause of the passage of the spark." [4]

While causal and scientific explanations have been continuously attempted in the social sciences, many people have questioned the possibility of discovering causal laws or causal interpretation in history

---

[2] E. H. Carr, *What Is History?* pp. 113, 115. An excellent relevant discussion can be found in Carey B. Joynt and Nicholas Rescher, "The Problem of Uniqueness in History," *History and Theory* 1, no. 11 (1961): 150–162.

[3] Bertrand Russell, "On the Notion of Cause," in *Philosophy in the Twentieth Century*, 4 vols., W. Barrett and H. D. Aiken (New York: Random House, 1962), 2: 684–685.

[4] Ernest Nagel, *The Structure of Science* (New York: Harcourt, Brace & World, 1961), p. 74.

and therefore the utility of these attempts. The argument centers around two basic issues: the nonrepeatability of historical events and the complexity of human behavior.

The problem of nonrepeatability is important in the sense that the difficulty of experimentation makes it impossible to observe a pattern, which is basic to the search for causes. This problem derives from the principle of causality itself, according to which "the same cause produces the same effect. . . . The principle of causality thus appears to assert the existence of causal laws that are independent of time and place. This implies that causal laws are significant because the order of nature is one in which certain patterns in phenomena recur." Although a state of the universe apparently never recurs, the physical scientist has created artificial repeatability by isolating phenomena in the laboratory.[5] It has been debated whether a similar isolation of phenomena by the social scientist is possible. It is held that "any set of relations of the partial system obtained while ignoring the rest of the system are really pseudorelationships that depend, to some extent, on historical circumstances." Nevertheless, even though "prediction in the strict sense is still out of the question . . . a theory of development and the estimates of its parameters should, in many situations, be able at least to explain some general trends."[6] This means that approximate repeatability can often be achieved by the artificial isolation of economic phenomena from the rest of the universe. It is in this sense that the economic historian can legitimately search for causes as does every other scientist.[7]

The problem of the complexity of human behavior is due to the fact that change can be influenced by human will or volition. Will or volition can become active before or during the process of change and be a causal factor in stimulating or inhibiting change. Human awareness of a causal force may interfere and slow down or even prevent the completion of its effect. Therefore, unless it is possible to lay down a psychological law regarding the behavior of the human factor in each class of relations between cause and effect, or unless the

[5] Victor F. Lenzen, "Procedures of Empirical Science," in *International Encyclopedia of Unified Science*, 2 vols., ed. O. Neurath, R. Carnap, and C. Morris (Univ. Chicago Press, 1955), vol. 1, nos. 1–5, p. 284.

[6] Harvey Leibenstein, "What Can We Expect from a Theory of Development?" *Kyklos* 19, no. 1 (1966): 7–12.

[7] Conrad and Meyer, *Economics of Slavery*, pp. 4–15.

relation is mechanical or deterministic, no general statement will be universally applicable to the class as a whole. Such assumptions or universal psychological laws have not been established.[8]

The problem may also be stated as one of relevance of causal factors. In the extreme case, to regard any or some factors as causal raises questions as to what caused those factors to act in the first place. However, there will be no attempt in this study to search for absolute or first causes, which falls more within the realm of philosophy. It is advisable for practical reasons to stop the investigation once the search for causes leads into the domain of another science; otherwise the search is apt to become dilettantish.[9] In other words, although "one can . . . avoid the pitfall of classical Greek logic by refusal to argue over a remote 'first cause' [and] . . . the fallacy of assuming a 'key' cause, one cannot, however, take refuge in explanations that seem, but only seem, to avoid causal imputation. The historical approach, observes Morris Cohen, involves 'an avowed or tacit theory of social causation.' "[10]

We are more concerned here with the causal relations that are related to the immediate environment and can be of importance in explaining empirical change and in implementing policies regarding economic behavior. The types of causes vary according to the subject matter under investigation. For example, causes can be classified as mechanistic, biological, and spiritual-moral. "The mechanistic involves the complete equality of cause and effect (causa aequat effectum). The biological seemingly permits the effect to grow beyond its cause through the full unfolding of a life in embryo to a life developed—with its own structure, purpose, and lawfulness. The spiritual-moral breaks through the purely mechanistic causal complex even more. Spontaneous and purposive impulses of personality—to be explained neither mech-

[8] John S. Mill, A System of Logic (London: Longmans, Green & Co., 1919), p. 598; Russell, "On the Notion of Cause," pp. 684–687, 693–698; another recent discussion of the concept of cause and its relevance is that of Sydney Hook, "The Problem of Terminology in Historical Writing," in Theory and Practice in Historical Study: A Report of the Committee on Historiography, Social Science Research Council Bulletin no. 54 (1946), pp. 110–115.

[9] Arthur Spiethoff, "Pure Theory and Economic Gestalt Theory," in Enterprise and Secular Change: Readings in Economic History, ed. F. C. Lane and J. C. Riemersma (Homewood, Ill.: Richard D. Irwin, 1953), p. 449.

[10] Hugh G. J. Aitken, ed., The Social Sciences in Historical Study, Social Science Research Council Bulletin no. 64 (1954), p. 146.

anistically nor biologically—effect the activities of men and thereby interrupt a mechanistic complex which otherwise appears to our thought as all-prevailing and continuous, excluding any interruption." [11]

Another system of classification considers the assumptions on which causality is based. One form of causal law is based on the assumed existence of "natural kinds," such that "there is an invariable concomitance of determinate properties in every object of a certain kind." The density of a substance is an example. A second type is based on an "invariable sequential order or dependence" among events. Two subtypes of this law have been noted. The first is causal in the sense that a rock thrown in the water causes ripples. The second subtype is developmental in the sense that the human lungs do not develop prior to the formation of the circulatory system. A third form of law is based on the asserted "invariable statistical (or probabilistic) relations between events," which are commonly used in biological and social sciences. The fourth type of law asserts a functional dependence, as in the physical sciences.[12] Causes, however, can be combinations of these types, which are hard to isolate or analyze. It is difficult, for example, to isolate or even identify the spiritual-moral type of causation. To avoid that difficulty the spiritual-moral type might be replaced by what can be called the social-psychological, thus indicating the behavioristic aspect that involves both the individual and the group.[13]

Economic empiricists, as well as theorists who attempt causal interpretation, look primarily for mechanistic causes and manage to regard the social-psychological relationships as given.[14] By this means they are able to formulate generalizations or theories of economic behavior. Even though they recognize and admit the limitations of their theories or generalizations in dealing with what apparently is due to social-psychological factors, they justify their methods by assigning these factors to disciplines other than their own. However, they continue to

[11] Friedrich Meinecke, "Values and Causalities in History," in *Varieties of History*, ed. Stern, p. 268.

[12] Ernest Nagel, *Structure of Science*, pp. 75–78.

[13] This modification is similar to R. M. MacIver's classification, though he presents the social and psychological in two separate classes; he also substitutes physical for mechanical causation (*Social Causation* [New York: Ginn & Co., 1942], p. 24).

[14] The biological is usually irrelevant. On the mechanistic nature of economic theory see Frank H. Knight, "Confusion on Morals and Economics," *International Journal of Ethics* 45 (1934/1935): 200–201, 215.

acknowledge the significance of these elements and therefore hesitate to predict on the basis of their findings; and when they do predict, they emphasize the highly tentative nature of their predictions.

In contrast, the economic historian cannot afford the luxury of holding the social-psychological phenomena constant, because these phenomena are historical and relevant to economic change. His field of inquiry commits him to the study of causation in its broadest sense.

The quest for causes raises questions about the relation between cause and effect, especially in complex situations that involve human behavior. John Stuart Mill formulated five canons as rules of inquiry.[15]

*Method of Agreement:* First Canon: If two or more instances of the phenomenon under investigation have only one circumstance in common, the circumstance in which alone all the instances agree is the cause (or effect) of the given phenomenon.

*Method of Difference:* Second Canon: If an instance in which the phenomenon under investigation occurs, and an instance in which it does not occur, have every circumstance in common save one, that one occurring only in the former; the circumstance in which alone the two instances differ is the effect, or the cause, or an indispensable part of the cause, of the phenomenon.

*The Indirect Method or the Joint Method of Agreement and Difference:* Third Canon: If two or more instances in which the phenomenon occurs have only one circumstance in common, while two or more instances in which it does not occur have nothing in common save the absence of that circumstance, the circumstance in which alone the two sets of instances differ is the effect, or the cause, or an indispensable part of the cause, of the phenomenon.

*Method of Residues:* Fourth Canon: Subduct from any phenomenon such part as is known by previous inductions to be the effect of certain antecedents, and the residue of the phenomenon is the effect of the remaining antecedents.

*Method of Concomitant Variation: applies to permanent causes to which none of the former methods applies:* Fifth Canon: Whatever phenomenon varies in any manner whenever another phenomenon varies in some particular manner, is either a cause or an effect of that phenomenon, or is connected with it through some fact of causation.

These five rules can be represented in symbols.
Let:

$E_i$ = events

$c_i$ = characteristics of events $E_i$

[15] Mill, *System of Logic*, pp. 255–263.

$a_i$ = antecedents to events $E_i$

$\leftarrow$ = anteceded or caused by

(1) Method of agreement:

$E_1$ with characteristics $c_1$, $c_2$, $c_3$, and antecedents $a_1$, $a_2$, $a_3$

$E_2$ with characteristics $c_1$, $c_2$, $c_4$, $c_5$, and antecedents $a_1$, $a_4$, $a_7$

Then $(c_1, c_2) \leftarrow a_1$

(2) Method of difference:

$E_1$ with characteristics $c_1$, $c_2$, . . . , $c_n$, and antecedents $a_1$, $a_2$, . . . , $a_n$

$E_2$ with characteristics $c_1$, $c_2$, . . . , $c_{n-1}$, and antecedents $a_1$, $a_2$, . . . , $a_{n-1}$

Then $c_n \leftarrow a_n$

(3) Indirect method or the joint method of agreement and difference:

$E_1$ and $E_2$ have $c_1$ and $a_1$ in common

$E_3$ and $E_4$ have no $c_1$ and nothing in common except absence of $a_1$

Then $c_1 \leftarrow a_1$

(4) Method of residues:

$E_1$ has characteristics $c_1$, $c_2$, $c_3$, $c_4$, and antecedents $a_1$, $a_2$, $a_4$

Since from previous induction $(c_1, c_2, c_4) \leftarrow (a_1, a_4)$

Then $c_3 \leftarrow a_2$

(5) Method of Concomitant variation:

If $E_i$ varies as $E_j$ varies such that $E_i\downarrow\uparrow$ as $E_j\uparrow\downarrow$

Then $E_i \leftarrow E_j$ | Either event may be a cause of the other or

Or $E_j \leftarrow E_i$ | both events may be related to the same cause.

Another set of rules, which applies mainly to the technique of isolating causes of specific events, has been proposed by François Simiand. His first rule is as follows:

A. *Define, in general terms, the specific effect* that must be explained. . . . The historian should search for a definition which in itself would already represent a scientific analysis. Such a definition, established by successive approximations, by gradual advancement, would focus on the relations to be considered: "the overthrow of a government by a small group of opponents"; "the overthrow of an unpopular government by a small group of opponents"; "the overthrow of an unpopular government by a small group of opponents who take advantage of this or that factor. . . ."
B. *Among the various antecedents of a phenomenon, the one which is linked with it by the most general relation is the cause.*
C 1. The first rule demands that we would *always make explicit the immediate antecedents.*
C 2. The secondary corollary leads to the rule: *Always try to establish the*

*kind of explanatory proposition of which the converse is also true.* This means, in final analysis, that the causality principle applies not only in the form "the same causes have the same effects" but also in the form "the same effects must have the same cause." [16]

In a recent statement of the method of difference, R. M. MacIver has expounded what he calls the "formula of causal investigation." According to MacIver: "Having first made our why specific, we identify the situation or type of situation in which the phenomenon occurs, as against a comparable situation or type of situation from which it is absent, and engage ourselves to discover how the phenomenon is related to the differential organization of the situation containing it. If x is the specific difference and it is found within the situation or conjuncture C we proceed to the consideration of $C_1$, the comparable situation of conjuncture lacking x. Sometimes we arrive at two closely comparable situations of this type. . . . Often, however, and particularly with respect to social phenomena, we cannot establish such clean-cut comparisons. But in all cases alike our question becomes: what is the causal series associated with x in the conjuncture C, such as does not obtain in the conjuncture $C_1$, where x is absent?" [17] However, the difference may be assessed as a matter of degree, which is equally true in the case of similarity.[18] Even when experimentation is not possible, as in the social sciences, "we still follow the same process of analysis, but now one of our alternative situations, C and $C_1$, usually remains hypothetical, a mental construct. We ask: What *would* have happened. . . . How *would* the situation have developed. . . . Or we ask: What did happen because x intervened which but for its intervention *would not* have happened?" [19]

To conclude, although various approaches can be used, the search for causes must be systematic, simple, and objective to the extent possible. Nevertheless, historical investigations will be imbued with difficulties that are unique to them. First, the great variability in human behavior renders causal interpretation tentative and probabilistic, regardless of how recurrent the same causes happen to be. Exceptions might still exist, and therefore universality can be regarded as only an

[16] François Simiand, "Causal Interpretation and Historical Research," in *Enterprise and Secular Change,* ed. Lane & Riemersma, pp. 477–482.
[17] MacIver, *Social Causation,* p. 251.
[18] *Ibid.,* p. 259.
[19] *Ibid.,* p. 258. This is reminiscent of the new economic history.

ideal. Second, the hypothetical approach that considers partial systems and tries to isolate phenomena or pose artificial alternatives may be acceptable or even necessary in other areas of investigation, but it can hardly be useful in history. The results would be not only tentative, but nonhistorical. Such an approach is certainly justified for generating hypotheses to be tested, but unless historical data can be found, the conclusion must remain incomplete. Third, the study of economic history involves the use of methods of agreement as well as of differences. It can also involve the use of given causes, even if the potential results are unverifiable, for the purpose of discovering what otherwise might remain uncovered. Whichever approach is used, the study of causation is an integral part of the economic historian's research objectives. Finally, the fact that universal laws cannot be discovered or that causation might involve a multiplicity of factors can only be complicating rather than prohibitive. To the extent that the economic historian deals with change and analysis, causal interpretation is indispensable.

### GENERALIZATION IN ECONOMIC HISTORY

The second basic question is whether the economic historian can legitimately discover laws of behavior or formulate generalizations. The debate centers around the adequacy of such generalizations for prediction, given the complexity of human behavior and the impossibility of exhausting the relevant data. Some critics go further by insisting on the uniqueness of historical events and therefore on the impossibility of observing patterns among unique events. The debate is in large part due to the use of different conceptions of generalization and hence to different expectations regarding prediction.

It may be true that historical events are unique in their totality, but they are not unique in every one of their features. Hence, similarities between events cannot be ruled out, nor can generalization. As Carr put it, "The very use of language commits the historian, like the scientist, to generalization. . . . The historian is not really interested in the unique but in what is general in the unique." [20] Furthermore, the subject matter with which the historian deals commits him to generalization. Easterlin has described the process of generalization in the context of economic development.

[20] Carr, *What Is History?* p. 80.

First, important similarities have been noted . . . between characteristics of today's underdeveloped nations and those of currently developed countries in their preindustrial stage—archaic taxes, laws, and land tenure conditions; unstable financial policies and currency management; political and military instability; preference of workers for leisure; of entrepreneurs for investment in inventories rather than fixed capital; unprecedented population growth. . . . Second, as has been shown particularly by Kuznets' studies, in every nation that has developed, a number of similar trends has appeared; decline of agriculture, rise of white-collar employment, shift to urban areas, growth larger units of economic and social organization, increased participation by the individual in nonfamily centered activities.[21]

From these similarities it should be possible to derive certain generalizations. It has been suggested that it is the researcher's ability to derive generalizations that makes him a historian, and not just a collector of facts.[22]

Karl Popper, the leading critic of generalization in history, suggests that causal explanation is possible only on the basis of two kinds of statements: "(1) *Universal statements of the character of natural laws; and* (2) *specific statements pertaining to the special case in question, called the 'initial conditions.'* . . . The initial conditions (or more precisely, the situation described by them) are usually spoken of as the cause of the event in question, and the prognosis (or rather, the event described by the prognosis) as the effect; for example, we say that the putting of a weight of two pounds on a thread capable of carrying only one pound was the cause, and the breaking the effect." [23] These causal explanations lead, according to Popper, to generalizations in the first case and only to trends in the second. These trends are dependent upon the initial conditions; they are not absolute trends, as the "historicists" including John Stuart Mill are said to believe.

Popper claims that he has refuted historicism, by which he means "an approach to the social sciences which assumes that historical prediction is their principal aim, and which assumes that this aim is attainable by discovering the 'rhythms' or the 'patterns', and 'laws' or the 'trends' that underlie evolution in history." [24] The historicists cannot make universal statements prerequisite for the formulation of laws

[21] R. A. Easterlin, "Is There Need for Historical Research on Underdevelopment?" *American Economic Review* 55, no. 2 (May 1965): 104–108.
[22] Carr, *What Is History*, p. 82.
[23] Karl R. Popper, *The Poverty of Historicism*, p. 123.
[24] *Ibid.*, p. 3.

or generalizations, and therefore they cannot formulate generalizations. However, Popper admits that trends can be observed and causally explained and even used for prediction, as long as it is recognized that these trends are conditional upon certain initial conditions.[25] It is obvious that Popper's position derives from his definition of historicism and of his conception of generalization. It is easy to start a debate with him on this issue, but a debate on definitions would be fruitless.

Objections have also been raised with respect to the process of generalization. Historians and other social scientists, for example, are usually confronted with the need to generalize from qualitative, imprecise, and often subjectively interpreted data. Their dilemma is aggravated by charges, like those of Karl Popper, chief spokesman of the school of the unique in history, that the observed similarities of unique events are more apparent than real. According to the pessimists, the validity of a generalization "varies in proportion as the proposition applies to posited entities, 'models,' and other 'unreal' abstract concepts. Of any concrete and particular social and human situation, historical, currently political, or other, I doubt whether any significant generalization can be shown by evidence to be wholly valid or wholly invalid. To put it another way, a generalization to be accepted as valid would have to be unencumbered by so many *ifs*, *ands*, and *buts* as to lose some of its hoped-for scientific precision." [26] More recently, William Aydelotte has opposed generalization in history by specifically arguing:

(1) that a "generalization" can take the form only of a general law, detachable from its context and applicable in all comparable situations and hence, because of the complexity of historical materials, entirely beyond the historian's grasp; (2) that no final proof can be given of any general statement because of the complexity of historical events, the limitations on the amount of information that can be recovered by the historian or digested by him, and the inescapable bias imposed either by the historian's own predilections or by the assumptions of the society in which he lives: that, since historical generalizations cannot be proved, historians who claim they can are merely deceiving themselves: that for these reasons no agreement can be achieved among historians about any general proposition: and that all generalizations, because of their inevitably flimsy character, should be relegated to a role wholly subordinate to the main business of the historian, which is telling a story based upon the facts; (3) that his-

25 *Ibid.*, pp. 126–129.
26 Robert R. Palmer, "Letter to Committee," in *Generalization in the Writing of History*, ed. Louis Gottschalk, p. 75.

torians should address their chief efforts to insight and speculation, not to the hopeless objective of achieving demonstrable generalizations; that the best of their insights have been achieved and will be achieved not through labored documentation but through judgment, wisdom, and maturity that comes only with experience; and that, therefore, such general statements as historians can make will be and should be personal, subjective, intuitive, speculative, and impressionistic; and (4) that, for these reasons, little can be gained from formal procedures, the hope that a recital of statistical evidence can take us deeper into the heart of reality is illusory, and the results of attempts to formulate general statements by these means have been trivial and inconsequential.[27]

It may be impossible to resolve the conflict on the basis of *a priori* considerations, since the respective attitudes are largely subjective. A more useful approach might be to try to evaluate the role of generalizations in history and see to what extent and how they can be generated.

A generalization, derived inductively from investigation, is a form of empirical law that is less than a universal truth but which may be a step toward discovering such a truth. Even though some generalizations may never be elevated to the rank of universal truths, Mill concluded, "there is a class of inductive truths avowedly not universal, in which it is not pretended that the predicate is always true of the subject, but the value of which, as generalizations, is nevertheless extremely great." [28] As an empirical law, or step toward empirical law, a generalization is a statement summing up the similarities or differences of a number of cases in which similar events have occurred. Defined differently, "generalizations . . . are commonly the summation by the historian of those views of historical explanation and causation which he has exhibited less obviously in the selection and arrangement of his facts. When one links a mass of events in different places or times by a connective tissue of generalization, the uniqueness of such historical events is thereby limited, for generalization is possible only if we can establish the presence of valid similarity." [29] Thus, the motivation to generalize derives from a view of generalization as "man's attempts to find uniformities and regularities in his own life and in the natural world around him. Without the formulation and acceptance of count-

[27] William O. Aydelotte, "Notes on Historical Generalization," in *ibid.*, p. 145.
[28] Mill, *System of Logic*, p. 387.
[29] Chester B. Starr, "Reflections upon the Problem of Generalization," in *Generalization in the Writing of History*, ed. Gottschalk, p. 3.

less generalizations, man could not create a stable society nor could he communicate ideas on more than a rudimentary level." [30]

Therefore, given the explanatory objectives of historical study and the common interest in understanding the present and controlling the future, generalization serves as a rule or a set of rules conceived as explanatory and predictive principles. Generalization is a shortcut method of summarizing observations of certain phenomena. The legislator writes a bill that is supposed to express the needs and desires of those to whom the bill applies. A generalization is a rule that suggests not what ought to be, but what seems and can therefore be expected to be. The degree of confidence in the predictive ability of a generalization only qualifies or suggests the degree of certainty with which the expectations can be held; this is determined by testing. It does not affect the methodological or philosophical premises on which generalizations are formulated. After a highly productive career in economic history, Alexander Gerschenkron concluded that "to predict is not to prophesy. Prediction in historical research means addressing intelligent, that is, sufficiently specific, questions as new materials are approached." [31] This means that predictive generalizations are means of identifying expectations in given circumstances. Put differently, "historical hypotheses are not general or universal propositions. They cannot be falsified by a single exception. Testing them largely means trying to discover the boundaries of the area within which they seem reasonably valid." [32] In other words, research simply shows whether the expectations have proved valid, and if not, why. This is true of all research guided by tendencies observed in previous investigations.

The interpretative function is closely related to the role generalization plays in the accumulation of knowledge for the purpose of discovering laws or universal principles. While generalizations may function as empirical laws, they are also stepping stones toward the more complex purpose of building theories and discovering universal truths. No researcher can repeat the studies carried out by all his predecessors, but generalizations formulated by these predecessors can be built on, refuted, or adopted as laws. In other words, generalization serves as means

[30] Derk Bodde, "Comments on the Paper of Arthur F. Wright," in *ibid.*, p. 59.

[31] Alexander Gerschenkron, *Economic Backwardness in Historical Perspective: A Book of Essays* (New York: Frederick A. Praeger, 1965), p. 359.

[32] *Ibid.*, p. 360. On generalization as abstraction see Gerschenkron, *Continuity in History and Other Essays*, pp. 40ff.

of communication between generations, disciplines, and environments. As means of communication, "general statements are useful to the historian not only as valid inferences and summations of specific historical facts but also as stimuli for further thought; the most useful generalizations are those which place the facts in a new light and lead to further generalizations based upon the facts." [33] It is enough to look at the bibliographies built around the studies of Marx and Toynbee to see the challenging impact of generalization. Certainly, a generalization is not justified if it only stimulates further study, but that function cannot be discarded.

The significance of generalization in the study of economic change is obvious. Economic change implies causation and therefore requires explanation. The observation of tendencies is a clue to causal explanation, but it can be useful in understanding change only if generalizations can be formulated. The study of economic change requires the building of generalizations on the basis of facts, since empirical laws are means of understanding, explaining, and possibly influencing economic change. The economic historian has no choice in the matter. As long as he applies inference to the data, he formulates generalizations. The question is whether he can apply inference and avoid mere speculation. This, however, is a function of the carefulness and competence of the individual scholar, rather than the wisdom or validity of generalization. At a later point we shall discuss the types of possible generalizations.

## METHODOLOGICAL CHOICES

A number of approaches can be pursued in the study of economic history, but regardless of the approach, the first step involves the selection and classification of the data. These two operations are, strictly speaking, a part of historiography.[34] Only a brief discussion of these operations will be presented here, to be followed by a discussion of various ways of analyzing the data.

[33] Starr, "Problem of Generalization," p. 12. Starr quotes R. G. Collingwood: "Statistical research is for the historian a good servant but a bad master. It profits him nothing to make generalizations, unless he can thereby detect the thought behind the facts about which he is generalizing, to warn against unwarranted generalization" (*The Idea of History* [Oxford: Clarendon Press, 1946], p. 228).

[34] For a good discussion see Marc Bloch, *The Historian's Craft*, especially chaps. 2, 3.

## SELECTION AND CLASSIFICATION

To record economic history means to specify and describe the conditions preceding economic change and the conditions following the change. Good recording requires acquaintance with the sources of information, the ability to distinguish facts from fable, and the skill to present these facts clearly and uniformly. To distinguish the facts requires familiarity with the environment and culture to which the data relate and an understanding of the conceptual framework according to which they were recorded. The recorder needs to verify any doubtful data, using all the available techniques for that purpose. Economic theory and statistics can be of great help in clarifying concepts and relationships represented by the data. For example, it might be questioned whether prices could have stood at a certain level at a given time and in a given economic situation. Information regarding the money supply, the levels of output, and knowledge of the relationship between these variables and the price level would be valuable. Similarly, knowledge of statistical techniques would be valuable in examining the methods by which the prices were gathered, standardized, or averaged, and in verifying these facts. Obviously the historian might have to call on other experts for help, since few can be expected to be expert in all areas.

Recording is in essence the selection of the relevant data. The recorder might choose to record not the raw facts at the given points in time, but the summary indicators or results of change. He might be interested in the differences between conditions before and after change, in which case classification and standardization of the data must precede the recording. The data describing change must be conceptually applicable to the whole period during which change has taken place. In the absence of standard concepts, new concepts may have to be devised to permit the measurement of differences between data collected in different periods and possibly different economic situations. For example, data on income in the sixteenth century might describe variables that are different from those described by income data of the nineteenth century. A standardized concept of income would have to be formulated, or the data of the two periods standardized to describe similar variables.

Classification of the data is a necessary step for comparison, inference, and the setting up of hypotheses. "In empirical science particular cognitions are organized into systems of knowledge. The particular cognitions of daily life already involve order: the perception of a thing involves the hypothesis that the actual perception is correlated with possible perceptions; the concept of a thing expresses a relatively invariable correlation of properties attributed to it. . . . A basic procedure for introducing order into knowledge is classification." [35] This phase of economic history can be applied to the facts of static conditions, or to the differences or indicators of change. The researcher could classify data derived from an investigation of one point in time and try to discover the relations then prevailing. In that case, he would be searching for what might be called the conditions of equilibrium at that given point in time, or, more realistically, for the apparent conditions of disequilibrium, since there is no reason to assume that the point of departure should be one of equilibrium. However, when the researcher classifies data of more than one period and compares them or classifies differences, he is dealing with comparative statics and therefore with economic change proper.

Classification involves grouping the data in categories based on similarity of meaning, function, or physical characteristics. "Classification is founded on the similarities between things and events; it is based upon the fact that things are similar in specific respects and dissimilar in others. . . . Scientific classification, however, eventually comes to be based upon essential characters which may be discovered only by careful observation and experimentation." [36] Therefore, classification implies an understanding of the conceptual basis of the data and a complete knowledge of the problem of the study.

Classification, however, cannot be separated from the analysis and treatment of the data because the conceptual scheme or theoretical framework for classification must be the same as the one used in the analysis. Even if these concepts are only definitions, they imply relationships that will influence the analysis if not taken into consideration, as will be shown below.

### DESCRIPTION, ANALYSIS, AND SYNTHESIS

Description, analysis, and synthesis are alternative ways of presenting and analyzing the data. The three approaches overlap, and it would

[35] Lenzen, "Procedures of Empirical Science," pp. 311–312.
[36] *Ibid.*, pp. 311–312.

hardly be possible to find a study that is a pure type of any one of them. Nevertheless, they should be discussed separately because there are major differences between them with respect to the questions asked, the tools used, and the results anticipated or realized. They differ from each other also with respect to the premises on which the study of history is undertaken.

## Description

Descriptive history deals primarily with what happened and to a certain extent with how it happened. It reconstructs the historical situation by narrating the facts as objectively as possible. Interpretation may be limited to describing how an event happened. At least in part, this is due to the common attitude that the interpretation of history is speculative and therefore cannot be regarded as history. A recession might be described by noting the magnitude of its impact, as represented by the facts, on employment, prices, production, or expenditure. Although correlations between the recession and other phenomena in the economy might be noted, this would not be interpretative in the sense of explaining why the recession took place. In other words, descriptive history does not venture into the area of prediction and would register very little interdependence between the past and the present or the future.

The presentation of descriptive history can be quantitative, qualitative, or both. While quantitative data render measurement more feasible, descriptive history is replete with qualitative information by which the situation is reconstructed. Historians have differed in their attitude toward the type of data they use, but these differences have primarily been matters of personal preference rather than reflections of conviction as to which type of data is more sound or useful in writing history. Neither type is regarded unanimously as best for good history, but it is agreed that whichever approach is pursued, the historian has the duty to be as objective, and as prudent as possible in judging the relevance, authenticity, and importance of the facts he uses. Judgment cannot be avoided, because no historian can exhaust all the information relating to his subject. In a sense, descriptive history can be considered an extension of the processes of data selection and classification. The main difference is that recording and classification as such can be general, whereas descriptive history deals with a given problem. For example, the bureau of census collects, selects, and

classifies data on a given economy, but it is the historian who writes
the history of the economy by relating the facts to the problems under
investigation, for which purpose he may discard many of the data of
the bureau or supplement them by data from other sources. The historian tells the story of what happened by noting the magnitude of
change and by emphasizing the functions of certain agents in the
economy. In short, the recorder presents the data, and the historian
makes them speak.

*Analysis*
Analytical history searches for the causes of events and tries to
answer the question why. It asks, for example, not only how deep a
recession was or what its effects were, but also why it took place;
not only whether or not production increased, but also why it did or
did not. In other words, analytical history is the explanation and
interpretation of events or changes in the economy or society under
study. This approach has been the most common among economic
historians, although the methods and expectations have not been
uniform. Some historians have dealt with limited problems or events,
while others dealt with broader questions relating to the same
economy. Analytical history is based on the premise that overt behavior may not tell the whole story; that every event must have a
cause; and that the facts by themselves require interpretation. The
historian searches for the causes and meaning of events in order to
understand change and discover the truth about behavior. The analysis
usually is guided by certain expectations. It is also controlled by
certain rules of analysis in order to arrive at valid conclusions. Some
of these assumptions and rules will now be discussed in some detail.

    CONCEPTUAL FRAMEWORK. The first requirement for meaningful
analysis is a conceptual framework by which potential relationships can
be identified. A conceptual framework is a set of concepts that define
categories and identify relationships relevant to the problem under
study. For example, before investigating price changes, it is important
to understand what is meant by *price* and to know, if possible, what
conditions could lead to price changes. In other words, the conceptual
scheme serves two functions: a definitional function that permits consistency and easy communication; and an explanatory function that
suggests possible explanations of the situation. The explanatory function
can be served by providing a general system of relations that applies to

a whole class of events, or by providing a system of relations that explains specific events within the class. These variants of the conceptual scheme will be treated separately.

A definitional system of concepts is basic to any meaningful study, especially if the study deals with variables and categories that allow subjectivity and arbitrariness to enter into the interpretation. The problem of terminology has afflicted all the social sciences and has often caused debate and confusion that could have been eliminated had a definitional scheme been introduced in the right context.[37] Though the terminology used may be only definitional, its efficiency in serving that function varies according to its applicability to the various stages of the study, and to its communicability. Dewey and Bentley have proposed that these functions would be served if:

(1) The names are to be based on such observations as are accessible to and attainable to everybody. This condition excludes, as being negligible to knowledge, any report of purported observation which the reporter avows to be radically and exclusively private. (2) The status of observation and the use of reports upon it are to be tentative, postulational, hypothetical. This condition excludes all purported material and all alleged fixed principles that are offered as providing original and necessary "foundations" for either the knowings or the knowns. (3) The aim of the observation and naming adopted is to promote further observation and naming which in turn will advance and improve. This condition excludes all namings that are asserted to give, or that claim to be finished reports on "reality." [38]

These rules for terminological clarity are operational in nature and are intended to systematize empirical analysis. However, not all terms can be based on observation, because some might have to be defined prior to observation. Even after observation, it is improbable that all possible characteristics of a term to be defined would have been observed and could be included in the definition. Furthermore, both the observations and the definition might be influenced by the purpose of the observer. Therefore, one might think of a definition in one of two ways: first, as a conceptual construct that designates an act and describes the process by which the act is carried out; or second, as a description of the real thing or act observed. Dewey and Bentley

[37] For example, R. Handy and P. Kurtz, *A Current Appraisal of the Behavioral Sciences*.

[38] John Dewey and Arthur F. Bentley, *Knowing and the Known* (Boston: Beacon Press, 1949), pp. 48–49.

have described these two types of definition as the "nominal" and the "real." [39] The real definition would be a subclass within the conceptual construct, or nominal definition, which is more general. Either type of definition may be adequate, as long as it is consistently usable and easily communicable.

A concept is not only a name; it is also a meaning. It designates a thing or an act; it also describes the process of that act or the implied relation of that thing or act to other things or acts within the relevant environment. For example, the term *price* designates a payment in exchange for some commodity and describes an act of transaction between at least two parties. It also represents, by proxy, the utility attached to the commodity by the buyer, and in that sense it may be an indication of the value system or of the psychology of the buyer and even of the seller. Although some of the implications of a term may be known, the investigator will save himself and others much confusion by making clear what is implied in his usage of a term, particularly when conclusions will be reached and need to be verified. Frequently, verification becomes impossible because of the vagueness of the researcher's terms. Most concepts have multiple functions, and therefore hold the potential danger of misuse or misapplication. As Alexander Gerschenkron put it, "a rigid conceptual framework is no doubt useful in formulating questions, but at all times it evokes the peril that those questions will be mistaken for answers." [40] Furthermore, dependence on such a scheme could be interpreted as determinism. Yet, how else can we "approach historical reality except through a search of regularities and deviations from regularities, by conceiving events and sequences of events in terms of constructs of our mind, of patterns, of models"? [41] A conceptual framework can be a fruitful tool of analysis, and the possible pitfalls avoided, if the framework is derived by empirical research, and if the limits of its applicability and the degree of its generality are carefully established.

RELATIONAL SYSTEMS. When we speak of an economy, a firm, or a household, we imply a unity of varying degree between the components of the unit. A conceptual framework is necessary to define the general relations that hold the unit together. In this study, a generalized frame-

[39] *Ibid.*, chap. 7.

[40] Gerschenkron, *Economic Backwardness in Historical Perspective*, pp. 67, 31–32.

[41] *Ibid.*, pp. 31–32.

work has been pursued as general systems analysis, according to which a unit is an organism whose components are interdependent. Each component affects and is affected by other components. For example, the central nervous system is central to an organism; or competition, self-interest, and a free market are indispensable to a capitalistic economy. A conceptual framework helps to explicitly identify both the system and the mechanics of its functioning. A system may be autonomous in the sense of being self-adjusting, as in cybernetics, or it may respond to external influences. Systems can also be described as "closed" or "open." "A system is called closed if no substance flows into it or out of it (an exchange of energy, however, is permitted). A system is called open if not only energy but also matter flows in and out. Equilibrium is a state of a closed system, independent of time, in which all macroscopic processes cease." A living organism, or a socioeconomic system, is an open system that "maintains a constant state while matter and energy which enter it keep changing (so-called dynamic equilibrium)."[42] A theory of systems analysis would establish the features of the constant state and the rate at which energy and matter flow in and out; that is, it would measure change in a system and explain the processes by which dynamic equilibrium is maintained.

A conceptual framework establishes the rules and procedures for the functioning of a system; it identifies the relations that hold together the members of an economy or society as a system. In other words, it provides possible explanations for the behavior of the members and for changes in the system as a whole. This is the function of a model describing the behavior of a unit.

Systems analysis is common in economics, even though a model is not always explicitly stated. In part this is due to the variability of the conceptions of a unit. It is also due to our ignorance of the actual functioning of these units and the difficulty of constructing a model. Finally, the lack of a model may be due to differences in approaching a unit of study. Some think of a unit in terms of structural relations; others in terms of functions. Still others suggest that an economic system can be distinguished according to the determining economic facts, in terms of such criteria as exchange or control.[43]

[42] V. A. Lektorsky and V. N. Sadovsky, "On Principles of Systems Research," *General Systems* 5 (1960): 73, 172.

[43] Walter Eucken, *The Foundations of Economics*, pp. 8off. For a discussion of systems see Alfred Kuhn, *The Study of Society: A Unified Approach* (Homewood,

Therefore, in specifying the background or the initial conditions of an economic unit, the investigator can follow one of two possible approaches. He can describe the main components of the economic system and their functional relations to each other and to the system as a whole, or he can concentrate on the effects of these relations.[44] As a strong proponent of economic systems analysis, Eucken insists that "a scientific investigation has to describe precisely the individual parts of the system, and show how these partial systems fit together into the whole. No partial system exists on its own, but is linked up by the division of labour with the rest of the economy." [45] Systems analysis has been recommended for the social sciences in general as well as for historical study. The analysis can be carried out in terms of the structure and process of the system under consideration. *Structure* means "the degree and mode of organization in a situation"; *process* relates to the pattern of change in a structure.[46] The specific approach selected for a given study will determine the variables to be observed. For example, a researcher might describe the components of a system, their scale of operation, and their scope of performance. This structural approach uses secondary indicators. In contrast, one might investigate the normative functions of the components of a system as sources of demand, supply, education or skill, or of employment and income. Or he might find it appropriate to consider primary indicators and assess only the effects of these economic functions by measuring variables such as the per capita income, distribution of income, price levels, amount and terms of credit, or the levels of consumption, saving, investment, and capital formation. More frequently a combination of these methods is necessary.

This functionalist approach may be objectionable to those who study economic change with the assumption that economic theory is mechanistic and therefore different from functional theory. Although both the functionalist and the mechanistic theories are regarded as equilibrating approaches, applicable to systems analysis,

Ill.: R. D. Irwin, 1963), chap. 3. For a discussion of an organization as a system see R. L. Ackoff, "Systems, Organizations, and Interdisciplinary Research," *General Systems* 5 (1960): 1–8.

[44] M. M. Postan ("Function and Dialectic in Economic History," *Economic History Review*, 2d s. 14, no. 3 [April 1962]: 397–407) discusses the appropriateness of function in the theory of economic history.

[45] Eucken, *Foundations of Economics*, p. 89.

[46] Aitken, *Social Sciences in Historical Study*, pp. 95–97.

they differ in basic ways. According to Krupp, "Functionalist theory focuses on the unity and directness of a total system, while mechanistic theory tends to concentrate on the precise determination of the relationships between parts of the system. Functionalist theory assumes a system to have a basic organizing principle of goals and self-regulating mechanisms. Mechanistic theory takes a system to be derived from the relationships between the parts." Perhaps the differences are only semantic and definitional. Indeed, Krupp discusses economic goals and self-regulating mechanisms in functionalist terms, thus casting doubt on the justification for juxtaposing functionalist and mechanistic theories to approach an economic system.[47] Mechanistic theory, to the extent it is applied to an economic system, regards a unit as goal directed and self-regulating. Whether it be a firm, an industry, or an economy, a system aims at achieving an objective, such as profit, growth, continuity, or redistribution, which are functions that help to sustain the system. When a goal is not explicitly stated, that is because the organization of the system is unplanned. The difference between planned and unplanned economic systems is that the goals and mechanisms of achievement are specified in the former, and anonymous in the latter. This suggests also that mechanistic theory, as applied to economics, is self-regulating, unless interfered with, as happens to be the case in functionalist theory. One might even go further and describe the economic system as a cybernetic system, in the sense that "no one ever worked a plan for such a system, or willed its existence; there is no plan of it anywhere, either on paper or in anybody's mind, and no one directs its operations. Yet in a fairly tolerable way, 'it works,' and grows and changes."[48] Therefore, functionalist theory and "mechanistic theory" can be equally applicable to economics.

Using a system as a unit of study is nothing more than using a macro model, which has been common in economics for many years. Most studies of economic history have approximated the systems or macro approach to a greater or lesser degree, although few have analyzed an economic system as a functioning unit. The German Historical Economists certainly tried; Marx succeeded; the American

[47] Sherman Roy Krupp, "Equilibrium Theory in Economics and in Functional Analysis as Types of Explanation," in *Functionalism in the Social Sciences*, ed. Don Martindale, American Academy of Political and Social Science Monograph no. 5 (Philadelphia, 1965), pp. 65, 81–82.
[48] Frank H. Knight, *The Economic Organization* (New York: Augustus M. Kelley, 1951), p. 31.

Institutionalists also intended it although their treatments were partial in application.

Systems-analysis models have differed in degree of abstraction, and have often been conceptual constructs of only limited relation to reality. This "degree of abstraction" is similar to what Boulding has described as the "theoretical level" of systematic knowledge, which belongs mainly to pure science. In contrast, he distinguishes systems according to three additional levels of empirical knowledge. "The first is that of purely empirical systems, based on frequently observed connections," such as observed bodily skills. The second is the "mechanical construction system," which involves knowledge of physical structures but not why each part should fit where it fits. The third level is the "engineering system," which involves knowledge of the design and why the parts should fit.[49] Economic history is concerned with the engineering and theoretical levels, but mostly with the former, which tries to explain the functioning of the system as it exists in reality and as the forerunner of the theoretical level. A systems approach that claims close relation to reality is the Gestalt method proposed by Arthur Spiethoff.[50]

Gestalt theory emphasizes real features and "aims at the closest possible approximation to observable reality . . . [and] considers the maximum number of relations in which the phenomenon to be investigated actually occurs. . . . By a process of induction, economic Gestalt theory arrives at discreet species of phenomena whose characteristics are the data from which it starts. . . . Its purpose is to consider all phenomena that actually and *uniformly* impinge on the one which is the center of attention." When applied to static situations, economic Gestalt theory is "theory in the true sense"; but when it is used to study change, "the border line between this theory and economic history becomes fluid," in which case the study may become "analytical economic history using the methods of economic Gestalt theory."

The relevance of Gestalt methodology to the study of change has been observed by Usher, primarily because of its comprehensiveness and empiricism.[51] The use of an economic system as one whole in

[49] K. E. Boulding, "Political Implications of General Systems Research," *General Systems* 6 (1961): 2.

[50] Spiethoff, "Pure Theory and Economic Gestalt Theory," pp. 444–456.

[51] A. P. Usher, "Significance of Empiricism," *Journal of Economic History* 9 (November 1949): 150–151.

historical study has been recognized as having another significant function. Since the "whole" consists of individual components subject to observation, the connecting relations between these components must be inferred by the observer. Alternatively, economic theory provides the guide by which these relations are identified and the whole constructed. Economic history, as the study of the pattern and causes of economic change in and of the system, can point out gaps in the theory and help in discovering and formulating laws of economic behavior. Thus the systems approach can be a connecting link between economic theory and economic history.[52]

The emphasis on realism side by side with the building of economic theory has been most strongly advocated by Eucken, who states that "the economic process goes on always and everywhere within the framework of an historically given economic system. . . . without a system no economy is possible." An economic system "depends on the determining economic facts, and on the forms in which the everyday economic process takes its course." Therefore the study of a system means the study of the facts and the forms of behavior, and the study of change must be a study of the variation in facts and forms. In the words of Eucken, "as every household and firm is part of a complete system, and every single economic action part of a complete process, it is necessary to understand the system and the process in their entirety." [53]

The use of an economic system as the unit of study has advantages, as has been indicated, but it also has complications; for example, how to identify or isolate a system, how to identify the connecting relations, and most serious of all, how to specify the boundaries when a system is complex and always in flux? In other words, how to deal dynamically with a complex that can hardly be measured or controlled? However, these complications are not insurmountable. Discretion, approximation, and carefulness can reduce these difficulties significantly, as will be shown below.

EXPLANATION OF CHANGE. The specific relations that form the third part of the conceptual scheme relate to the explanation of change. For example, to understand the causes of a price rise, it is necessary to formulate general explanatory statements about price changes. These

[52] F. A. von Hayek, "Scientism and the Study of Society," *Economica*, n.s. 10 (February 1943): 56.

[53] Eucken, *Foundations of Economics*, pp. 80, 85, 304.

statements may or may not explain the actual change, but they should be potentially capable of doing so, depending on their origin and premises. Explanatory statements may be derived either by deduction or induction; in most cases, however, they result from a combination of both.

Two points have usually been debated in this respect: (1) which of these approaches is truly scientific? and (2) which of them is applicable to economic history and other social sciences? Regarding the first question, there has been much misunderstanding primarily because there is no accepted definition of *scientific method*. "The practice of scientific method is the persistent critique of arguments, in the light of tried canons for judging the reliability of the procedures by which individual data are obtained, and for assessing the probative force of the evidence on which conclusions are based." [54] Therefore, as long as clarity and systematic procedures permit critical evaluation, the method should be considered scientific, regardless of whether it is deductive or inductive. The economic historian, and the social scientist in general, do not need to commit themselves to one approach. They should be ready to use any approach appropriate for their research and explanation. To clarify this conclusion, it is necessary to discuss the meanings of deduction and induction.

Deduction is generalization from the universal to the particular, or from general to individual facts. An explanation or prediction of individual or specific events is hypothesized on the basis of certain universal laws or relations governing a class of behavior. Price fluctuation in a given period is usually explained according to the laws of supply and demand as standardized and accepted in the literature. Whether the actual fluctuation is truly explained can be verified by investigating the facts surrounding the price movement. If the facts support the hypothesis, it will not be rejected; otherwise it will be rejected, and a new hypothesis formulated. In a sense, economic inquiry tends to follow this approach, although not always rigorously. These investigations state certain causes as premises and infer from them certain consequences, which are then compared with empirical observations for verification. A search for explanation thus moves from the universal laws to the initial conditions antecedent to a change, as in the inquiries of Adam Smith, Ricardo, Marx, and Schumpeter.[55]

[54] Nagel, *Structure of Science*, p. 13.
[55] B. S. Keirstead, *The Theory of Economic Change*, chap. 4.

Whether or not a hypothesis is rejected, given the criteria for rejection, will have little effect on the universal law a hypothesis is based on. A universal law is true by definition since it is logically consistent in the sense that its conclusions are logically derived from its premises. A law itself might never be tested as true or false by empirical investigation because all the necessary conditions might never be present in the empirical situation. However, the relevance of a law might be evaluated by its power of explanation and prediction of empirical events.[56]

Deductive analysis is controlled by certain rules that govern the relations between the premises and derived conclusions, namely a universal law. Deduction is generalization from a universal law in the sense of "if . . . then," such that an explicandum follows logically from the premises, but not otherwise, or else, the explanation would be tautological. When a conclusion is to explain single events, it is sufficient that the premises from which the conclusion logically follows include only one universal law. However, to explain another universal law, the premises must contain more than one universal law.

A universal law will not explain events unless the initial conditions of these events are specified. Initial conditions are statements "which assert that certain events have occurred at indicated times and places or that given objects have definite properties. . . . More generally, initial conditions constitute the special circumstances to which the laws included in the explanatory premises are applied." It is possible, however, that the premises not include a universal law. The minimum condition is that the premises include at least one relation more general, conceptually, than the explicandum. The premises of a law are subject to further qualification. In classical thought, it was considered essential that premises be "true, . . . known to be true, and that they must be 'better known' than the explicandum." More recently this rigid restriction has been relaxed. Now it is considered sufficient that premises be "compatible with established empirical fact," and be supported by data other than those supporting the explicandum.[57] Furthermore, it is possible that laws be established empirically without reverting to premises from which to derive them logically. This is

[56] On how these ideas apply in economics see Frank H. Knight, in *Economic Anthropology: A Study in Comparative Economics*, ed. M. J. Herskovits, 2nd ed. (New York: A. A. Knopf, 1952): 511–512.
[57] Nagel, *Structure of Science*, pp. 31–32, 42, 43.

equivalent to induction and will be treated below. It is sufficient to add here that empirically established laws are experimental laws and are different from theories, which are usually associated with universality.

Deductive analysis, then, requires a universal law, premises from which the law follows logically, and initial conditions precipitating an explicandum. The applicability of deductive analysis depends on all these conditions.

The economic historian, like any other social scientist, may have problems in using the deductive method in historical analysis. First, universal laws might not be available to guide him. Second, the premises of any applicable laws might not be true, or known to be true, or verifiable by observable facts. And, third, the premises the law is based on might not coincide with or even approximate the empirical situation under study. It is doubtful there are sufficient universal laws governing the economic and social behavior that the economic historian investigates. Many scholars have doubted that any such laws can be discovered or formulated, as has been mentioned above. Even where such laws exist, it is not certain they are universal in the sense mentioned above; the laws of supply and demand do not comply with the "if . . . then" condition of universality. There are no universal laws to explain inflationary movements, nor are there such laws dealing with monetary behavior, with unemployment, or with investment. It is true that experimental (probabilistic) laws exist, but these are not universal nor do they exist for all economic behaviors.

A more serious problem is that not all the premises economic laws are based on are empirically verifiable or adequately supported by empirical evidence. For example, it would be an exaggeration to claim that economic rationality is adequately supported as a common human characteristic on which to base economic laws. It is equally debatable that maximization is a true and known premise, unless the specification of maximizing behavior is relaxed enough to include various types of behavior, including maximization of security, permanence, and economic advantage. Although such relaxation may be conceptually permissible, it has the disadvantage of rendering the empirical observation and verification of a premise virtually impossible.

It follows that the economic historian cannot depend solely on deductive analysis. He must use his discretion as to when it is appropriate to apply deduction, and should seek alternative approaches to deal with the material he studies. Induction is one alternative.

Economic historians have tended to generalize from the particular or individual to the universal or general. They begin by observing the facts, and then try to explain change or the events by inductive inference from these observations. "An argument is called inductive . . . if from the evidence that a specified predicate is true of certain members of a class, it proceeds to a conclusion which is a generalization concerning the composition of the whole class with respect to that predicate or to a conclusion which is a prediction about whether this predicate applies to some particular unexamined member of the class." [58] The logic of induction is basic to the philosophy of empiricism; that is, generalization must be based on observation rather than on intuition.

Inductive analysis and its philosophical foundations have been perennial issues of debate, going back at least to the Greeks. Although the debate concerning the validity and justification of inductive statements and conclusions has continued, the inductive method has been the backbone of the sciences, both natural and social. In a sense, it might be argued that the only questions warranting debate should relate to the rules and principles of induction, all other questions of validity or justification being academic in the sense that the method has no substitute and has been in use in all research. A more positive attitude, however, would question the significance of the debate by arguing that the value of induction, or any other method, lies in its ability to explain and predict, and that whether or not the logic of the method can be justified is hardly relevant. Only the correctness of the results can justify a method. On this basis, inductive analysis has earned its justification in most, if not in all, fields of empirical research. Nevertheless, before reaching any conclusions on the subject, we should discuss briefly some of the basic problems of induction.

The first problem is one of justification: how to justify generalizing from a part to a whole, or from the observed to the unobserved and possibly unobservable. Many answers have been proposed, all of which center around probability theory and the law of large numbers. According to this law, "if M is a class, and MQ a subclass, and P is any predicate, then if [MQ] is large, MQ is a class of subclasses of M, all

<hr />

[58] S. F. Barker, *Induction and Hypothesis* (Cornell Univ. Press, 1962), p. 49.

of the same size [MQ], among which the great majority are statistically similar to M with respect to P, and . . . consequently an inference that the composition of the population M is similar to the composition of the given sample MQ is one of a great number of inferences, with true premises, in which the great majority have true conclusions." [59] Given this law, it becomes legitimate to generalize from a sample to a population, from one sample to another sample, or from a population to a part of it. However, this approach, which premises the law of large numbers as universal, may seem more deductive than inductive, but it is different from deduction in two ways: the results or conclusions do not follow from the premise as a logical necessity, and the truth or falseness of the conclusions is probable only to degrees that cannot be determined on the basis of the law itself; the law of large numbers is not true intuitively or logically, but is regarded as an empirical law and verifiable by empirical observations.[60]

A second problem involves the rationale of induction, which derives from other assumptions, two of which require discussion. The first is John S. Mill's "principle of the uniformity of nature." According to this principle, there is enough uniformity and continuity in nature to justifiably expect similar behavior if given similar antecedents or initial conditions. Therefore, it is justified to generalize from a subclass to a class and from the observed to the unobserved. In other words, it is legitimate to use induction as a basis for prediction. Another version of this principle is that probability "matures" so that eventually the similarity between a subclass and a class, with respect to a given property, will be nearly complete.[61] Yet, this principle, which appears to be a universal law, renders the analysis deductive, unless it is considered an empirical or inductive generalization subject to observation. If such considerations are entertained, "this approach to the problem appears to resolve it only by generating an issue that is identical with the one it claims to settle." [62]

The second assumption has been proposed by the "reductionists,"

[59] Donald Williams, *The Ground of Induction* (New York: Russell & Russell, 1963), p. 138.

[60] This position has been challenged on the ground that the law is logical and need not be verified empirically, which may be impossible to do (*ibid.*, pp. 138–139).

[61] *Ibid.*, pp. 119–120.

[62] Henry E. Kyburg, Jr. and Ernest Nagel, eds., *Induction: Some Current Issues* (Middletown, Conn.: Wesleyan Univ. Press, 1963), p. xviii.

who contend that induction does not generalize from the observed to the unobserved, but only to the already observed or at least observable; that is, the unobserved is reduced to the observed on the assumption that it is observable and hence verifiable. And, when a statement is made concerning the unobservable, it is not an inductive generalization or hypothesis, but a logical construct that is neither verifiable nor a conclusion. For example, there is no such thing as "the average American," and therefore it cannot be verified. A logical construct is formulated as a convenience and should not reflect on the methods of induction.[63] However, it is doubtful that all statements generalized to the unobservable are only logical constructs. Is generalizing with respect to human feelings only a logical construct? Furthermore, suppose a hypothesis deals only with the observed or observable, does that mean that all hypotheses or statements associated with it deal only with the observed or observable? What if one of them does not? These questions remain unanswered.

A third, more serious problem relates to the confirmation of statements or generalizations that cannot be proved by deduction or verified by induction. Even if specific events can be observed and verified, the conclusions might be impossible to confirm. Probability theory allows an estimate of the probability that a given statement is true, given the law of large numbers. But such a degree of correctness is only probable and not confirmed deductively. One suggestion for avoiding the problem is to repeat the observation or experiment and estimate the frequency with which the same observation of similar subclasses gives the same results. Frequency theory, however, does not confirm the results. It only increases the subjective confidence in the validity of the results, since probability estimates are not cumulative. Furthermore, frequency theory tries to avoid dependence on the logical explanation inherent in the use of the law of large numbers. It is doubtful, therefore, that the mere recurrence of an event can be used as confirmation.[64]

A different approach to confirmation is induction by elimination, advocated by Keynes and others of his time. This approach suggests that the confirmation of a hypothesis or statement can be carried out only by eliminating rival hypotheses or statements. The greater the number of rival generalizations eliminated, the more confirmed the given hypothesis should be. The principle involved is the "principle of limited

[63] Barker, *Induction and Hypothesis*, chap. 6.
[64] *Ibid.*, pp. 65–67.

variety" of properties and groups in any given population. All possible hypotheses as to which groups are characterized by a given property, or which property characterizes a given number of groups, will have equal probabilities of being true. However, as evidence accumulates, those hypotheses falsified can be eliminated—thus increasing the probability that the remaining hypotheses are true—until one hypothesis is confirmed. This theory has been criticized on the basis of its assumptions. For example, it has been argued that the principle itself cannot be verified. Futhermore, as used by Keynes, the principle applies only to properties, and does not seem to apply to relations.[65] This latter argument, however, is not very destructive because there is no evidence that the theory cannot be extended to relations just as it is applied to properties.

In view of these problems, a recent approach to empirical research has been the method of hypothesis. Generally, this method consists of "deducing consequents from a hypothesis and in verifying them; the hypothesis is regarded as confirmed if some consequents are verified and none is falsified; and one hypothesis is regarded as better confirmed than is another if more consequents of the former than of the latter have been verified and none falsified." [66] The hypothesis need not be inductively derived, nor does the method allow for hypotheses, such as universal laws, that cannot be verified empirically because they are not observational.

A more recent version of this method reverts to the theory of elimination, namely the hypothetico-deductive method. According to this version, a hypothesis is verified by falsifying its rivals. This modification, however, renders the method noninductive. For instance, a hypothesis is confirmed or not on the basis of indirect evidence, namely the consequences of a rival hypothesis. Yet, it is not even stipulated that these consequences are themselves empirical. For all practical purposes, they might be hypothetical consequences that should have followed from the hypothetical rival hypothesis. In the absence of these hypothetical consequences, the rival hypothesis is rejected, thus adding confirmation to the given hypothesis. This approach does not solve the problem of how to confirm or reject a rival hypothesis itself. In other words, the rejection or acceptance of a rival hypothesis and consequently of a given hypothesis assumes that the two hypotheses

[65] *Ibid.*, pp. 55ff.
[66] *Ibid.*, pp. 153–154.

are mutually exclusive as true or false. Yet most hypotheses in the social sciences cannot be either true or false in absolute terms. Furthermore, this method suffers from the complication that a hypothesis could have so many rivals that falsification of all these rivals would be impossible. In other words, the method is limited to singular hypotheses derived from more general premises, which is the reverse of induction.[67]

Finally, compare the hypothetico-deductive method with current practice in widely accepted circles of the philosophy of law. An accused person is considered innocent until he is proved guilty, since guilt is the object of analysis. The method of hypothesis regards the hypothesis that contains the object of analysis as nonrejected until the opposite is nonrejected. The differences are vital. In legal procedure, the accumulated evidence relates to the object of analysis, whereas in the method of hypothesis the evidence is related to a rival hypothesis that does not contain the object of inquiry. Furthermore, the premises in legal procedure are inductive, derived from observation of human behavior over extensive periods of time. The premises of the hypothesis method are not stipulated as inductively derived. Therefore, it seems that the proponents of the hypothetico-deductive method have not yet made their case strong enough for application, especially in the social sciences.

All these problems are especially serious when related to human behavior and to historical data. For example, unless a certain degree of uniformity of nature is assumed, it is impossible to induce any generalizations from history, particularly since past experiences cannot be observed and verified. Nevertheless, induction remains the basis of research in history and the other social sciences, especially induction by enumeration on the basis of the law of large numbers. As for confirmation, two approaches seem appropriate. The first is confirmation by probability estimate through direct evidence, not by eliminating rival hypotheses. The second is a positivist approach, namely, to generalize and predict and watch for the correctness of these predictions as a test of confirmation, regardless of the logical validity of the results.

STATISTICAL ANALYSIS. We have seen that inductive analysis may be the economic historian's most useful approach. However, induction has been shown to be closely related to probability theory, which requires quantitative data for precise estimates. Therefore, the economic historian would find himself in a dilemma if he were to depend on statistical data that might not always be available. One result has been

[67] Williams, *Ground of Induction*, pp. 112–117.

a tendency to restrict research to only those problems for which there are statistics. Yet, there is no obvious reason why statistical data should be the only basis for inference, nor are statistics free of complication.

Inference can be based on either qualitative or quantitative data, but inference from quantitative data is more precise, more objective, and more critical, because the use of quantitative data permits the application and use of statistical theory. In turn, statistical theory renders interpretation more systematic, permits the significance of results to be tested, and reduces the probability of misinterpreting results. Even though certainty is never achieved, the probability of occurrence by chance can be estimated and a degree of confidence established.[68]

Statistical inference is simply a method by which findings can be presented with more precision than would otherwise be possible. Economic historians should thus be highly receptive to the use of statistics. Any reluctance to resort to statistical theory ought to be due only to insurmountable obstacles. For example, it might be difficult to obtain statistics, adequate samples, or data on a period long enough to permit the observation of tendencies. For these reasons the economic historian might be reluctant to commit himself to statistical methods, given the potential and unavoidable errors of observation and omission.[69]

There are situations in which statistical methods can be invaluable, and the economic historian should be ready and able to take advantage of them. Foremost among these situations is research focused on a short-term phenomenon for which both statistical and economic theory have provided the necessary tools. For example, the effects of farm subsidy on income distribution or on the level of prices within a given period can be analyzed statistically, assuming the data are accessible. The profitability of an enterprise or the growth of a firm are equally amenable to statistical analysis. Such cases are different from those cases dealing, for example, with the impact of farm subsidy on farm income in general, which reach for generalizations that must be based on the observation of a large number of short periods—on trends too long to be subjected to rigorous statistical analysis. The same difficulty would arise in the attempt to explain the relation between colonialism and economic change. Therefore, statistical analysis is recommended primarily for short-term, well-defined periods and events. It can hardly

---

[68] On the problem of uncertainty see Michael J. Brennan, *Preface to Econometrics* (Cincinnati: South-Western Publishing Co., 1965): 16.

[69] *Ibid.*, pp. 250–252.

be recommended for long periods, at least until new tools have been developed.

The second circumstance in which statistical analysis can be applied is the search for facts to generate relations or hunches. Sometimes it is necessary to establish a relation, or to clarify it as a fact. For example, whether or not slavery was profitable might be established by analyzing the available records, assuming the slave can be regarded as a commodity and the slave holder an entrepreneur. However, statistical analysis can hardly be recommended if profitability has already been accepted as an established fact, unless assessment of the degree of profitability is an objective of the study. In many cases, and certainly for purposes of generalization, the mere fact of profitability might be adequate regardless of its magnitude.

A similar situation arises when the impact of a certain technique on economic change is under investigation. If statistical analysis can establish the relation between the given technique and economic change, it should by all means be used. However, if it is acknowledged that the given technique had certain effects, of what consequence is it to establish the probable results of alternative techniques that were not introduced? To discover that the contribution of the horse to communication was less than it could have been is of little consequence from a historical standpoint, as long as it is acknowledged that the use of the horse was positively related to economic change in a given environment. These findings and discoveries may be of academic interest, but are of little historical significance. They may be useful in improving the methods of analysis, but not in increasing our knowledge of economic history. The only case in which these discoveries would be of historical significance is when the purpose of a study is evaluation of the efficiency of the entrepreneur or the horse, which is different from explaining economic change.

Third, statistical analysis should be used when economic phenomena can be isolated from social and political phenomena and when the event under consideration can be studied statistically. Profitability can be studied as a statistical value, in which case statistical analysis is indispensable. However, when profitability means reward in a broader sense —security, certainty, power, prestige, and influence—statistical analysis is extremely inadequate. It is hardly possible to analyze statistically the behavior of "traditional" estate holders, or of those who receive indirect economic benefits because of the influence and prestige of holding an estate. It is equally difficult to apply statistical analysis when intervening variables have made economic behavior subjective, arbitrary, or nonrational.

Finally, statistical analysis should be applied whenever possible as supportive evidence, for verifying relations, or for testing hypotheses. Especially in verifying general relations, statistical analysis must be used, but only as a complementary tool rather than a substitute, and only when the basic nonstatistical approach fails to indicate the proposed relations with a high degree of certainty. Probabilistic evidence gained by statistical analysis can then be quite helpful in establishing the facts about the relations under consideration.

In conclusion, statistical analysis should be used whenever possible. It should also be clear that the nature of historical research precludes total dependence on statistics. Even if data are available, they must be interpreted with extreme care. The predictive capacity of statistical analysis depends, to a large extent, on the representativeness of the sample, and the accuracy and comprehensiveness of the data. Given the breadth of economic history, the variability in meaning of concepts and the historian's probable unawareness of these meanings, and also the limited comprehensiveness of statistical data, prediction from statistical inference can be as shaky as prediction or inference from imprecise qualitative data. In using statistical inference for historical explanation, Conrad and Meyer warn that "one must be careful: we are not talking about predictions that *were* made, obviously. Neither are we talking about predictions that *could* have been made. We are saying of observed events only that they would have confirmed predictions that *might* have been made." [70] If so, careful inference from qualitative data can be equally, if not more dependable than inference from inadequate statistical data. The researcher, therefore, must use his discretion regarding the approach he follows.

ECONOMETRICS IN HISTORY (CLIOMETRY). A recent tendency in economic history has been to use econometrics for the measurement and evaluation of economic change. There is no precise and accepted definition of econometrics. Writing a survey on the subject, Leontief decided to choose what he considered a middle course, "that of interpreting 'Econometrics' as a special type of economic analysis in which the general theoretical approach—often formulated in explicitly mathematical terms—is combined—frequently through the medium of intricate statistical procedures—with empirical measurement of economic

[70] Conrad and Meyer, *Economics of Slavery*, p. 39.

phenomena." This general conception would imply the application of statistics to economic data and the interpretation of the results in the light of economic theory. If that were all, there would be no argument with nor novelty in this recent trend in economic history. However, Ragner Frisch asserts that "experience has shown that each of these three viewpoints, that of statistics, economic theory, and mathematics, is a necessary, but not by itself sufficient condition for a real understanding of the quantitative relations in economic life. It is the *unification* of all three that is powerful. And it is this unification that constitutes econometrics." Given this conception, the first complication arises when econometrics is limited to quantitative relations. A second complication is implied in the view that "the function of statistical analysis in application to econometric research is that of an intermediary between a general theoretical hypothesis and the directly observed facts." [71] Finally, a difficulty arises when it is necessary to use mathematics as part of econometrics in history. These complications will be treated separately.

The first complication has already been covered, in a sense, under the previous heading, "Statistical Analysis." The absence of quantitative or quantifiable data can be a limiting factor. This is not a reflection on statistics but on the availability of data. Without further detail, it should be reiterated that statistical analysis is invaluable whenever it is possible to apply it.

A second complication is that econometrics is difficult to use when statistical analysis serves mainly as an intermediate step between formulating a hypothesis and then testing it by observing the facts. Such a conception assumes the existence of general premises from which hypotheses can be derived. However, if the facts are to be analyzed statistically as a step toward formulating hypotheses, the complication will be avoided. The analysis would be inductive in the sense of generalizing from the observed facts. The intermediary role of statistical inference limits its applicability and shifts the focus of research. First, the research has to be limited to those areas for which hypotheses can be formulated; there are many areas of economic behavior for which general premises have not been established. Second, this procedure focuses attention on theory and hypotheses rather than analysis of historical facts: unless the facts happen to support a hypothesis, they are discarded and new facts gathered to test the same hypothesis. This pro-

[71] Wassily Leontief, "Econometrics," *A Survey of Contemporary Economics* 2 (1948): 388, 391, 392.

cedure may be justifiable for the theorist whose objective is to formulate theoretical relations expressed by a hypothesis, but not for the historian whose objective is to interpret historical facts and discover new relations. Although this difference is only a matter of emphasis, it is significant enough to alter the whole research objective. It is sufficient to review the research sponsored by the National Bureau of Business and Economic Research to see that significant contributions would not have been possible had the research been contingent on ready-made hypotheses. Even the statistical analysis that preceded the theoretical generalizations might have been premature if nonquantitative "analytical insights" had not already been achieved.[72] In other words, although the hypothesis approach might be recommended, the economic historian need not be bound to it and might actually find it inapplicable to the problems and data he is dealing with.

A similar conclusion can be reached with respect to the complication of using mathematics. As a tool of systematic and logical analysis, mathematics can be indispensable. However, the use of mathematics in economic analysis requires certain preliminary achievements. The function of mathematics lies in building definitional models that are behavioral or analytical. The latter eventually lead to the formulation of axioms of economic behavior. As for definitional models, they are a convenience and a source of economy, and are especially useful in the measurement of economic change. Therefore, there should be no hesitation in using them. The same is not true of relational models, because these imply that the relations described are already well known —that the relevant economic theory is well understood and can therefore be formulated mathematically as a step toward deriving further theories or axioms. It is true that such relations can be formulated intuitively and in a form general enough to be almost universalistic. However, unless these intuitively derived relations approximate reality, they are of little empirical use. Nor can these theoretical relations be understood unless the empirical conditions have been carefully explored. Intuition alone is not sufficient. " 'Intuition' is the step that leads from historical-statistical-experimental research to the first stage of theoretical interpretation." [73] Only when the concepts are made clear through historical-statistical-experimental research is it feasible to theorize and

---

[72] *Ibid.*, p. 393.

[73] O. Morganstern, "Limits to the Use of Mathematics in Economics," in *Mathematics and the Social Sciences*, ed. J. C. Charlesworth (Philadelphia: American Academy of Political and Social Science, 1963): 24–25.

branch out into mathematics for further development. These first stages are the domain of the historian. Whether or not he happens to be treating problems for which the first stages have been completed will determine the extent to which relational mathematical models can be used.

We have seen that complications arise with respect to each of the three components of econometrics: statistics, theory, and mathematics; and these complications are compounded when all three aspects are united. Few problems in economic history fall in a category that satisfies all three of the conditions required for econometric research. Vast areas of research lack the quantitative and theoretical qualifications that permit a mathematical treatment. These areas need to be explored by more traditional, if less sophisticated, methods. The economic historian must use his discretion in these cases since "the primary task is to discover the true nature of the underlying economic phenomenon and to concentrate efforts in that direction, instead of stopping short and branching out into the mathematical treatment of an ill-defined and vaguely described situation." [74]

COMPARATIVE METHOD. Comparison may be undertaken for two reasons: to explain certain events, or to synthesize findings for purposes of generalization. The latter will be treated later in the context of synthesis.

It has been argued that historical investigations are essentially concerned with causal interpretation, and also that the search for causes implies comparison. Therefore, historical research must be greatly dependent on the comparative method.[75] Generally speaking, every kind of research that involves evaluation is comparative in one form or another. Even when a researcher has not explicitly stated or intended his position to be so, and even when his evaluation is limited to data on one specific case, he is actually evaluating the data on the basis of an implicit set of rules or standards.[76] The tools of measurement he uses imply an ideal against which he measures his results. When he con-

[74] Ibid., p. 19.

[75] For a general discussion of this method see Marc Bloch, "Toward a Comparative History of European Societies," in Enterprise and Secular Change, ed. Lane & Riemersma, pp. 494–521.

[76] Sylvia L. Thrupp, "The Role of Comparison in the Development of Economic Theory," Journal of Economic History 17 (1957): 554–555; the rest of the article is a historical survey of the uses of comparison in the social sciences. Professor Thrupp's paper was a contribution to a symposium on comparative method, thus indicating economic historans' renewed interest in its uses.

cludes that certain conditions prevail or fail to prevail, he implicitly betrays his expectation that these conditions should or should not have prevailed. For example, when a researcher concludes that the level of prices in a certain period did not rise, he is suggesting in effect that there was a possibility prices would rise. It also implies that on the basis of his conception of the behavior of the market, prices have failed to behave according to his expectations and therefore require explanation. Or he might observe that a national economy has undergone change in a certain direction or pattern, but as soon as he tries to explain that change, he immediately conveys his implicit assumption that the change was not obvious and therefore needs explanation. In either of these cases, he will usually base his evaluation on a theory of change against which to evaluate his empirical findings.

These implicit assumptions become explicit as soon as a researcher makes known his intentions on comparison by stating the method and objectives of his study. His explicit assumptions might be formally stated or only loosely put; they might also be expressed by partial models relating to a given sector of an economy or society, or take the form of a comprehensive model of a total environment in which the relevant phenomena are being observed. Finally, a model itself might be an abstract ideal type, or it might be a real type based on empirical findings of research in similar cases.[77] The real type of explicit model is the most common in traditional, formal comparative analysis in the social sciences.

The difference between implicit and explicit applications of the comparative method is that in the former case many of the requisites of the method might be slighted and the advantages of comparison, therefore, less than fully realized. Furthermore, to the extent that the assumptions are not known in advance, ambiguity or confusion can result. A researcher may consider it permissible to use his data to support his views without abiding by the requirements of a method he is implicitly using. In this discussion, however, we are concerned with the explicit use of the method as applicable to two or more empirical situations.

There are many advantages of comparison. The comparative method makes it necessary to account for all the relevant data in all the cases under study. Commenting on the beginning of historical and statistical

[77] For the difference between ideal and real types see Spiethoff, "Pure Theory and Economic Gestalt Theory."

studies in England, Alfred Marshall saw a "certain narrowness" due mostly to the limited use of comparison. "Hume, Adam Smith, Arthur Young and others had been led by their own instinctive genius and the example of Montesquieu occasionally to compare social facts of different ages and different countries, and to draw lessons from the comparison. But no one had grasped the notion of the comparative study of history on a systematic plan. In consequence, the writers of that time, able and earnest as they were in their search for the actual facts of life, worked rather at haphazard. They overlooked whole groups of facts . . . of vital importance, and they often failed to make the best use of those which they collected. And this narrowness was intensified when they passed from the collection of facts to general reasonings about them." [78] Systematic comparison precludes incomplete analysis or the inadequate and biased selection of variables. The larger the number of relevant cases in the social sciences, or experiments in the physical and biological sciences, the higher the probability that all the significant factors will be detected and observed. In any one case, certain factors can be observed and others overlooked, but in the comparison of a large number of cases many more factors will be observed and less are likely to be left out altogether.

Comparsion is particularly advantageous in the study of economic change because it tends to bring to attention the significance of the noneconomic factors that might be overlooked or left out in a more isolated case study. In an isolated study, a researcher might justify holding the noneconomic factors constant, but he can hardly do so in a comparative approach because of the inevitable need to clarify relevant concepts, to standardize data, and to interpret and explain differences within the relevant context. This means that should similar initial economic conditions fail to be followed by similar results, the inconsistency might be found in the influence of noneconomic factors. For instance, inflationary tendencies could be found favorable to development in one country, but not so in another. The reason could be differences in the psychology or attitudes of the entrepreneurs in these countries. Without camparison, these influences would be difficult to observe.

One of the most important advantages of comparative method is that it sidesteps the difficulty of experimentation in the social sciences —it permits scientific analysis of social and economic change without

[78] Alfred Marshall, *Principles*, 8th ed. (London: Macmillan & Co., 1922), p. 762.

complying with the rigid requirements of repeated experimentation. Comparative method removes the need for repeated experiments to the extent it increases the number of cases studied, either by comparing different segments in the life span of the same unit, or by comparing apparently relevant phases of a number of units. Each of these phases can be regarded as an experiment in which the same conditions are set up by following a uniform pattern of observation and analysis. In other words, comparison can be longitudinal or cross-sectional. The biological or physical scientist does the same thing when he conducts a number of experiments simultaneously to avoid the difficulty of repetition and the time lag entailed in repeated experimentation. The social scientist deals with conditions that change slowly and cannot be subjected to experimentation. Therefore, by use of the comparative method he may be able to overcome these problems and hope for scientific results in his research.

However, certain conditions must be fulfilled before comparison becomes possible. The first prerequisite for comparison is a common conceptual framework within which all systems or subsystems can be compared.[79] A conceptual scheme is essential for the uniform selection and classification of data and for the identification of the expected explanations of the events under study. The conceptual scheme is not necessarily a theory or even a hypothesis. It is closer to the conceptual scheme described above as a definitional set of concepts; the only difference is that the concepts used for comparative analysis tend to be more general and more abstract so they will be applicable to a wider range of empirical data. What is stipulated here is only an analytical system of concepts or definitions to standardize and guide the search for the explanations of given events.[80] These concepts obviously must express certain relations, but these relations need not be universal or proven theories. They need only be relevant, logical, and applicable to the data, and can be created especially for the specific purpose of the study or studies being undertaken. Actually, these concepts or definitions might be derived on the basis of comparison such that a generalizable meaning can be expressed in the concept.[81] A system of ideal

[79] Gunnar Heckscher (*The Study of Comparative Government and Politics* [London: Allen & Unwin, 1957], pp. 67–79) discusses the principles of comparison.

[80] On the analytical scheme see Leibenstein, "What Can We Expect . . . ?"; and Crane Brinton, *The Anatomy of Revolution* (New York: Vintage Books, 1952), chap. 1.

[81] Eucken, *Foundations of Economics*, pp. 301–302.

types might also be perfectly appropriate for the purpose, even if the relations deriving from it are neither proven nor universal.[82]

This prerequisite has often been interpreted in ways that tend to undermine comparison. It has been asked, for example, how we can justify comparison between unique events across cultures or intertemporally. What significance does the experience of the Greeks and Romans have for present-day society? Or, more relevant, what significance does the experience of the industrialized societies have for present-day developing countries? The conditions have changed and the behavioral expectation should have too. Therefore, comparison is possible only if the principle of uniformity of nature and if a theory of evolutionary development of societies are assumed, which may not be valid.[83]

It is true that unless a certain degree of uniformity of human behavior can be assumed, no comparison can be undertaken. *Uniformity* means that people in similar situations facing similar problems can be expected to seek and find similar solutions. The assumption of uniformity, however, is not true *a priori*; it is a historical observation. For example, when people outgrow the land potential they colonize new territories, emigrate, or conquer. Changes in technology that may add another alternative solution do not invalidate the proposed pattern of alternatives, but simply enlarge the scope of the search. Therefore, if the model for comparison stipulates that under certain circumstances people search for alternatives for survival, it is meaningful to ask why certain societies failed to do so, or what alternatives were tried, which were not, and why. In other words, comparison requires only fundamental similarities and a certain degree of uniformity. On the other hand, as long as historical events are not considered to be unique, in which case the relevance of historical study might be questioned, comparison can usefully proceed by considering the similarities and differences between apparently unique experiences. In fact, unless a certain degree of uniformity of behavior is assumed, the prediction of behavior would be impossible, and empirical research would lose much of its value.

The assumption of uniformity has also been interpreted as the

---

[82] This is different from comparison with an "idealized" situation, regarded by Rondo E. Cameron as one of the pitfalls of the method ("Summary of Discussion," *Journal of Economic History* 17 [1957]: 596).

[83] Kenneth E. Bock, "The Comparative Method of Anthropology," *Comparative Studies in Society and History* 8, no. 3 (April 1966): 272, 275.

acceptance of the evolution, gradualism, and stage development of societies; therefore, all societies should be expected to evolve progressively through similar stages, and the history of certain societies may be reconstructed on the basis of the experiences of better-known societies. Whether the assumption of uniformity and its implications can be justified will not be treated here. It is enough to suggest that this particular interpretation is extreme: uniformity of behavior need not be a zero-sum proposition. It is adequate to assume that when societies face similar conditions, uniformity applies and similar behavior patterns can be expected. It does not follow that such similar conditions should prevail in all societies or at all given stages.

Nor is it correct to stipulate an evolutionary theory for the application of comparative method.[84] Comparison can be applied to isolated events or to classes of events in different societies as long as the initial conditions include certain similarities. Whether war, prosperity, or famine are aspects of an evolutionary development is irrelevant, but when facing these similar conditions, different societies can be expected to take similar measures, and any deviation must be explained by differences in initial conditions or intervening factors.

Most researchers use the comparative method in empirical research without assuming an evolutionary or stage theory of development. The apparent difficulty may be due to the proposed research objective. If the objective is to reconstruct history, a theory of history may be necessary, but this is not true of all forms of application of the comparative method, and certainly not when only certain events or classes of events are being compared. Therefore, neither an evolutionary nor a stage theory assumption is necessary for comparison as long as a certain degree of uniformity of nature is taken as a premise.

The second prerequisite for comparison is that the cases to be compared have not only similarities but differences. The failure to observe similar results from similar conditions should be explicable from evident differences in the conditions leading to the different results. The similarities, however, must be related to fundamental features of the cases to be compared, and the differences should be observable among the results. Alternatively, similar results should be attributable to differences in the initial conditions. For example, similar tenure arrangements might lead to different results, or similar results might follow from different tenure arrangements. Comparison would be useful to explain these variations.

[84] Kenneth E. Bock, *The Acceptance of Histories*, pp. 106–107.

The relevant comparable features could be structural, functional, or organizational, such that variation in these features should be expected to influence the events under consideration, but not exclude them from the class under study. For example, two economies could be compared on the basis of their fundamental institutions—land tenure, degree of competition, structure of government, or the institutions of money and credit. Comparison could also proceed on the basis of similarities in the structure of these institutions by describing their organization. Or it could be based on a study of the functions of these institutions in different economies. Another possible basis of comparison might be the objectives of economic behavior and the processes by which these objectives are realized. A comprehensive comparative analysis can take more than one set of criteria into consideration. In all cases, however, the similarities and differences must be identified and the expected results specified.

The assumptions and prerequisites of comparative method bring into focus additional problems associated with its application. These problems are in many ways similar to those faced by any other research method in the social sciences, but are more serious. The data must be available for more cases; selection and classification are more difficult; standardization of the material is more complicated; and the researcher must be familiar with more than one social and cultural environment.[85] The problem becomes more complicated when the conceptual scheme used as a point of departure seems to be inapplicable to all the cases under study, in which case the data and recorded information could mean different things in the different observations. These are technical difficulties that might render a comparison impossible or of limited usefulness. Care, ingenuity, and experimentation, however, will overcome most of these problems. At least it is tempting to try to overcome them, knowing that the advantages of successful comparison can hardly be exaggerated, regardless of whether the method is utilized in the physical, biological, or social sciences.

In conclusion, comparative method is an indispensable tool in the study of economic change, all the difficulties and implications notwithstanding. To render the study of economic change as useful and as scientific as possible, it is imperative to (1) recognize and apply comparative method as a necessary tool, (2) make all the assumptions

---

[85] For a historical critique of the method see *ibid.*, pp. 37–40, 55–56. The critique, however, is based on assumptions that are not essential or even useful to comparison.

explicit, (3) maintain uniformity and consistency in using these assumptions in all cases being compared, and (4) take as a point of departure the principle of uniformity of behavior, at least in a general way.

## Synthesis

The explanation of single events or groups of events is central to economic history. However, the ultimate objective is to discover laws, formulate generalizations, or—which is the same—to be able to predict behavior from more general principles. Although general principles can be intuitively or deductively derived, empirical research studies are a major source. From these can be synthesized the findings of pertinent research that relates to a class of events and has provided general rules of behavior. Synthesis, in this context, is primarily the comparison of results, rather than of initial conditions explaining single events. The latter will have been done by the monograph writer or the analytic and interpretative historian. The synthesizer, because of the immensity of his undertaking, must depend on the findings of others. Thus his results can be only as good as the results he compares.[86]

Comparative analysis is based on the conviction that generalization is possible and that causal laws can be discovered. It implies also, at least in the social sciences, that the uniformity of and similarity between events is frequent enough to permit induction from the unique to the general. Put more broadly, synthetic comparison implies that a philosophy of history, or at least a general theory, is ultimately possible. Whether a researcher starts with a hypothesized philosophy or a theory of history, or whether he attempts inductively to formulate one, the possibility of such a philosophy is stipulated.[87]

Comparison implies almost by definition that knowledge can be acquired from the observation of similarities and contrasts between these events.[88] Should trends or tendencies be observable, it is necessary

[86] Some might question the possibility of synthesis just as they question the suitability of tools "perfected for short-period analysis to the study of particular events or problems of the past" (W. T. Easterbrook, "A Long-Period Comparative Study: Some Historical Cases," *Journal of Economic History* 17 [1957]: 572). This pessimistic view, however, has little historical evidence to support it.

[87] There seems to be confusion in the statement that "genetic studies are fundamentally comparative" (N. S. B. Gras, "The Present Condition of Economic History," *Quarterly Journal of Economics* 34 [February 1920]: 215–216).

[88] Formally, *comparison and contrast* means inference through eliminative induction, advocated by Keynes and others, as preferable to enumerative induction, which

to explain these trends or discover the causes underlying them in the hope that future events can thereby be predicted. That is, prediction is implied as a possibility. It is almost natural to regard as a necessary objective of comparative history the accumulation of knowledge leading to the formulation of generalizations.[89] If a historical generalization could be adopted as universal, the result would be a philosophy of history.

The stipulation of a philosophy of history as a necessary objective is apt to cause misunderstanding. The idea that the "use of the comparative method involved acceptance of some principle on which culture differences could be arranged in a presumably temporal series" led Comte and his contemporaries to regard their acceptance of the philosophy of continuous progress as an adequate precondition for application of that method.[90] What if no such objective exists, or what if no such philosophy is possible? Synthesis and the comparative method can still be applied as long as there exists a possibility of the discovery of trends and the formulation of generalizations. In other words, a philosophy of history or universal laws are only ultimate goals that may never be realized. It is adequate to stipulate the possibility of discovering a partial philosophy or theory of history or change in a narrow environment, if not in the world at large. If it is possible to generalize that in a certain type of environment and in a given set of conditions certain events may take place, synthesis and comparison are fully justified. This flexibility is an obvious and necessary condition, because exhaustive comparison in any area of the social sciences would be an immense undertaking. Therefore, comparison can be undertaken to any degree of exhaustiveness, without undermining the implicit assumptions regarding generalization or philosophy of history, which require exhaustive observation. The inevitable results of a less-than-exhaustive comparison are findings that must be viewed as tentative and limited in application.

On the other hand, the stipulation of a philosophy of history does not mean a researcher must be committed to any such philosophy. It does not mean his commitment, for example, to a cyclical theory of history, or to the evolutionary approach, or to any deterministic or

simply enumerates supportive or comparable events for evidence (S. F. Barker, *Induction and Hypothesis*, pp. 50–52).

[89] On the relation of comparison to generalization see Bock, *Acceptance of Histories*, pp. 124–127.

[90] *Ibid.*, p. 10.

nondeterministic interpretation of events.[91] The possibility of discovering a philosophy or universal law of history relates only to the
objectives or results of a study, not to a presupposed hypothesis; and
whereas commitment tends to bias research, acceptance of the possibility of discovering a philosophy requires only that research remain
open-ended and that a researcher be receptive to the possibility.[92] It
should be noted that the possibility of generalizing is not a novel
requirement of research. It has been accepted to the extent that the
prospect of discovering universal laws has been a prime mover in the
study of history.[93]

## THE RESULTS

It may be a truism to say that the conclusions of research are determined to a large extent by the nature of the data and the method of
analysis. These in turn are determined by the objectives of the research,
the availability of data and appropriate tools, and the philosophical
inclinations and training of the researcher. Once the objectives have
been decided and the data and methods chosen, however, the generality
and explanatory power of the results may be determinate. Conclusions
or generalizations cannot be classified as pure types or as mutually
exclusive, but certain types of generalization can be specified for and
roughly identified with certain types of data and methods of analysis.

The variety of types of generalization has been explored by several
historians. M. I. Finley divides generalization into three types.[94] The
first type of generalization classifies as either a noun or an adjective.
The word *Greek*, for example, is a generalization. "It is literally impossible to make any statement including *Greek* which is not a
generalization." The second type classifies by period. *Classical, neoclassical, ancient, modern,* and *archaic* are all classifications indicating

[91] See above references to Gerschenkron (chap. 2, fn. 11; chap. 3, fns. 31, 32).

[92] Thrupp has suggested that the reason the results of the comparative approach
in the area of growth were limited in the nineteenth century "lies in the philosophies of history that made nineteenth-century comparativists beg the question of
growth, in the limited use they made of continuous series of documentary evidence,
and in their consequent frequent failure to identify the agencies that were responsible for new turns of development" ("Comparison in the Development of Economic Theory," p. 570).

[93] Isaiah Berlin, "History and Theory," *History and Theory* 1, no. 1 (1960): 4.

[94] M. I. Finley, "Generalizations in Ancient History," in *Generalization in Writing History,* ed. Gottschalk, pp. 21ff.

similarity among members belonging to the same period and non-similarity between those belonging to different periods. When economists speak of the classical school, they have in mind a certain group of economists who have common doctrines, philosophies, or methodologies, even though each member of the group may have unique beliefs or approaches of his own. The third type is the "kind of generalization on which attention is usually concentrated—[it deals with] *interrelations* of events and, beyond that . . . causes, . . . [and provides] answers to the question Why?" This is the type of generalization usually under attack because of the nature of historical and social phenomena.

Louis Gottschalk's more detailed classification divides the various types of generalization into six categories: (1) The School of the Unique, whose members "maintain that the historian's purpose should be to emphasize differences rather than similarities, to deal with the special rather than the comparative and general." According to Gottschalk, members of this school "make generalizations only if they are unaware that they are doing so," because they assume that events are unique and generalization is impossible. In essence, these historians emphasize the compilation of facts and chronicles. (2) The School of the Strictly Limited Generalization, to which belong the "purely narrative-descriptive historians." Members of this school do generalize "knowingly but intend to limit their generalizations strictly to the exposition of the historical subject matter under investigation and of that subject matter only in its own setting." For example, if they were dealing with the British economy in the first quarter of this century, they would limit their generalization to that place and period. (3) The School of Generalization on the Basis of Trends includes the "interpretative historians, those who strive to establish some hypothesis or theory that will help to explain a number of interrelated historical events." They take into consideration the relations between "antecedent, concurrent, and subsequent events" in the hope of interpreting the events. Thus, in the example study above, they would look into events of the periods before and after the quarter century for information. However, they too limit their interpretative synthesis to the period and environment under study. (4) The School of Generalization on the Basis of Comparison, or the comparative historians, who are ready to go beyond their subject matter. They find "parallels and analogies to it in other times or places of the past, whether or not otherwise interrelated." This is synthesis by comparative illustration with past experience in other settings. (5) The School of Predictive Generalization, whose generalizations are intended for prediction of the future. The members of this school "venture propositions about past trends or analogies in such general or abstract terms as to leave the implications, if they do not indeed state explicitly, that their propositions may well be extrapolated to events in the future." These may be described as the "nomothetic historians," or the seekers of laws in history. (6) The School of Cosmic Generalization, or the philosophers of history. The members of this school seek to discover *the* laws of historical development, and "propound philosophies that are intended to provide a cosmic understanding of the course of human events past and to come." [95]

Gottschalk summarized these categories from a survey of past generalizations and opinion, and they are intended only as a convenient system of classification, for they are imprecise and most of them overlap with each other. For example, the third through sixth schools are rarely followed strictly, and a member of any school may belong more or less to one or more of the other schools. A generalization on the basis of a trend can be formulated either from a longitudinal study of one environment or comparatively from a cross-sectional study of several environments. In either case, a generalization based on observed tendencies serves as both a hypothesis and a guide for prediction, depending on the degree of validity attached to it. Finally, any interpretative generalization is cosmic to a certain degree and contains elements of a philosophy of history. The difference between an empirically derived generalization aiming at a philosophy of history and one of more limited aim is a matter of degree. This overlapping is best illustrated by the examples given by Gottschalk to elaborate his categories. Among members of the Interpretative School are Weber, Pirenne, and Turner. Yet, Gottschalk himself admits that the theories of these scholars pertain to wider and more general environments. And are they not predictive and comparative? Similarly, the nomothetic historians were also comparative, since they found "some basis for prediction or possible control of future behavior" and examined "seemingly comparable sets of past events." The universalists, also, were not a pure type uniform in approach. There were those who, like Machiavelli,

[95] Louis Gottschalk, ed., "Categories of Historiographical Generalization," in *ibid.*, pp. 113–114.

desired to control behavior less than did others, but on a universal basis. Others like Hegel and Marx were interested in the "overall course and the end-product of the historical process." [96] But was not Marx predictive, interpretive, comparative, and also interested in capitalist economic behavior as an economic system?

Nevertheless, Gottschalk's system of classification has important implications; that is, a method or approach is colored by a researcher's objectives, which are based on his conception of historical analysis. There is an important element of subjectivity in choosing objectives, but once they are chosen, the method becomes determinate. Therefore, by observing the relation between type of generalization and method of analysis in the studies by economic historians, it may be possible to predict a generalization from the method, or to control a generalization by controlling the method. It may also be possible to evaluate the contribution of a given study by assessing the consistency between method and conclusions reached, as is proposed in the following chapter.

[96] *Ibid.* pp. 122, 123, 124.

# 3

# An Evaluative Model
# of Historical Research

As a summary of Part One, a model, of framework, will be proposed which may serve as an evaluative standard for research and writing in economic history. This model is based on four assumptions. First, there is a direct relation between the data, method of analysis, and the generality of results obtained. Second, the relation between these variables can be formalized to serve as a standard of evaluation and as a tool for predicting the nature of the results. Third, it is possible to suggest an ideal combination of data and method for each type of generalization. Finally, it is possible to estimate the degree to which research in economic history validates this model, and to determine to what extent the actual results are consistent with the potential results. These assumptions will be further elaborated below. Table 2 represents the proposed model.

The entries in table 2 have been discussed and with one exception need no further explanation. Gottschalk's six categories of generalization have been reduced to five: the comparative and the predictive, or categories 4 and 5, are combined, since both go beyond our subject matter and form a basis for prediction. This applies whether the study is cross-sectional or diachronic.

The degree to which each feature is represented in a particular study will vary according to its relevance and the degree to which a researcher has used it. For convenience, we have assumed that each feature may be represented to one of three levels of degree—high, medium, or low— and a numerical ranking will be adopted for each level of degree, ranging downward from 3 to 1. In other words, a feature ranked 3 is one used with high frequency, regardless of whether such use is appropriate or not. For example, one might use quantitative data extensively and thus assign a rank of 3 to that feature, only to find that these data tell nothing about the problem unless combined with a qualitative study of the relevant institutions.

To render these classifications useful, the relation between the data,

84

method, and results might be formalized such that a certain combination of data and method would be prerequisite for and should lead to a certain type of generalization. Thus, the type of generalization to be formulated would become predictable; also a given type could be purposely chosen as the appropriate data-method combination. Table 3

TABLE 2
Evaluative Framework of Historical Research

I. Data
    Relevance (defined unit of study)
    Primary indicators
    Secondary indicators (institutional)
    Historical-hypothetical
    Quantitative
    Qualitative
    Interdisciplinary
    Comprehensive-selective
II. Methodological Choices
    Descriptive
    Analytical
        Conceptual scheme
        Systems analysis
        Deduction *
        Induction
        Statistical inference *
        Econometrics *
        Comparative
    Synthetic
III. Results
    Generalization
        Unique
        Limited
        Trend (interpretive)
        Comparative-predictive
        Cosmic
    Conclusive (valid)
    Verifiable

Note: In an ideal study, each feature would be represented to a high degree, or rank 3.
* The feature is useful but not essential.

represents the possible data-method combinations. The numerical rank of each feature is what seems to be the ideal degree of use required for deriving each type of generalization. These combinations and ranks are presented as an ideal framework and proposed here as a hypothesis, pending evaluation below. From table 3 we see, for example, that a primarily "unique" generalization would require rank 3 on relevance, 3 on primary data, and so on down the column. Each type of generalization can then be associated with the appropriate combination of numerical ranks for data and method and for degree of conclusiveness and verifiability. The rationale of these rankings should be briefly noted.

Regardless of the type of generalization to be derived, it is necessary to define the unit of study in order to establish the relevance of the data. (Although this may seem obvious, the problem of relevance often causes confusion and difficulty in historical research.) However, primary data tend to be important only for unique and limited generalizations, whereas secondary data are more relevant for the broader generalizations. The rationale of the proposed association is that generalizations answering the "what" and "how" questions require more descriptive (primary) data than do the generalizations answering the question "why." The latter must depend greatly on (secondary) data associated with institutions and other explanatory factors.

The problem of historical *versus* hypothetical data is troublesome because of the ambiguity of what economic history aims at. One might argue that history deals with experience and therefore only historical data are relevant. This, however, does not preclude hypothetical situations or counterfactual hypotheses. It only implies that the hypothetical situation must be constructed on the basis of historical data and knowledge. Therefore, regardless of the type of generalization, the ideal in economic history is historical data.

Whether quantitative or qualitative data should be used depends on the research objectives and on which sort of data is more available. For unique and limited generalizations, quantitative data are more relevant and possibly more accessible. However, as a generalization becomes broader, it becomes more difficult to obtain quantitative data, and also such data become less indispensable. This qualification is not a matter of convenience; broad generalizations, which are usually explanatory or predictive, must take into consideration factors that cannot be quantified. That is why qualitative data are re-

TABLE 3
Ideal Data-Method Combination
by Type of Generalization

| FEATURES OF STUDY | GENERALIZATIONS | | | | |
|---|---|---|---|---|---|
| | Unique | Limited | Trend | Comparative-predictive | Cosmic |
| *Data* | | | | | |
| Relevance (unit of study) | 3 | 3 | 3 | 3 | 3 |
| Primary indicators | 3 | 3 | 2 | 1 | 1 |
| Secondary indicators | 1 | 1 | 3 | 3 | 3 |
| Historical-hypothetical | 3 | 3 | 3 | 3 | 3 |
| Quantitative | 3 | 3 | 2 | 2 | 1 |
| Qualitative | 2 | 2 | 2 | 3 | 3 |
| Interdisciplinary | 1 | 1 | 2 | 3 | 3 |
| Comprehensive-selective | 3 | 3 | 3 | 3 | 3 |
| *Method* | | | | | |
| Descriptive | 3 | 2 | 1 | 1 | 1 |
| Analytical | | | | | |
|   Conceptual scheme | 3 | 3 | 3 | 3 | 3 |
|   Systems analysis | 1 | 1 | 3 | 3 | 3 |
|   Deduction | 1 | 2 | 2 | 1 | 1 |
|   Induction | 1 | 3 | 3 | 3 | 3 |
|   Statistical inference | 1 | 2 | 3 | 3 | 3 |
|   Econometrics | 1 | 3 | 2 | 1 | 1 |
|   Comparative | 1 | 1 | 2 | 3 | 3 |
| Synthesis | 1 | 1 | 3 | 3 | 3 |
| *Results* | | | | | |
| Conclusive | 3 | 3 | 3 | 3 | 3 |
| Verifiable | 3 | 3 | 3 | 3 | 2 |

garded as more relevant for the broader than for the limited generalizations. The distinction in the degree of relevance of quantitative and qualitative data is based in part on the proposition that the broader generalizations require interdisciplinary data more than do the narrower generalizations. Some of the interdisciplinary data simply cannot be quantified, and yet they are indispensable for the broader generalizations. Finally, regardless of the generalization type, a generalization is more defensible the more comprehensive the supporting data are. Conversely, more selective data permit a less defensible generalization.

Therefore, the more comprehensive the data, the closer they are to the ideal of research in history.

As for method of analysis, description is more appropriate for the limited than for the broader generalizations, which is the reverse of the relation between synthesis and generalization. The relationship between the analytical method and generalization is less straightforward. As in the case of data relevance, a conceptual scheme or framework is necessary, regardless of the type of generalization. Obviously, the framework should vary according to the generalization expected, but the principle remains applicable. A systems approach is not important, however, in seeking unique or limited generalizations, but is essential for broader generalizations that establish trends or serve for predictive purposes. The logic of this stipulation is simply that trends and predictive conclusions cannot be made without consideration of the various interdependent factors that relate to the event under consideration.

Deduction and induction are not easily separated. Ideally, economic history is based on inductive inference, except in deriving unique generalizations, for which description is adequate. In contrast, deduction, which relies on premises more general than the expected explanation, can be of relevance mainly for the limited and trend generalizations, for which a pertinent theory may be available. Even in these cases, an explanation can be only partially deductive since the objective is to explain historical situations that are less perfect or logical than the theory. The same kind of relation has been proposed for econometrics and generalization, primarily for the same reasons. The relation is different, however, in the case of statistical inference. Although the lack of quantitative data might hinder the application of statistical theory to the broader generalizations, controlled use and analysis of the data is indispensable. Statistical theory is less relevant for the limited generalizations, because inference is generally not required.

Comparative method is indispensable for the two broadest types of generalization, because comparison is the only meaningful substitute for experimentation in historical research. Where narrower generalizations are concerned, comparison may still be useful, but it is less essential.

There is little need to explain the relevance of conclusiveness and verifiability. Both are integral parts of any sound method of research and scholarship. The only imperfect relation proposed here is that between verifiability and cosmic generalization; a cosmic generalization is never derived from complete and fully verifiable data. An element of speculation persists and it is therefore not subject to complete verification or testing.

The extent to which this model applies will be explored in the next two chapters.

# PART TWO

## Traditional History:
## Illustrations and Critique

# 4

# Observations on
# Traditional Methodology

Part Two of this book may seem presumptuous in referring to Traditional History when, in fact, it deals with only a small number of contributions as illustrations. Even as illustrations they cannot possibly represent all the varieties of history and the approaches to it. My objective is much more modest. It is primarily to pinpoint some of the more conspicuous problems met with in economic history as they are illustrated by representative studies that have been chosen to include works from various chronological periods, cultural environments, and schools of thought and works of a variety of topics and objectives. The selection may have been somewhat arbitrary, but this could hardly be avoided. With few exceptions the contributions have already left an impact on research in economic history and in the social sciences in general, and they may be responsible in part for some of the methodological problems common in these fields.

The contributions under study are: (1) Karl Marx, *Capital* (only volume one will be analyzed because it contains a large part of the substance of his contribution in *Capital*, but mainly because it embodies the methodological features of all the volumes combined; the other volumes add no new methods or approaches); (2) Max Weber, *The Protestant Ethic and the Spirit of Capitalism*; (3) Henri Pirenne, *Mohammed and Charlemagne*; (4) John Clapham, *The Economic Development of France and Germany, 1815–1914*; (5) Frederick J. Turner, *The Frontier in American History*; (6) Eli F. Heckscher, *Mercantilism* (only the first volume has been included because, by his admission, the second volume deals with the history of economic thought rather than with economic history; furthermore, volume one contains all the methodological problems with which this critique is concerned); (7) Paul Mantoux, *The Industrial Revolution in the Eighteenth Century*; and (8) Rondo Cameron, with the collaboration of Olga Crisp, Hugh Patrick, and Richard Tilly, *Banking in the Early Stages of Industrialization*.

A few points of clarification are appropriate at this stage. First, this critique does not consist in book reviews as far as substance is concerned, except to illustrate problems of analysis or of the derivation of conclusions. My concern is primarily with the ways the conclusions have been reached in each of the works.

Second, I am not concerned with critiques or reviews by other scholars, although an extensive bibliography of these critiques is appended for the benefit of the reader. The field of observation is restricted to the contributions themselves and not to the contributors, who might have made different methodological contributions in other works. The frame of reference is the scheme, or model, presented as the summary of Part One.

Third, this approach is empirical and comparative, and it assumes that a comparison of the features of the representative contributions can shed light on the usefulness of the model and on the basic problems of research and writing in history. Admittedly, there are grave dangers in comparing these studies, which might have little in common. Hence, each contribution is treated in terms of its own objectives and the consistency between the data, the methods of analysis, and the conclusions reached.

The critique will be presented in four chapters. This chapter will investigate the methodology of the representative contributors and present a summary of the findings in table 4. This will constitute a frame of reference for the discussion of the following three chapters, which deal respectively with data, methodological choices, and results.

Although none of the studies to be considered is primarily a study of methodology, invariably the authors have something to say on the subject, sometimes to defend their own approach, but more frequently because they have thought of the problem and have taken a stand on it. Marx, of course, was a philosopher and therefore, to nobody's surprise, was interested in the problems of logic and inference. His comments on methodology are brief but revealing. For example, he explicitly associates his choice of England as case study with the availability of better statistics, thus revealing his interest in empiricism and precision. However, he defends his choice on more fundamental grounds, namely that England provided a laboratory for the study of capitalism, which did not at the time prevail in any other country. He explains his position by analogy. "The physicist either observes physical phenomena where they occur in their most typical form and most free from disturbing influence, or, wherever possible, he makes experiments under conditions that assure the occurrence of the phenomenon in its normality. In this work I have to examine the capitalist mode of production, and the conditions of production and exchange responding to that mode. Up to the present time, their classic ground is England." [1] Although Marx's argument seems logical, it raises basic questions. How well formulated should be the phenomenon under investigation before it is put to the empirical test of observation, and how well known should be the case study before it is selected for study? In other words, how perfect a model should the investigator have before proceeding to observation, and how familiar should he be with his case study before selecting it? Both questions are relevant to the debate as to whether Marx derived his theory before or from observation, and whether he chose the empirical examples only to illustrate and support his theory.

Marx draws attention to the methodological differences between presentation and inquiry. "The latter has to appropriate the material in detail, to analyze its different forms of development, to trace their inner connection. Only after this work is done, can the actual movement be adequately described. If this is done successfully, if the life of the subject-matter is ideally reflected as in a mirror, then it may appear as if we had before us a mere a priori construction." [2] This means that unless the inquiry is included in the text, the presentation can be evaluated only on logical grounds or as a matter of trust in the writer or both. This renders verification of the detail and the connections between these details almost impossible.

Marx believed that empirical inquiry demands a certain degree of conceptualization and abstraction to render the many variations and details manageable. Thus, the term *capitalist* is a conceptual construct. [3] The capitalist is the expression of a mode of production and is, therefore, a generalized phenomenon, as is the capitalist mode of production itself. A conceptual construct may be based on empirical observations, but it is not observable. It is not reality, but is as close to reality as possible. In other words, a conceptual construct is derived by a combined effort of deduction and induction in order to understand the motions of the phenomenon under investigation, in this case the total society.

[1] Karl Marx, *Capital*, 1:vii, 644.
[2] *Ibid.*, pp. xxix–xxx.
[3] *Ibid.*, p. xix.

In these methodological observations Marx addresses himself to one of the most controversial issues in the social sciences, namely the contradictions between determinism and free will. If, as he suggests, "society can only shorten and lessen the birth-pangs" of the new order, then the pattern of social evolution is fairly set.[4] Therefore, the objectives of social investigation should be to discover the laws of evolutionary change by combining empirical observation with deductive inference. Marx tries to redefine determinism and free will in order to reconcile them. For example, he accepts as predetermined only the general pattern and direction of change, but insists on the flexibility of detail or the rate of change. This definitional freedom of action apparently is a legitimate tool of the researcher.

It is probably unrealistic to evaluate Weber's involvement in methodology on the basis of The Protestant Ethic, since he devoted a whole volume to the methodology of the social sciences. On the other hand, there is no reason why the reader of a certain contribution should be familiar with all other contributions of an author before he can appreciate a particular one. Therefore, in consistency with the plan of this critique, and on the assumption that a given contribution is complete in itself unless otherwise stated by its author, only the particular works will be explored.[5]

In The Protestant Ethic Weber emphasizes the impact of environment on the historian, the difficulty of dealing with universal problems, and the significance of both subjectivity and empiricism in deriving universal concepts. Taking himself as an example, he asserts that one who is "a product of modern European civilization, studying any problem of universal history, is bound to ask himself to what combination of circumstances the fact should be attributed that in Western civiliza-

[4] Ibid, p. xix.

[5] For those interested, the most relevant points can be found in Max Weber, The Methodology of the Social Sciences, pp. 56–90. One methodological observation seems quite pertinent in this context; namely, the relation between economic theory and history, which was problematic in Weber's time as it is today. Weber concluded that "the 'abstract' theoretical method . . . shows unmediated and ostensibly irreconcilable cleavage from empirical-historical research." Abstract theory fails to encompass all the relevant facts necessary to explain historical events and, moreover, seems to be deducible from fundamental psychological laws which are themselves unknown. Therefore, economic theory can serve only for ideal types which cannot explain reality but are indispensable for heuristic and expository objectives. In that sense, "the ideal typical concept will help to develop our skill in imputation in research; it is no 'hypothesis' but it offers guidance to the construction of hypotheses" (Methodology of the Social Sciences, p. 90).

tion, and in Western civilization only, cultural phenomena have appeared which (as we like to think) lie in a line of development having *universal* significance and value." Although Weber indicates his intention of dealing with universal phenomena, he insists that the phenomena be put in historical perspective and the concept be derived empirically. "It must be gradually put together out of the individual parts which are taken from historical reality to make it up." In any case, investigation must be guided by a concept, which cannot be defined *a priori*, but for which a convenient meaning can be specified "in order clearly to understand the object of the investigation." [6]

Weber distinguishes, as Marx did, the requirements for different types of research. Certain study problems require accuracy and detail; others are satisfied by general observations. For example, in dealing with the concept of rationality, he states that "so far as the transactions are rational, calculation underlies every single action of the partners. That a really accurate calculation or estimate may not exist, that the procedure is pure guess-work, or simply traditional and conventional, happens even today in every form of capitalistic enterprise where the circumstances do not demand strict accuracy. But these are points affecting only the degree of rationality of capitalistic acquisition." For the purpose of establishing rationality as a fact or tendency, it is enough to establish as fact that money income and expenditure are compared before the transaction.[7] In other words, to observe tendencies requires less accuracy than does measuring the intensity of the tendency.

Weber is aware of the difficulty of analyzing human behavior and motivation with precision or by primary indicators. Therefore, he suggests that overt behavior should be related to the underlying phenomena. "Just as the Christian is known by the fruits of his belief, the knowledge of God and His designs can only be attained through a knowledge of his works." [8] Hence, interest in empiricism is a means to understanding the essence of such phenomena as rationality or asceticism, which is not subject to observation. Nor can a Protestant's interest in physics and technology be taken at face value.

Compared with Marx and Weber, Pirenne was more a historian than an economist or social scientist. Direct contribution to methodology in *Mohammed and Charlemagne* is almost nonexistent. (This, however,

[6] Max Weber, *The Protestant Ethic*, pp. 13, 47, 48.
[7] *Ibid.*, p. 19.
[8] *Ibid.*, p. 249.

can be misleading; Pirenne has been a contributor to the methodology
of history and the social sciences.[9]) To the extent that Pirenne makes
no direct statements in this particular work, our evaluation will be
confined to the example he set.

Turner is almost equally silent on methodology in *The Frontier in
American History*. His only direct mention of method is his criticism
of economists and others who formulate theories and laws on the basis
of the present but resort to history for illustrations.[10] He seems to insist
that the right approach is to observe historical processes and to induce
therefrom the theories and laws that might be relevant. This suggests
Turner's commitment to empirical investigation and his conviction that
theories and laws can be formulated from historical research.

Like Pirenne, Clapham has made a direct but separate contribution
to methodology.[11] However, in his *Economic Development of France
and Germany* he is more conversant than Pirenne on the subject, especially when he tries to explain or justify his approach. For example,
he states in the introduction that the history of a country can be studied
only within its larger context, even though the economic forces of an
era or a region may be studied by illustrations from shorter periods or
smaller areas. Thus, "all the economic forces which were at work in
Western Europe during the long peace can be illustrated in French
and German history. That history must be put into a European, and
in its later phases an international, setting if it is to be thoroughly
understood." In other words, history can be understood through the
study of a sample but only in relative terms. The effects of the French
Revolution, for example, can be studied only relative to its objectives
and to what prevailed before its occurrence. Similarly, changes in agriculture can be understood only if the "starting point" and the "point
of arrival" are clearly stated.[12]

Clapham often speaks of *testing* his conclusions, but there is little
consistency in the meaning he attaches to the term. *Test, indicator,
illustration,* and *index* are all used interchangeably.[13] Nevertheless, his
interest in testing his conclusions and in using an index for standardiza-

[9] Henri Pirenne, "What Are Historians Trying to Do?" in *Methods in Social
Science*, ed. Stuart A. Rice (Chicago: Chicago Univ. Press, 1931), pp. 435–445.
[10] Frederick Jackson Turner, *The Frontier in American History*, pp. 330ff.
[11] J. Clapham, "Economic History as a Discipline," in *Encyclopedia of the Social Sciences* 5–6 (1957), p. 328.
[12] J. Clapham, *The Economic Development of France and Germany*, pp. 5, 6, 27.
[13] *Ibid.*, pp. 53, 70–71, 82, 126.

tion of the data cannot be mistaken. Like the other contributors, Clapham associates method with objective, but somewhat differently. For broad surveys he finds it appropriate to omit "minor" sectors of the economy, even though the minor sector might be from sixteen to eighteen percent of the total.[14] This illustrates Clapham's conception of the immensity of history and the necessity of condensation to cope with the problem.

Although Clapham says hardly anything in this study about the objectives of studying history, some implications are apparent. "At the end of any economic survey of history, it is right to stop and ask—and what have the developments of this time and these places done for the common man? The answer cannot be in terms of happiness, for which the economist has no measuring rod. And it cannot be precise, whatever the terms. Still it can be attempted." Clapham thus introduces the study of welfare as the objective of history. He also expresses an opinion regarding measurement and precision. He advises that in the absence of the means to be precise, comparison and relative estimates are the only alternatives, to which he resorts in this study.[15]

Heckscher has contributed to debates on methodology, both in *Mercantilism* and elsewhere.[16] In many ways his studies represent the beginning of what has been called the new economic history. To begin with, Heckscher expresses dissatisfaction with the "insufficient attention to economic theory" by economic historians. His remedy is to use theory more often, to combine it with facts, and to always give a reason for any conclusions presented. Like Marx and Weber, Heckscher considers it essential to use concepts that represent the phenomenon under investigation, such as the concept of mercantilism. However, a concept is only a tool to identify certain phenomena and implications, regardless of time and place. In other words, abstraction is necessary for convenience, even though it entails oversimplification. Heckscher defends abstraction as a way of simplifying complex problems and as a means of isolating economic from noneconomic aspects. Abstraction provides "some selective principle" without which historical phenomena become a mere conglomeration of data. In other words, Heckscher asserts the need for a model, or framework, by which facts can be understood and explained.

[14] *Ibid.*, p. 199.

[15] *Ibid.*, pp. 402, 407.

[16] Eli F. Heckscher, "A Plea for Theory in Economic History," *Economic History*, o.s. 1 (January 1926): 525–534.

He explains the need for abstraction and for a model as means to put a study in the right perspective. In studying economic policy, for example, the content of policy is more relevant from the economic standpoint; whereas from an administrative standpoint, only the form is relevant. Furthermore, the economic historian has to consider both ends and means, while other researchers may be satisfied with one or the other. The reason, according to Heckscher, is inherent in the meaning of economics as "the adaptation to given non-economic ends and the apportionment of means to such ends." [17]

Heckscher is concerned with theory, but his concern is with "scientific" theory, by which he means that a body of ideas must form a "consistent whole," and the discussion of the problem be "intellectually 'autonomous,' . . . aimed at objectively accurate solutions, irrespective of their practical outcome." [18]

Heckscher's modernity is expressed in his explicit statement about the application of the counterfactual approach to historical research. In his own words, "to understand clearly the reconstruction of the states after their dissolution in the Middle Ages, it is best to ask what might have happened had their renascence never occurred. It is, undoubtedly, a severe mental test to try to remould history in this fashion. But to form a conception of what part one of many contributing factors played in historical development, it is necessary, in every such attempt, to make the tacit or explicit assumption that one or the other of these factors was absent and then to ask what the result might have been." [19] Heckscher is emphatic in this position, as he asserts in another context. "Every investigation of the consequences of an individual factor involves a train of experimental reasoning and an answer to the question of what conditions would have been like had the particular factor not been present, or had it taken some different form. Historians who have no use for such conjectural reasoning must therefore refrain from passing judgment on the effects of individual forces in a common development." [20] These statements render the "new economic history" not so new after all, at least with respect to the counterfactual hypothesis.

Although Heckscher emphasizes concepts and theory, he does not

[17] Eli F. Heckscher, *Mercantilism*, pp. 14, 19, 22, 26.
[18] *Ibid.*, p. 27.
[19] *Ibid.*, pp. 41–42.
[20] *Ibid.*, pp. 436–437.

ignore facts. He criticizes those who reach conclusions on the basis of partial evidence, but he warns against taking facts at face value, for the facts might be misleading. For example, policy measures do not always mean that these measures have been implemented or that the results are obvious. The economic historian should be able to judge the fact from the fable.[21]

Mantoux's interest in methodology, at least as represented in *The Industrial Revolution in the Eighteenth Century*, is indirect and emanates from the need to justify his approach. Nevertheless, his comments relate to basic issues of method. For example, Mantoux stresses the role of empiricism in proposing definitional concepts, which must describe reality. "Is it not better to choose the most inclusive one [definitional concept], the one which not only indicates the origin or one of the origins of the phenomena it describes, but which comprises the phenomena in their entirety and thus makes use of their actual interrelation to define them?" Comprehensive definitions may not be elegant or clear, but neither would they be artificial or arbitrary classifications. Economic phenomena are easily put in clear and distinct classifications only by rendering them artificial and remote from reality. Therefore, to cope with reality, definitions should center around a characteristic tendency of a phenomenon, rather than be specific and precise but far from the real world.[22]

Mantoux's interest in empiricism is expressed by his emphasis on facts, "even if only a partial observation of the facts were possible." Without precluding abstraction, he warns against misunderstanding the role of abstraction, which tends to oversimplify reality. "Marx, when he applied to this study all his faculty of abstraction, reduced the movement to much simplified terms and divided it into too sharply defined epochs. Moreover, we must beware of accepting as accurate descriptions of facts what, in Marx's mind, had chiefly an explanatory value." In other words, what is appropriate for theory may not be appropriate for history. This point is more explicitly treated. "When we have to define and classify phenomena from the economic or philosophical point of view, it is enough if we only consider their characteristics. But, from the historical point of view, we must also take into consideration what we may call their volume and their weight, their actual effect on surrounding phenomena, everything which determined the material rela-

21 *Ibid.*, pp. 71, 102, 133, 265–266.
22 Paul Mantoux, *The Industrial Revolution*, pp. 40–41.

tionship of facts, so different sometimes from the logical chain of principles and consequences." Economic laws are needed to help explain complex phenomena, but one should be aware of the danger of oversimplifying through abstract laws. Furthermore, to be scientific, laws can be discovered "only by patient inductive work conducted on strictly scientific lines," not by intuition and abstract deductive analysis. Only facts and observation can lead to a clear understanding of historical analysis.[23]

For weighing evidence or evaluating facts, Mantoux advocates the use of counterfactual argument, and postulates the need to back conclusions with economic law. The counterfactual is primarily a way of arguing an issue such that one is innocent until the opposite is proved. In other words, positive evidence is invoked rather than arguments supporting the counterfactual.

Cameron et al., authors of the most recent study included in this critique, *Banking in the Early Stages of Industrialization*, have had the advantage of experiencing current debates on the problems facing economic history and historical research. They have made explicit statements on methodology at least in defense of their work and its relevance. They observe, for example, that "historical experience is revelant to the problems of the contemporary world. Recorded history is to the human race what memory is to the individual: it is the 'collective' memory of society." [24] Although the authors do not state the basis for these statements, they seem to accept, at least in broad terms, the principle of uniformity of nature. Otherwise, what is the function of memory or the relevance of past experience to the present or the future? Only if one accepts this principle will memory help in shedding light on the present or in deriving generalizations or laws of behavior. The analogy with memory has another important implication, namely that society is an integral unit just like the individual. Otherwise, "collective" memory becomes meaningless. This implication is important in the sense that a given society must be studied as a unified body or unit. Thus, the analogy between society and individual is taken as a premise for studying an economy in the aggregate.

The authors do address themselves to this question when they try to justify the choice of nations as units of study. Their reasoning, however, does not do justice to their cause. They choose nations as units of study

[23] *Ibid.*, pp. 42, 89, 196, 347.
[24] Rondo Cameron et al., *Banking in the Early Stages of Industrialization*, p. 3.

because legislation is usually introduced on the national level, and because the statistical data are collected in the aggregate.[25] Although these reasons are based on truth from a practical point of view, they do not justify the approach. Legislation is national because a country is already a unit. Statistics are collected in the aggregate because an economy is already a unit. To think otherwise is to mistake the effect for the cause. Unless an economy can be regarded as a unit from a behavioral standpoint, it would be unjustified to study its movements in the aggregate, regardless of the form of legislation or the manner in which statistics are collected.

The authors advocate comparative method in history as being "particularly valuable in that the comparison of a number of cases not only reveals the variety of combinations by which development can be achieved, but also offers the possibility of observational controls, the closest approach to laboratory techniques available in most of the social sciences." The main precondition for successful comparison is to choose cases that are "really comparable in some meaningful sense." Unfortunately, we are not told what would make "meaningful sense" as a general guide to selection. It is also not clear why the cases should be comparable but not also in contrast to each other. It is doubtful that the authors have intentionally disregarded the contrast aspect of comparative method, but no explicit statement is made except to regret the omission of cases different from those chosen.[26]

The authors seem committed to the study of history, but they caution against misuse of the results. "A knowledge of history, although useful in understanding social processes in general, cannot be used for purposes of prediction except in a most cautious and qualified sense. In the final analysis one discovers the limitations on the uses of history from history itself. But the theorist or policy maker who dismisses historical experience as irrelevant to the problems of the present with some such phrase as 'everything is different now' is himself indulging in a historical generalization of very doubtful validity." [27] Although the caution may be justified, the reasoning behind it is quite brief or even lacking. If no prediction of some sort is possible, what relevance has history to the present. Every explanation and generalization implies the ability to predict. What is the rationale for comparison, synthesis, and generali-

25 *Ibid.*, p. 5.
26 *Ibid.*, pp. 4, 5.
27 *Ibid.*, pp. 5–6.

zation if not to increase the ability to predict. Again, the authors tend to hint at their interest in method and the philosophy of historical study, but much is left unexplained.

The authors are also brief and vague when they assert as obvious that "the historical search should be guided by theoretical notions," and that if no theory is available, a sort of normative set of principles or theoretical relations can be stipulated.[28] In other words, they seem to specify the questions of historical research in the form, Did event *e* happen, assuming it could have happened? This, however, leaves no room for questions such as, What did actually happen? and How did it happen? even though no theoretical notion of the happening may exist. In view of their silence on these issues, it is sufficient to draw attention to what they say, leaving out what they do not say.

This brief survey suggests that problems of the method or philosophy of history have been on the minds of all the contributors we have considered, and that the degree of their involvement in these problems varies from one to another, at least to the extent that such involvement is set out in writing. Nevertheless, the questions dealt with are basic. Furthermore, although no definitive solutions of the methodological problems have been proposed, the comments and statements are indicative of the pattern of research in economic history. For example, all the authors emphasize the indispensable role of empirical observation, the need for facts, and the right perspective. Much attention has been paid to abstraction and concepts, and to theory as a guide in research, but little is said about how theory should be derived. Only Mantoux makes an explicit statement; namely, that laws of behavior must be derived by scientific induction. On the other hand, there is an apparent wariness toward the role of theory because of the oversimplification inherent in theory and abstract concepts. There is also an awareness of the difficulty of precise measurement and exhausting the data. In fact, there is a tendency to accept illustrations as sufficient to establish general trends. The problem of relevance—how to define the unit of study and what questions to ask—also occupies a great deal of attention, particularly because there is a danger of mistaking the potential for the actual, and the symptom or effect for the cause. In at least two cases there is direct reference to the counterfactual approach, even though these two contributions are more than a generation old. Finally, there is an awareness

[28] *Ibid.*, p. 7.

TABLE 4
Relation Between Data, Method, and Results

| Features of Study | Marx | Weber | Pirenne | Heckscher | Clapham | Mantoux | Turner | Cameron | Fogel * |
|---|---|---|---|---|---|---|---|---|---|
| *Data* | | | | | | | | | |
| Relevance (unit of study) | 2 | 2 | 3 | 2 | 2 | 2 | 1 | 3 | 3 |
| Primary indicators | 2 | 1 | 3 | 2 | 2 | 3 | 1 | 3 | 3 |
| Secondary indicators | 3 | 3 | 2 | 3 | 3 | 1 | 2 | 3 | 1 |
| Historical-hypothetical | 3 | 3 | 3 | 3 | 3 | 3 | 3 | 3 | 2 |
| Quantitative | 2 | 1 | 1 | 2 | 3 | 1 | 1 | 3 | 3 |
| Qualitative | 3 | 3 | 3 | 3 | 3 | 3 | 1 | 3 | 1 |
| Interdisciplinary | 3 | 2 | 3 | 3 | 2 | 2 | 3 | 1 | 2 |
| Comprehensive-selective | 2 | 2 | 2 | 2 | 2 | 2 | 1 | 3 | 1 |
| *Method* | | | | | | | | | |
| Descriptive | 2 | 1 | 1 | 2 | 3 | 1 | 1 | 3 | 1 |
| Analytical | | | | | | | | | |
|   Conceptual scheme | 3 | 3 | 1 | 2 | 1 | 2 | 2 | 2 | 3 |
|   Systems analysis | 3 | 1 | 2 | 2 | 1 | 2 | 2 | 2 | 2 |
|   Deduction | 2 | 1 | 1 | 2 | 1 | 1 | 1 | 2 | 3 |
|   Induction | 3 | 3 | 3 | 3 | 2 | 3 | 2 | 3 | 2 |
|   Statistical inference | 2 | 1 | 1 | 1 | 1 | 1 | 1 | 1 | 3 |
|   Econometrics | 1 | 1 | 1 | 1 | 1 | 1 | 1 | 2 | 3 |
|   Comparative | 2 | 2 | 3 | 3 | 2 | 2 | 1 | 3 | 1 |
| Synthesis | 3 | 3 | 3 | 3 | 1 | 3 | 3 | 3 | 1 |
| *Results* | | | | | | | | | |
| Type of generalization | | | | | | | | | |
|   Unique | 1 | 1 | 1 | 1 | 3 | 1 | 1 | 1 | 1 |
|   Limited | 1 | 2 | 2 | 3 | 2 | 3 | 1 | 1 | 3 |
|   Trend | 2 | 3 | 3 | 2 | 1 | 1 | 3 | 3 | 2 |
|   Predictive-comparative | 3 | 2 | 2 | 1 | 1 | 2 | 2 | 3 | 1 |
|   Cosmic | 2 | 1 | 1 | 1 | 1 | 1 | 1 | 1 | 1 |
| Conclusive | 3 | 2 | 2 | 1 | 2 | 2 | 2 | 2 | 2 |
| Verifiable | 2 | 1 | 2 | 2 | 2 | 2 | 1 | 3 | 3 |

Note: The numerical rankings represent the relative frequency of use or representation of a feature in the study.

* The contribution of Robert W. Fogel is representative of the new economic history and will be discussed in chapter 9.

of the difficulty of experimentation in historical research. As a substitute
for experimentation, the contributors tend toward comparative method.
In the following chapters we will explore the extent to which problems
have been avoided and the various methods of handling them. A brief
summary of the findings is presented in table 4, which will serve as a
focal reference for subsequent detailed evaluation.

The results represented in table 4 must be interpreted with great
caution for four reasons. First, the chart does not indicate the objectives of each of these studies. Since there is a relation between the
objectives and the data and method of analysis, the rankings shown may
represent an oversimplification, but this will be remedied in later discussion. Second, the numerical rankings represent only an impression
of the degree to which the various features are used or represented in the
case studies; they do not represent the quality or proficiency of use.
For example, a rank 3 for comparative method means that great
emphasis has been put on comparison; it does not indicate the degree of
perfection in implementation. Third, the ranking, even after a thorough
study of each of the contributions, nevertheless involves a certain
amount of unavoidable subjectivity. However, to reduce this impressionism, the ranking has been checked against rankings made independently by three generations of graduate students in their capacity as
members of my graduate seminar in economic history. Fourth, the table
indicates one of the most common problems in economic history and
the other social sciences, namely, the disparity between the ideal type,
or model, and the real world. In my ideal model (see table 3) each
type of generalization is associated with a certain data-method combination. In reality, none of these representative contributions is
restricted to one type only. Most of them reach a combination of at
least two types of generalization and thus render almost impossible a
clear association between the three main classes of features in the table.

In comparing table 3 with table 4 it will be seen that of five of the
component features that should be ranked 3, regardless of the generalization type, only one has been given that rank in table 4. As in table 3,
relevance, historical emphasis, and comprehensiveness of the data, a
conceptual scheme, and conclusiveness are all ideal features that should
be ranked high in any study. Yet, only the historical emphasis has
achieved that rank in all the contributions. They all emphasize empirical
data that are historical, not hypothetical or simulated. On the other
hand, it seems the other features that should have ranked high could

not be so ranked despite the intentions of the contributors. One might even suggest that it is in the nature of historical and social research that perfection in these fields can be only an ideal, since it cannot be realized without compromising the scope, content, or objectives of such research. This observation will be elaborated in the separate discussion of each of these features.

# 5

# The Data

## DATA RELEVANCE AND THE UNIT OF STUDY

The value of data depends in large part on their relevance to a problem under investigation. Relevance, however, is determined by the degree to which the problem is well defined and the unit of study clearly identified. The degree of clarity and the precision of identification are in part functions of the problem itself. Phenomena relating to human behavior, especially if viewed over a relatively long period, may be difficult to delimit or identify in the form of units of study. These difficulties are well illustrated in the studies we are considering. Despite the contributors' interest in specifying their problems of study, only two have attained a rank 3 on relevance. One ranked 1, and all the others ranked 2. Whether this low level could have been avoided is not certain, but the negative impact this has on the results, especially for purposes of communication and verification, cannot be mistaken.

Marx, for example, is interested in studying capitalist enterprise to discover the laws of motion on society. The place is England; the period is the era of capitalism up to his time. In his words, "I have to examine the capitalist mode of production, and the conditions of production and exchange responding to that mode." [1] Given these problems as the topic of study, all kinds of data may seem generally relevant. What is the unit of capitalist production or enterprise to be studied? Or does the whole of England form a unit? Do data from any place in the country serve the same function? Put differently, if England is the unit, then the data must be aggregates; otherwise the unit must be smaller than the whole of England. Is the unit a type of business enterprise? This is not clear either. The phenomenon studied is a relationship and all data that may shed light on that phenomenon would be relevant, whether these are consistent with or contradictory to that relationship. However, even this general framework is still vague because the geographical and chronological boundaries of the study are not specified. Would an example from 1760 be relevant, or should the period be limited to after 1800? Unless the time period is

[1] Marx, *Capital*, pp. xvii, 664.

specified, it is difficult to determine whether certain data are relevant or not. Marx is aware of the problem of data relevance; he thus tries to illustrate by examples.

Marx speaks of units of unskilled labor as his theoretical standard of measurement. However, to illustrate the declining number of laborers employed, he counts persons regardless of their skills, the remuneration they receive, or the number of hours they work.[2] Similarly, some data cover two decades, whereas other data relate to one or two years only. This renders any estimate of the weight to be given to the illustrations very difficult. Although it may be difficult to define the phenomenon clearly as a unit of study, it is possible and necessary to specify the boundaries from which data drawn will be relevant.

The same observations apply to Weber, who ranks moderate on relevance. Weber studies "the spirit of capitalism," which cannot be defined except by observation of the historical reality. If so, what should one look for when observing? Weber complicates the problem further by suggesting that for a study such as his, accuracy is not necessary and general observations may be sufficient, but that even these general data should not be taken at face value.[3] However, no criteria are given for determining the degree of accuracy or direct relevance to be adopted. This leaves room for each individual to decide which data are relevant, as he himself does.

Weber is aware of the need to specify the unit of study as a step toward establishing data relevance. However, he asserts that no geographical or chronological boundary can be specified until either a hypothesis regarding a phenomenon has been formulated or until the existence of the phenomenon has been empirically observed. In other words, it is up to the researcher to select the data that he himself regards as relevant. Thus time and geography are not important in his case; only the phenomenon itself is important for relevance. Even after Weber formulated a hypothesis, the boundaries remain unclear. That subjectivity is an important element of his contribution is suggested by the fact that Weber discounts the relevance of apparently similar capitalist developments in other environments simply by asserting that certain fundamental features of Western capitalism were missing in those environments.[4]

[2] *Ibid.*, p. 450.
[3] Weber, *Protestant Ethic*, pp. 4, 19, 249.
[4] *Ibid.*, pp. 13–17.

Similar problems characterize Pirenne's contribution, even though his topic is more amenable to specification. He speaks of Europe, of the Roman world, and of the Mediterranean basin as if they were all his unit of study. He tries to define his unit of study as an economically united area centering around the Mediterranean, which tied Rome to its provincial sources of supply and to the centers of commerce and trade. Africa provided wheat; Constantinople, manufactured goods; and the eastern Mediterranean area, the entrepreneurs who carried out the Roman trade. "Thanks to the Mediterranean, then, the Empire constituted, in the most obvious fashion, an economic unity. It was one great territory, with tolls, but no custom houses. And it enjoyed the enormous advantage of a common monetary unit." [5] Pirenne also tries to establish the temporal boundaries. The period begins prior to the barbarian invasions and ends with the revival of European trade and the redirection of economic activity northward in the ninth century.

Thus, the economic, geographical, and temporal boundaries leave much room for vagueness. For example, was the unity Pirenne speaks of a reality? What magnitude of interdependence existed between Rome and the provinces? Or how many slaves, entrepreneurs, or bushels of wheat would have to have been traded for interdependence and unity to exist or cease to exist? On the other hand, the barbarian invasions extended over three or more centuries. How does one describe these centuries as the beginning of a period, given the amount of change that might have taken place? Pirenne is aware of these complications and the difficulty of precision. Therefore he searches for processes rather than for specific events as data. Specific data are then relevant only as benchmarks. The search for processes need not be easier; in fact it can be much more difficult unless the researcher allows himself too many liberties. Despite these ambiguities, Pirenne's attempt to define this unit of study deserves a high ranking.

Heckscher's *Mercantilism* involves as many difficulties of specification as do the three preceding topics. Heckscher describes his study as being concerned with Europe, but mostly with Britain and France. The subject is not economic development but the history of the policy influencing it, "not the economic system in itself but with the attempts to influence or mould it consciously in one way or another." Economic policy is considered both a cause and an effect of economic conditions. The period covers "the time between the Middle Ages and the age of

[5] Pirenne, *Mohammed and Charlemagne*, p. 19.

*laissez-faire,*" which begins and ends at different times in different countries. This definition "presents the time factor with sufficient clarity." [6] These boundaries may seem specific enough to determine the relevance of the data, but Heckscher does not specify the criteria for identifying policy or the relevant effects. In fact, he does not define policy; nor does he define the Middle Ages, *laissez-faire,* or the beginning or end of either of these periods. Instead, he finds it sufficient to use examples from a period of over six centuries to support one point or another, as if they all belonged to the same period or phase of policy development. In a sense, Heckscher knows he has not resolved the problem of relevance, and he therefore finds it necessary to specify again and again what his plan is. For example, he plans to "deal with policy in the sphere of feudal disintegration, that is, simply with the circumstances of disruption, without considering its special economic import . . . [and] then go on to the attempts made to nationalize the consciously designed and firmly co-ordinated policy of the towns." Yet neither *feudal* nor *disintegration* are clarified. He also wonders, when speaking of England, whether "we understand the territory taken as a whole, ruled by the king." He leaves the reader wondering, and deals with England, Great Britain, or a portion of each as seems convenient. Again he specifies the area of study as "concerned not with fiscal policy in itself but with its influence on industrial regulation." [7] However, *fiscal policy* is not defined, nor is it clear how its influence can be measured. Many interpretations of this statement can be made, and the relevant data will vary according to the interpretation adopted.

Heckscher tries at several points to establish relevance criteria or to define the unit of study, but the results remain unclear and difficult to specify objectively. The unit relevant to the phenomenon he is studying could be a motive, a policy, or a body of thought. Presumably all will be clear when the phenomenon itself is clarified. Therefore, Heckscher devotes many pages to the discussion of mercantilism as the phenomenon, but with little success in removing subjectivity as the means of data selection.

In contrast, Clapham's study should permit the precise and accurate delimitation of a framework and unit of study. If this were done, the problem of relevance would be resolved. However, Clapham's view of history complicates the issue. The history of a country must be viewed

[6] Heckscher, *Mercantilism,* pp. 13, 20.
[7] *Ibid.,* pp. 44, 52, 182.

in a larger perspective that includes the international environment. The area under study is France and Germany; the period, 1815–1914, which forms a political unity. Yet, because "in continental Europe political and economic boundaries rarely coincide," it is not certain how relevant political unity is, or whether the unit is the political or the economic environment.[8] In practice, he deals with nations, segments of nations, and even specific villages and towns in each country. He also deals with Spain, Italy, England, and sometimes America. In a sense it may be misleading to speak of a unit of study in this context. The study deals with various sectors of the French and German economies as separate entities, and it may therefore be more accurate to speak of the railways in France or of steel in Germany than of the French and German economies. Furthermore, no way is specified by which these individual sectors can be combined as parts of the same unit. Apparently, the objective is to study the parts as units, which may be consistent with his times, because the tradition of national accounts and aggregate economies was not yet established when his book was first published. Nevertheless, given these individual units, the data are economic variables that describe change in each of them. There is no uniform checklist as to what one should look for to describe, measure, or explain change. The author follows his intuition as to what constitutes change and relevant data.

In order to delimit the scope of his investigation and establish data relevance, Mantoux defines his field of interest in terms of geography and time, both of which are determined by the process of change itself. For example, the midland and northern counties of England were selected as "the chief home of the events which are the object of our study." The chronological limits were dictated by the substance of change. "Arnold Toynbee . . . wanted to begin it [the Industrial Revolution] in 1760 and carry it on until 1820 or 1830. We have preferred, for reasons which seem to us conclusive, to close with the first years of the nineteenth century. By then the great technical inventions, including the most important invention of all, the steam engine, had all become practical realities. Many factories were already at work which, apart from certain details as tools, were identical with those of today. Great centers of industry had begun to grow up, a factory proletariat made its appearance, the old trade regulations, already more than half destroyed, made way for the system of *laissez-faire*, itself even then

[8] Clapham, *Economic Development of France and Germany, 1815–1914*, p. 29.

doomed through the pressure of already half-perceived necessities. The law which inaugurated factory legislation was passed in 1802. The stage was ready set; there was nothing left but to follow the working out of the drama." [9] Thus the component topics of the study, the location and timing of the phenomenon, are specified from practical considerations. These classifications, however, are too broad and vague in that they leave it up to each author or reader to decide which data are relevant and which are not. Which industries should be studied and what kinds of change are not specified. It is not even clear whether we are dealing with the aggregate economy or with certain sectors as independent units.

The lowest degree of data relevance is evident in Turner's study of the American frontier. Turner seems concerned with a process, a movement, or an idea which he connects with the frontier. The frontier or section is a unity he stresses frequently.[10] The unity is not political, and state boundaries can be ignored because they create only artificial unity. The unity of the Middle West lies in the "physiography, in the history of its settlement, and in its economic and social life, a unity and interdependence which warrant a study of the area as an entity." However, no evidence of this unity is given, nor is it even suggested what criteria of each of these factors are relevant. If evidence is given, it is in the form of opinion or assertion. For example, "the acquisition of Louisiana was a recognition of the essential unity of the Mississippi Valley." The problem studied is the impact of the frontier on American life, but it is not clear how the impact should be studied. Actually, the variables observed vary from frontier to frontier and from period to period, as will be shown below. Even though the book is a collection of essays, these essays deal with a common theme which requires uniform criteria to establish relevance of the data. Such criteria are nowhere to be found in any of the essays.

Unlike Turner, Cameron et al. present a good example of successful unit specification and data relevance. All the case studies in the collection follow the same theme. Cameron et al. have taken good advantage of a topic quite amenable to specification. To ensure relevance of the data, the authors formulate and seek answers to a number of questions relating mainly to the relation between banking and industrialization; [11] they specify the geographical areas and time period for

[9] Mantoux, *The Industrial Revolution*, p. 42.
[10] Turner, *The Frontier*, pp. 68–69, 127, 188–189.
[11] Cameron et al., *Banking in the Early Stages*, pp. 6–7.

each of the case studies, and the questions raised in each of the seven
case studies are used in the synthesis. To that extent, there is little ambiguity as to what data are relevant or to what area or period they apply.
A problem that allows some vagueness and reinterpretation centers
around the role of banking in industrialization. The theoretical relations
adopted as guiding principles are themselves based on broader assumptions that have not been empirically verified and are therefore
inadequate to guide the interpretation. For example, what constitutes
the contribution of banking to growth? Did the banks cause growth or
were they an outgrowth of economic expansion? [12] These questions are
relevant in this context only to the extent to which wrong data may be
gathered or right data left out. The authors, however, have been candid
in their interpretations to allow for margins of error that may be due to
low relevance.

In conclusion, in the majority of cases it appears a problem of
relevance exists. The topic or objective of study is not always well defined. The unit of study is somewhat vague. The criteria of relevance
or the questions investigated are not well specified. Consequently, the
authors in most of these cases tend to follow their intuition in gathering and classifying data and in deriving therefrom answers to their
self-styled questions. On the other hand, knowing the thoroughness and
care of most of these contributors, one might wonder whether the problem of relevance could have been solved more satisfactorily, given the
nature of the topics dealt with. The two contributions in which
specificity or relevance were high dealt with relatively narrow and
primarily economic variables. In other words, the weakness might be
due more to the complexity of the subject matter than to the quality of
scholarship. If so, as I tend to believe, it may be hopeless to expect a
higher degree of specificity and relevance unless the research is redirected toward topics that can be handled with more specification and
relevance.

## PRIMARY AND SECONDARY DATA

The problem of data relevance is closely related to most other research
features of the representative contributions. This is well illustrated in
trying to determine the degree to which primary or secondary data are
used. We have defined as primary data those directly related to the

12 *Ibid.*, pp. 7ff.

event, whereas secondary data relate indirectly and indicate only potential events. There is no visible trend as to when primary or secondary data have been used. Table 4 suggests that secondary data are used more frequently than primary, regardless of the type of generalization. It would seem that most primary data are never complete and must therefore be supplemented by indirect information for a full understanding of the phenomenon under investigation. A corollary of this interpretation is that the contributors are too sophisticated to take primary data at face value and thus seek additional evidence related indirectly. Furthermore, the use of secondary data may indicate a belief that historical phenomena are too complex to be observed directly or by means of data from any one discipline, and that although indirectly related, data from other disciplines are necessary because of the interdependence that characterizes human behavior, as in fact several contributors have stated explicitly.

Looking at table 4, we notice that the use of primary data is high in three cases, low in two cases, and moderate in three cases. In contrast, secondary data are used intensively in five cases, moderately in two, and to a limited degree in one. As stated earlier, primary data relate more to description or the "what" question, whereas secondary data relate to the "why" and "how" questions. This can be seen in the individual contributions.

Marx's objective is to study the laws of motion of society in a capitalist framework. Capitalism was already a reality in England. Therefore, his primary data are mainly to illustrate the existence of capitalism and some of the dynamics of that system. However, he was also and primarily interested in explaining why these dynamics prevailed and what was to come next. Therefore, he needed both primary and secondary data, the first to illustrate and the second to explain. For example, to illustrate the misery of the proletariat he goes into a detailed description of the conditions of workers in the factories, the concentration of incomes, the accumulation of capital, and the exploitation of the workers. He gives quantitative and qualitative data on these happenings for at least certain years and localities. Then he shows how all that was possible. Although the economic laws of capitalism necessitate these processes, he seeks further evidence about the institutions of society which could, at best, suggest the possibility that these processes would prevail. The best example is his elaborate discussion of the Factory Acts, passed between 1833 and 1864, to show how economic and noneconomic forces interact—how the conditions of work related to health, and the hours of work to the power of the employer, the laxity of law enforcement, and the influence of the capitalist in the law courts. In discussing the Act of 1850, he says that "whilst the bill was under discussion, the Factory Inspectors laid before Parliament statistics of infamous abuse due to this anomaly. To no purpose. In the background lurked the intention of screwing up, during prosperous years, the working day of the adult males to 15 hours by the aid of the children." [13] Thus, Marx shows how his data on misery are relevant, and how the economic forces were reinforced by social and political factors, all of which could not be seen by a mere estimate or description of the conditions themselves. This approach is further enchanced when direct data are not available, as for conditions in agriculture, in which case Marx resorts to institutional changes for support of his thesis.

Weber is even more in need of secondary data than Marx, because his topic leaves little room for direct, or primary indicators. Weber is admittedly in search of the underlying motives of capitalism, having observed it as a reality. His problem is the spirit of capitalism as represented by rationality, methodical and systematic business management, and a high propensity to save and invest—characteristics that Weber believed were the result of worldly asceticism, a calling, and the desire to prove one's worth, since the essence is known by the fruits of one's labor. Therefore, by showing that these motivating preconditions were developed by Protestantism prior to the development of capitalism, he concludes that a positive relation exists between the two developments, and proceeds to show how Calvinism made these motivating factors common. In other words, he does not use primary data to show the relation between Protestantism and capitalism, such as the number of Protestants who went into business after conversion, or the number of Catholics who failed in business because they did not convert. Nor does he estimate the number of savers and investors in each group, or the number of actual believers of the Protestant ethic, relative to the non-believers, in and out of business. Such figures might indeed be impossible to obtain. In any case, the data he uses are indirect evidence that, if dependable, would show only that Calvinism and Protestantism did promote asceticism, rationality, and hard work. Such evidence would not suggest the actual development of capitalism, only its

[13] Marx, *Capital*, pp. 263–264, 500ff, 281.

potential development, unless supported by an analysis of the mechanism by which the spirit and the behavior are connected, and by evidence that the mechanism was actually implemented.

This argument, however, may be objectionable on the grounds that Weber was interested in establishing the relation between Protestantism and the "Spirit of Capitalism" rather than capitalism as an economic behavior, in which case the number of businessmen or the figures on actual saving would not be important. Even though this interpretation may be admissible, the data used would still seem to be secondary. Primary indicators would include the degree to which Protestants had in fact acquired the spirit of capitalism in comparison to those among Protestants and non-Protestants who did not. That asceticism, rationality, and hard work were preached and written about would indicate only the possibility that these values were adopted, but not that they were or to what extent.

Pirenne's contribution is a closer mixture of primary and secondary data, with more emphasis on primary than on secondary sources. His problem centers around the economic unity of the Roman Empire, the breakdown of that economic unity, and its revival, which he directly observes in terms of the volume and composition of trade, which he specifies as indicators of unity, through the Mediterranean at the beginning of the period. Pirenne also studies as direct indicators changes in the volume and direction of flow of coins and taxes before and after invasion by the Moslems—whether currency changed, and to what extent Rome was still the capital. But Pirenne is aware that unity depended on other criteria that would show indirectly whether such unity was possible. Therefore, he deals with various factors that might suggest why the barbarian invasions could not have disrupted the unity of the empire; why the barbarians could be absorbed and assimilated, whereas the Moslems disrupted the unity and objected to assimilation. Thus, he deals with religious and cultural institutions—the Church, language, literacy, and the arts. He also observes demographic changes and property rights that might indicate change or potential change in the structure of the empire. For example, the invading Germans "were not a conquering army, but a people on the move, who settled down on such fertile soil as was available." [14] Therefore, so runs the conclusion, they could not have disrupted the unity of the empire.

[14] Pirenne, *Mohammed and Charlemagne*, p. 35.

However, this does not mean that they did not, unless all the premises on which such a statement is based are accepted a priori, rather than empirically derived.

Because of the indefinite nature of his unit of study, Heckscher encounters problems in trying to isolate primary from secondary data. If policy measures constitute his topic of study, then a discussion of legislation represents primary data and direct evidence. However, if his topic is the impact of these measures on development, then legislation becomes a secondary indicator and actual changes in the economy need to be investigated as primary indicators of that impact. Nevertheless, differentiation between primary and secondary data is essential in that secondary indicators suggest only potential rather than actual changes, as Heckscher himself recognizes.[15] To avoid this dilemma, Heckscher uses both kinds of indicators. He points out attempts at unification and then tries to evaluate the success of these attempts. He discusses legislation in detail and then goes on to evaluate the effectiveness of its implementation. A few examples will illustrate. Although England had a uniform system of customs duties, Heckscher observes that its application was neither uniform nor complete. There is evidence that in the third quarter of the seventeenth century the king of France attempted unification by denouncing "the encroachments of the tolls, but the general impression is that no positive result was achieved," as Heckscher proceeds to illustrate. Attempts to unify weights and measures in France were made over a number of centuries, but the outcome was modest until the French Revolution achieved unification.[16] Heckscher uses both types of data intentionally. In fact he makes such a sweeping statement on this point that it deserves quotation. "The description of the mercantilist system given hitherto has been confined solely to statutes and ordinances. But these, at most, express intentions. To determine their influence on actual economic development it is necessary to go beyond the written ordinances. In thousands of instances, the prescriptions alone must have had no effect whatever when applied throughout a large country with a low standard of social development and with the poor administrative machine of the *ancien régime*." [17] Heckscher provides several examples to support this statement.

[15] Heckscher, *Mercantilism*, pp. 115, 166, 196, 215, 239.
[16] *Ibid*., pp. 52, 83, 97, 110–114.
[17] *Ibid*., p. 166.

Clapham's contribution is confusing because he does not define his problem. What does *economic development* mean and, more specifically, what constitutes *economic*? The answers to these questions would make it possible to differentiate between primary and secondary data. To begin with, Clapham presents direct indications of economic change in the form of output, prices, interest rates, credits, transportation, and other detailed data on specific changes in the economy. He goes further by treating institutional changes that might suggest economic change. It is not clear, however, whether these institutional changes are treated as part of economic development, in which case they would be primary data, or as contributing factors, and thus secondary indicators. These institutions could have been treated as a part of social history and as related only indirectly to economic development. Clapham does not explicitly differentiate these uses of the data, although certain implications can be attributed to his approach. For example, he deals with emancipation of the peasantry, commercial policy, and the cooperative movement as they relate to agricultural reform and rational farming. He deals with agricultural societies, exhibits, shows, and fairs as means of spreading information beneficial for advanced farming, but all these suggest only potential changes. He also treats in detail the role played by the government.[18] In fact, he devotes almost a third of his study to a discussion of institutional changes, both those with positive and those with negative effects on the economy. In all cases, however, the potential impact is taken for granted; the relation between these institutional changes and development is not presented. The reader is expected to know that relation.

Mantoux is more analytical than Clapham, and he therefore discusses the relation between the various factors of the Industrial Revolution more elaborately. He tries to explore all possibilities to obtain data, knowing that data are not easily accessible. His interest lies mainly in primary data—the actual size of industries, price levels, or the location and distribution of industry and production. However, when such data are not available, he resorts to secondary indicators. For example, he notes the dispersion of industry prior to the Industrial Revolution by following travelers in various districts and by showing the distribution on maps. He also resorts to population distribution as a secondary indicator: the more widely dispersed the population the more widely dispersed the industry, because people live where there are jobs. In

[18] Clapham, *Economic Development of France and Germany*, pp. 47, 76–77.

another instance he illustrates the expansion of trade by observing the growth of commercial centers and the development of ports. However, when direct data on the port towns are inaccessible, he resorts to tax assessments on these towns as an indirect indicator. Nevertheless, Mantoux always searches for primary data and only when these are not accessible or when he wants to explain the expansion would he use secondary data. Thus, even though communications can be investigated for their own sake as a part of the economy, Mantoux investigates improvements in communication as means of possible commercial expansion.[19] Because of his emphasis on primary data, relative to his interest in secondary indicators, his contribution has been ranked high on primary and low on secondary, in contrast to the ranking of Clapham's contribution.

Turner's contribution is so lacking in data evidence that any classification must be superficial; his arguments are supported by opinion and assertions. For example, he asserts that the frontier was a safety valve for the socially discontent, but gives no estimates of internal migration or of emigration of the discontent. To the extent any evidence is given, it is in the form of institutional arrangements that indicate only indirectly a relation between the frontier and American life. For example, he uses the land tenure system rather than the actual distribution of farms by size or title—or market facilities in general—rather than actual price levels as evidence.[20] It may be that due to the nature of the topic, direct evidence is impossible, but such an assumption could be reached only if the data from which his conclusions were derived were available.

Cameron et al. provide us with an example of a balanced emphasis on both primary and secondary data. They use data indicating the growth of banking and discuss the policies and institutions affecting that growth. For example, they discuss the number of financial institutions, their relative size, and their assets and liabilities, both absolutely and as a ratio of the national income. They estimate the role of banks in providing credit and expanding the means of payment as measures of banking development. They also explore the governmental laws and regulations that made possible the development of banking.[21] Thus, to the extent the study centers around the development of banking, both primary and secondary data are equally and greatly emphasized.

[19] Mantoux, *The Industrial Revolution*, pp. 52–55, 105–108, 112.
[20] Turner, *The Frontier*, pp. 51, 59, 110.
[21] Cameron et al., *Banking in the Early Stages*, pp. 112, 136, 211ff, 249ff.

A problem arises, however, when their focus shifts to the role of banks in industrialization. In most cases, only the direct participation of banks in industrialization would be a primary indicator of their role; all the other activities mentioned above would indicate only the potential, not actual contribution of banks, because there is no reason to believe that the growth of banking automatically represents a contribution to industrialization. Such a conclusion must derive either from a postulated premise, or it must be shown to be empirically true. For example, a measure of the ratio of credit to the demand for capital, or the degree to which capital supplied by the banks was directly responsive to demand both in volume and distribution, would be direct indicators of the contribution of banks to industrial development. However, to the extent that the meaning of *contribution* is not generally well defined, this criticism can easily be exaggerated.

Although there is no definite pattern in the use of primary and secondary data, there seems to be a tendency shared by all the authors of these studies to try to explain events as well as to record them. There is great emphasis on secondary data in all cases of explanation, except in Mantoux's contribution, where primary data are given much more preference, and in Clapham's contribution, mostly because he treats institutions for their own sake; if his framework is taken into consideration, the shift of emphasis would be toward primary data. It is more significant to note, however, that regardless of the type of generalization, it is possible and fruitful to combine primary and secondary data, especially when primary evidence is not easily and fully accessible.

## HISTORICAL–HYPOTHETICAL DATA

As contributions in economic history, all these studies invariably emphasize historical data, as indicated by the uniform rank 3 assigned to each of them. This should not be surprising since all the contributors were interested in what happened, how it happened, and why. The fact of happening is the point of departure. Their interest does not lie in the proposition "What would, or what might, if . . . ?" This does not mean they do not ask such questions. Indeed, as will be seen presently, some of them raise the question of what might have happened in the absence of a given factor. It is important, however, that their hypothesized answer is itself based on historical data. It would serve no purpose to illustrate here the types of historical data used; it is sufficient to discuss only data that are mere estimates or that relate to hypothetical situations.

To begin with, we shall exclude from this account information derived indirectly, information that is not observable and must be deduced from observation data. Weber, for example, treats attitudes and behavioral patterns on the basis of the motives underlying them. These we shall regard as historical to the extent that the motives are expressed by historical events such as literature, preaching, saving, or investment. The closest we can come to hypothetical data in Pirenne's contribution is when he resorts to the elimination of an alternative hypothesis: when the available data do not prove the existence of event $E$, he tries to show that the nonexistence of $E$ was improbable and that its existence cannot therefore be rejected. In a sense, his apparently hypothetical data are historical, but not sufficient for the derivation of a relevant conclusion. This can be illustrated by an example already used above. The barbarians did not shatter the unity of the empire, nor did they dominate the majority. The data, however, are not sufficiently accessible to show this. Therefore, Pirenne tries to prove that they would not shatter the unity because they had a less established culture, a less fanatic and absorbing religion, and little organization for domination. The opposite conclusion is reached with respect to the Arabs. They would not let themselves be absorbed, they would not adopt Christianity, and they were highly organized. Therefore, they would shatter the unity of the empire and try to dominate the majority. The basic data in both cases are historical and relate to observable factors such as religion, language, and organization. In other words, the hypothetical alternative is rejected on the basis of these historical data, thus leaving the original hypothesis to be adopted.

Heckscher's contribution, although it depends strictly on historical data, comes closest to making use of hypothetical data. This might sound like a contradiction in terms, but Heckscher manages to reconcile the historical and the hypothetical without infringing on the methodological integrity of either approach. His data, even when hypothetical, are based on experiences of another area in which a particular factor is absent. Thus, to hypothesize the absence of a certain factor or policy, and to discover what the effects would be, he resorts to analogy with some other experience in which that factor or policy was missing, and assumes similar results for his own area of study. In other words, what is hypothetical in one context is actually historical in another. Data of this type, however, raise problems of relevance. How can we assume similarity of results, in the absence of evidence, as he actually does? Heckscher applies various methods to establish the relevance of these apparently hypothetical situations. For example, in evaluating the impact of territorial fragmentation, he suggests that "there might nevertheless have been a different shaping of events, if the larger and more powerful states had employed their superior position to compel their numerous neighbours of the smallest size, petty principalities and cities to obey the imperial regulations." [22] As it stands, this hypothetical statement is almost true by definition, since the only hypothetical condition is that the alternative result might be different. Thus, one way of avoiding the problems of hypothetical or counterfactual assertions is to propose harmless and truistic assertions.

Another form of hypothetical alternative is to assume something different from what "might have been expected." [23] Thus, the difference between the toll systems of France and Germany was less than might have been expected, given the great differences in the historical conditions prevalent in these countries. Because the difference is an indefinite quantity, the conclusion seems justified to the extent that the historical dissimilarities have been established as data.

A third approach is implied in the proposition that "it would be the reverse of true to say that the French state built up its whole system of industrial regulation on the cooperation of the gilds. Had that been the case, the system of medieval regulation could certainly have broken down, just as it did in England." The hypothetical alternative is based on two sets of historical data: the experience of England, and the fact that the French state did not delegate enough power to the guilds to enable them to supervise regulations in a country as large as France. Given these two historical conditions and assuming a certain uniformity of behavior in France and England, the hypothetical alternative is rendered admissible. Finally, Heckscher resorts to a more modern method of deriving the alternative on the basis of hypothetical conditions. For instance, "if the industrial development of the world had taken the same course after the beginning of the eighteenth century as before, it may be taken for granted that France might have become one of the first industrial countries." [24] All that Heckscher is doing is assum-

[22] Heckscher, *Mercantilism*, p. 66.
[23] *Ibid.*, p. 78.
[24] *Ibid.*, pp. 151, 192.

ing a constant pattern or rate of industrialization before and after the beginning of the eighteenth century. In other words, France was a leader; had she continued to lead, or had the other countries not accelerated their rates of industrial development, France would have continued to be a leader. The inference is logically sound, and the initial condition is historically established.[25]

It is interesting to note that when historical bases for the hypothetical alternative do not exist, Heckscher chooses to be more cautious. For example, he concludes that "it will never be possible to determine what would have been the course of French development had it continued along these lines. The possibility must not be altogether discounted that, without the intervention of the Great Revolution, the work of reform might have brought about an increasing adaptation of industrial policy to altered ideas and circumstances. This is not very probable, however, since at the outbreak of the Revolution so little had been achieved." Thus, whereas the English experience might have supported the alternative hypothesis, the historical experience of pre-Revolution France disputes it. Heckscher leaves it to the reader to speculate on what might have happened. In at least one case, however, the historical basis for the hypothetical alternative is unclear. According to him, "the whole system [of agreement among Dutch companies] would have been impracticable had Amsterdam not been so important."[26] Either the system was practicable because Amsterdam was important, in which case the converse is true by definition and the statement becomes a tautology, or the system needed a strong member, in which case the statement is false because any other strong member would have rendered the system practicable. Though Heckscher depends on the historical fact of Amsterdam's importance, he does not clarify this. Nevertheless, throughout Heckscher sticks to the historical, even when making use of the hypothetical.

The same conclusion can be reached regarding Clapham's contribution. He depends on historical data even when he resorts to hypothetical alternatives, which he does at several points. For example, "it is most doubtful . . . whether the cotton trade of the North could have grown had it been exposed to Lancashire competition." Given the impact of competition and the historical fact that the North was weaker than Lancashire, the statement cannot be rejected. Sometimes Clapham

[25] *Ibid.*, p. 218 for a similar example.
[26] *Ibid.*, pp. 219, 365.

indulges in speculation and applies techniques similar to those of Heckscher. For instance, it is difficult to evaluate the impact of the Zollverein because "many things which happened might have happened without the Zollverein." Here Clapham simply raises a question but does not give an answer because no historical data are available to suggest an answer. Where historical data are available, Clapham is more specific. For example, rural progress in France "was not so great as it might have been, given the possibilities of modern scientific agriculture" and the historical experiences of Belgium, Holland, Germany, and England. In other words, since these countries had developed agriculture, why had France not? The same approach is applied to the electrical industries. "On the balance it is hard to see why the French electrical industries should not have been at least as efficient as those of, say, Switzerland." [27] The hypothetical data are the obstacles that prevented similar development in France.

Clapham also applies a modern approach by assuming a certain pattern or rate of development and then estimating the possible consequences. Had Russia kept pace with Germany "in the development of waterways, as Austria-Hungary very nearly did, the figures would have been somewhat different." In other words, had Russia developed at a given historical rate the results would have been different. In one case, though depending on historical data, Clapham seems to have derived hypothetical alternatives from a certain kind of determinism. For example, "had the French company completed its task [in Panama], there can be little doubt that the history of Suez would have been repeated, with America in place of England." [28] Apparently the pattern is predetermined although the actions might be different.

Finally, we find some use of nonhistorical or hypothetical data in the contribution of Cameron, et al. The objective in such instances is not to deal with a hypothetical situation, but to uncover some of the historical facts by estimation. In a sense, this is one of the main objectives of the new economic historians when they speak of econometric history. Cameron et al. use different ways of estimation, as the following examples will show. An estimate of the size of the banking sector in England is based on the capital of an "average" country bank and of a "typical" London bank. Given the number of banks at various dates,

---

[27] Clapham, *Economic Development of France and Germany*, pp. 71, 97, 177, 257.

[28] *Ibid.*, pp. 355, 357.

an estimate of bank capitalization is possible. However, the authors add in a footnote that because "the figure of £30,000 for the average capital of London banks in 1800 is probably too low, and for 1825, it certainly is, I have, accordingly, raised it to £50,000 (which may still be too low) since the purpose of the calculations is to give merely a rough approximation. As noted above, the estimate of £10,000 for country banks in 1825 is also probably too low. The number of both London and country banks have been rounded." [29]

They resort to estimation in measuring the stock of money, means of payment, national income, and velocity of circulation in England for selected years between 1688 and 1913. The sources and procedures of estimation are given in full detail, and the authors are aware of the roughness of some of the estimates. In estimating bank notes, the authors admit that "the figure is hypothetical, derived by multiplying the demand notes of the Exchange Bank of Bristol outstanding on 17 June 1779 (£18,874 from Pressnell, *Country Banking,* 142) by 100, which is the estimated number of country bankers (no allowance is made for issues of the London private bankers, which may now be regarded as negligible), adding the result to the circulation figure of the Bank of England for 1775 (£8.76 million) and rounding downward." Usefulness of such a rough estimate will depend on the purpose of the study. A whole table is used to illustrate "the declining relative importance of specie and the correspondingly increased number of bank-created money." [30] Even though such a conclusion is relatively safe to make, it is rather trivial because the mere issue of bank money, regardless of its volume, already implies the conclusion.

Again the authors make estimates of the evolution of the French banking structure. However, they add that "no sources are cited, for the simple reason that for more than half the 'total resources,' and for a still larger proportion of the number of banks, there are no sources properly speaking, only guesses." Nevertheless, the authors reach some conclusions from these guesses which are misleading, as will be indicated below. The author of the case study on Germany also resorts to estimation by assuming the same uniform average for the region, or state, as for the land as a whole. In this case the regional or state averages, which are historical, are simply generalized to the rest of the country.[31]

[29] Cameron et al., *Banking in the Early Stages,* p. 33.
[30] *Ibid.,* pp. 43, 46.
[31] *Ibid.,* pp. 110, 173.

These various approaches to data suggest that economic historians have tended toward historical data; they have resorted to hypothetical data only when historical information was inaccessible; the methods of estimation have ranged from mere guessing to an involvement with the counterfactual and econometric methods advocated by the new economic historians. In general, these estimates have been used with care and awareness of the difficulty of deriving dependable conclusions from them.

## QUANTITATIVE–QUALITATIVE DATA

Economic historians have often been reminded of the need to use quantitative information. As table 4 shows, there is a tendency toward using qualitative more than quantitative data in the contributions under study. Quantitative data are used at the low rank of 1 in four cases, and only once at rank 3. In contrast, qualitative data are emphasized in six cases, whereas the low rank of 1 exists in one case only. This differential emphasis might be due to the individual interests of the contributors, to the nature of the problems under study, or to the lack of quantitative data. It might also be due to the type of generalization anticipated. It is difficult to observe a trend from table 4. Even a scatter diagram would shed little light on the possible relation between type of data and generalization because of the small number of cases and the narrow range of classification.

Marx's contribution illustrates some of these relations clearly. It deals with economic values such as incomes, houses, prices, machines, all of which are quantifiable. It also deals with power, class conflict, quality of life, misery and exploitation, and revolution, most of which can hardly be quantified. It is not surprising, therefore, that Marx in this contribution uses both quantitative and qualitative data, though more frequently the latter. His search for quantitative data, when attempted, is thorough and detailed. To illustrate the concept of surplus value, Marx considers a spinning mill with "10,000 mule spindles, spinning No. 32 yarn from American cotton, and producing 1 lb. of yarn weekly per spindle." With a waste of 6 percent, 10,600 pounds would be produced, of which 600 pounds would be wasted. Given the price of cotton in April, 1871, as 7¾ d. per pound, the raw material cost would be £342. The spindles, assuming £1 per spindle, would cost £10,000. Assuming wear and tear at 10 percent; rent of the building at £300 a year; coal consumption calculated per horse power at £4½ a week; gas at £1 a week; oil and co. at £4½ a week. Thus the constant cost would be £378 and wages at £52 a week. The price of yarn, at 12½ d. per pound would amount to £510. The surplus value would be £510 − £430 = £80. The rate of surplus value, $s/v = {}^{80}\!/_{52} = 153^{11}\!/_{13}$ percent. Marx footnotes this example by explaining that "the above data, which may be relied upon, were given by a Manchester spinner." [32] Even more detailed quantitative data are used in the discussion of the general law of capitalist accumulation, as a glance through the pages would show. Marx searches for figures on wages, population, housing, wealth, and social conditions for different years, tax returns providing an important source of quantitative data. One example may be sufficient to illustrate.

The increase of profits liable to income tax (farmers and some other categories not included) in Great Britain from 1853 to 1864 amounted to 50.47% or 4.58% as the annual average, that of the population during the same period to about 12%. The augmentation of the rent of land subject to taxation (including houses, railways, mines, fisheries, and c.), amounted for 1853 to 1864 to 38% or 3⁵⁄₁₂% annually. Under this head the following categories show the greatest increase:

| Excess of annual income of 1864 over that of 1853: | Increase per year: |
|---|---|
| Houses, 38.60% | 3.50% |
| Quarries, 84.76% | 7.70% |
| Mines, 68.85% | 6.26% |
| Iron-works, 39.92% | 3.63% |
| Fisheries, 57.37% | 5.21% |
| Gasworks, 126.02% | 11.45% |
| Railways, 83.29% | 7.57% |

If we compare the years from 1853 to 1864 in three sets of four consecutive years each, the rate of augmentation of the income increases constantly. It is, e.g., for that arising from profits between 1853 to 1857, 1.73% yearly; 1857–1861, 2.74%, and for 1861–1864, 9.30% yearly. The sum of the incomes of the United Kingdom that come under the income tax was in 1856 £307,068,898; in 1859, £328,127,416; in 1862, £351,745,241; in 1863, £359,142,897; in 1864, £362,462,279; in 1865, £385,530,020.

The accumulation of capital was attended at the same time by its concentration and centralization. Although no official statistics of agriculture existed for England (they did for Ireland), they were voluntarily given in 10 counties. These statistics gave the result that from 1851 to 1861 the number of farms of less than 100 acres had fallen from 31,583 to 26,597, so that 5016 had been thrown together into larger farms. From 1815 to 1825 no personal estate of more than £1,000,000 came under the succession duty; from 1825 to 1855, however, 8 did; and 4 from 1856 to June

[32] Marx, *Capital*, p. 202.

1859, i.e., in 4½ years. The centralization will, however be best seen from a short analysis of the Income Tax Schedule D (profits, exclusive of farms, and c.), in the years 1864 and 1865. I note beforehand that incomes from this source pay income tax on everything over £60. These incomes liable to taxation in England, Wales, and Scotland, amounted in 1864 to 95,844,222, in 1865 to 105,435,579. The number of persons taxed were in 1864, 308,416 out of a population of 23,891,009; in 1865, 332,431 out of a population of 24, 127, 003.[33]

Marx continues in the same form, presenting statistics derived from official and unofficial sources, but in each case the source is carefully cited. However, he is equally detailed in the qualitative description of conditions which he uses to illustrate his points.

In the hardware manufactures of Birmingham and the neighborhood, there are employed, mostly in very heavy work, 30,000 children and young persons, besides 10,000 women. There they are to be seen in the unwholesome brass-foundries, button factories, enameling, galvanizing, and lackering works. Owing to the excessive labour of their work-people, both adult and non-adult, certain London houses where newspapers and books are printed, have got the ill-omened name of 'slaughter-houses.' Similar excesses are practiced in bookbinding, where the victims are chiefly women, girls, and children; young persons have to do heavy work in rope-walks and night-work in salt mines, candle manufactories, and chemical works; young people are worked to death at turning the looms in silk weaving, when it is not carried on by machinery. One of the most shameful, the most dirty, and the worst paid kinds of labour, and one on which women and young girls are by preference employed, is the sorting of rags. It is well known that Great Britain, apart from its own immense store of rags, is the emporium for the rag trade of the whole world. They flow in from Japan, from the most remote states of South America, and from the Canary Islands. But the chief sources of their supply are Germany, France, Russia, Italy, Egypt, Turkey, Belgium, and Holland. They are used for manure, for making bed-flocks, for shoddy, and they serve as the raw material of paper. The rag-sorters are the medium for the spread of small-pox and other infectious diseases, and they themselves are the first victims. A classical example of over-work, of hard and inappropriate labour, and of its brutalizing effects on the workman from his childhood upwards, is afforded not only by coal-mining and miners generally, but also by tile and brick making, in which industry the recently invented machinery is, in England, used only here and there. Between May and September the work lasts from 5 in the morning till 8 in the evening, and where the drying is done in the open air, it often lasts from 4 in the morning till 9 in the evening. Work from 5 in the morning till 7 in the evening is considered 'reduced' and 'moderate.' Both boys and girls of 6 and even of 4 years of age are employed.

[33] *Ibid.*, pp. 665–666.

They work for the same number of hours, often longer, than the adults. The work is hard and the summer heat increases the exhaustion. In a certain tile field at Mosley, e.g., a young woman, 24 years of age, was in the habit of making 2000 tiles a day, with the assistance of 2 little girls, who carried the clay for her, and stacked the tiles. These girls carried daily 10 tons up the slippery sides of the clay pits, from a depth of 30 feet, and then for a distance of 210 feet. 'It is impossible for a child to pass through the purgatory of a tile-field without great moral degradation . . . the low language, which they are accustomed to hear from their tenderest years, the filthy, indecent and shameless habits, amidst which, unknowing, and half wild, they grow up, make them in after life lawless, abandoned, dissolute. . . .'[34]

It is doubtful whether this qualitative description could be completely quantified, although it might be partly so, not only because of the nature of the subject matter, but also the inaccessibility of data. If this is true, it appears that these two variables, the availability of data and the nature of the topic, determined whether Marx would use quantitative or qualitative data.

In contrast, Weber leans heavily toward the qualitative and very little toward the quantitative. Weber knows the importance of statistics and objectivity in social science; in fact, he makes assertions as though they were statistically valid and significant. For example, "a glance at the occupational statistics of any country of mixed religious composition brings to light with remarkable frequency a situation which has several times provoked discussion in the Catholic press and literature . . . , the fact that business leaders and owners of capital, as well as the higher grades of skilled labour, and even more the higher technically and commercially trained personnel of modern enterprises, are overwhelmingly Protestant." However, he illustrates all this in a footnote in which he observes that in Baden in 1895, tax returns show that taxes collected per 1,000 Protestants were 954,000 marks, compared with 589,000 marks per 1,000 Catholics. He adds, "it is true that the Jews, with over four millions per 1,000, were far ahead of the rest." He also uses quantitative data to support the view that Protestants were more inclined toward technical and business education than were Catholics, although Jews were ahead of both groups in seeking education.[35] Strangely enough, it does not seem to make any difference to his conclusions how extensive in detail or coverage the data are.

Weber's data, however, are primarily qualitative and often impres-

[34] *Ibid.*, pp. 466–467.
[35] Weber, *Protestant Ethic*, pp. 35, 188–189.

sionistic, as statements chosen at random would show. For example, "The universal reign of absolute unscrupulousness in the pursuit of selfish interests by the making of money has been a specific characteristic of precisely those countries whose bourgeois-capitalistic development, measured according to occidental standards, has remained backward. As every employer knows, the lack of *conscienziosità* of the labourers of such countries, for instance Italy as compared with Germany, has been, and to a certain extent still is, one of the principal obstacles to their capitalistic development." In another statement he observes that "the joy and pride of having given employment to numerous people, of having a part in the economic progress of his home town in the sense referring to figures of population and volume of trade which capitalism associated with the word, all these things obviously are part of the specific and undoubtedly idealistic satisfactions in life to modern men of business." [36] Both statements might be measured quantitatively, but would be hard to justify in statistical terms. Weber chooses to present them qualitatively.

Pirenne's contribution covers areas that certainly can be quantified, in addition to his observations on language, religion, and social solidarity which may be difficult to quantify. Yet, like Weber, Pirenne tends to emphasize the qualitative and de-emphasize the quantitative. In part, we can discount the nature of the topic as a reason for this bias. Given the period and area covered, the lack of data might be a more relevant factor. Pirenne, as has already been noted, is aware of the significance of statistics for scientific accuracy. Therefore, he tries to provide figures whenever possible, even if only in the form of estimates. For example, he estimates the population of the empire to be large enough such that the invading Germans "disappeared in the mass of the population." He also estimates the number of invading warriors, relative to the resident population, as too small to change the native population except by domination, which he rules out for other reasons. In all these cases, however, no precise quantitative data are given, and the tendency toward qualitative statements is conspicuous. For example, "Spain and Gaul had not suffered so greatly from the invasions, and, moreover, were not so completely Romanized as Italy and Africa." Neither the degree of suffering or of Romanization is specified even as an approximation. Even more quantifiable variables are presented in similar terms. Discussing the continuation of trade, Pirenne mentions the slave trade.

[36] *Ibid.*, pp. 57, 76.

"We read of their being offered for sale at Narbonne. There is mention of them also in Naples, whence they came, no doubt, from Marseilles, which was the great slave market." [37] Thus a mere mention is used as evidence, and even as proof. An even broader statement is that the continuing similar trend is a "final proof" of the continuity of the preinvasion society, just as mention of slave trade is a proof of the continuation of trade. In part, of course, Pirenne's objective is responsible for this use of the data; he is interested in a trend rather than in a degree or absolute measure. Yet he allows no room for a "more or less," since he talks of cessation of trade, unity and disunity of the empire, and continuity of secular power. At the same time he accepts a single trade item as sufficient evidence of trade continuity or the lack of it. Consequently, despite his intentions, Pirenne's contribution tends to be highly biased toward qualitative data at the expense of quantitative.

Heckscher's contribution is similar to that of Marx in that he uses both quantitative and qualitative data, but the lack of statistics and the nature of his topic render emphasis on the qualitative. The difficulty of quantifying unification, power, disintegration, and other social institutions or policy concepts is an apparent problem, let alone the absence of data for the period he considers. For instance, "the strengthening of the corporations furthered local exclusiveness, so that at any rate from the middle of the 16th until the end of the 17th century, it even proved to be on the increase, until at length the distinction between employers and employed led to a change-about. One gild after the other clamoured for a compulsory period of training in the town for apprentices and journeymen, sometimes even for those who had already acquired the status of master in another town." Or take the statement that "the J.P.s occasionally showed a tendency to oppose the orders of the Council, for their own interests as corn producers were often involved, but this policy corresponded on the whole to what the great majority considered right, and therefore found willing helpers . . . In other ways the justices were not only unable to carry out everything demanded by them, but were even able sometimes to offer successful resistance." [38] Both statements could be quantified or supported by quantitative data, but no attempt to do so is apparent.

When the attempt is made, Heckscher succeeds in securing quantitative data, as is shown by the following example, which is on the order of the above statements. "When reforms were carried out in Baden in

[37] Pirenne, *Mohammed and Charlemagne*, pp. 35, 36, 49, 99.
[38] Heckscher, *Mercantilism*, pp. 149, 260.

1810, earlier than in other places, there were found within that small territory, 112 different measurements of length, 92 different square measures, 65 different dry measures, 163 different measures for cereals, 123 different liquid measures, 63 different measures for liquor, and 80 different pound weights. This was certainly a record which was difficult to beat." Also when speaking of privileged industrial positions in France, Heckscher notes that the number increased rapidly following the fifteenth century, "especially during the reign of Henry IV who, in 1606 introduced no fewer than 320 such industrial positions and 47 various industrial groups. It seems that this number must be added to the 169 privileged positions which had already been invested by Francis I, six years before." [39] These examples suggest that it is not only the nature of the topic that prevents the use of qualitative data, but more frequently the lack of ready data and the inaccessibility of sources. This combined with his topic and comprehensive interest seems to have forced Heckscher to use qualitative data more often than quantitative.

Clapham's contribution is a little harder to evaluate on the use of quantitative or qualitative data, because though he uses both extensively, there are many areas that could have been more quantitatively or more qualitatively expressed than they were. Nevertheless, Clapham gives detail whether the data are qualitative or quantitative. In particular, he tends to use both kinds of data as a check or at least to support each other. As has been suggested, about a third of the contribution is devoted to institutional topics and is mostly qualitative in form. On the other hand, detailed quantitative information can be found on at least forty-five pages, including fairly comprehensive tables like the following example.[40]

### Output in Metric Tons

|      | Great Britain | Germany | | France | Belgium |
|------|---------------|---------|---------|--------|---------|
|      |               | Coal | Lignite |        |         |
| 1871 | 118,000,000 | 29,400,000 | 8,500,000 | 13,300,000 | 13,700,000 |
| 1880 | 149,000,000 | 47,000,000 | 12,100,000 | 19,400,000 | 16,900,000 |
| 1890 | 184,500,000 | 70,200,000 | 19,100,000 | 26,100,000 | 20,400,000 |
| 1900 | 228,800,000 | 109,300,000 | 40,500,000 | 33,400,000 | 23,500,000 |
| 1910 | 268,700,000 | 152,800,000 | 69,500,000 | 38,350,000 | 23,900,000 |
| 1913 | 292,000,000 | 191,500,000 | 87,500,000 | 40,800,000 | 22,800,000 |

[39] *Ibid.*, pp. 118, 185.
[40] Clapham, *Economic Development of France and Germany*, p. 281.

Clapham goes further than most of his generation of economic historians in making use of quantitative data. Only when such information is not available, or when he is dealing with nonquantifiable material, does he resort to qualitative data. This observation can be explained in terms of the factors we have already mentioned. Clapham tends to be interested in the quantitative approach, and his topic, the period, and the availability of data for the countries dealt with, make that approach possible. The economic variables of his study are quantifiable; the nineteenth century tends to have good records, especially for France and Germany, which may be surpassed only by those of England, and Clapham successfully makes use of these data in accordance with his interests. In addition, as we shall discuss in detail below, Clapham's objectives regarding analysis and generalization are such that detailed quantitative data are quite appropriate.

Mantoux's contribution represents extremes in the quality of the data. He uses precise quantitative data, but also data in the form of poetry as evidence. Quantitative data are scattered throughout his contribution, but the bulk of information is qualitative, and the quantitative data are used more to support his views and impressions. In describing the old type industry, for example, he tells us that

in the western villages the weavers, who still combined agricultural with industrial work, earned their living fairly well. In 1757 a Gloucestershire weaver, with his wife to help him, could earn, when work was good, from 13s. to 18s. a week—2s. to 3s. a day. This was much more than the average weekly wage, which probably approximated to the 11s. or 12s. noted a few years later by Arthur Young. In the Leeds district, where the industrial population had preserved less of its rural character, a good workman earned about 10s. 6d. a week; but frequent unemployment reduced this to an average of 8s. In the Norfolk worsted industry, where the capitalist employer played a greater part, wages were lower still: in Norwich they were only 6s.—hardly 1s. a day. Thus as we pass from a scattered industry, still connected with agriculture, to an industry which had reached a higher stage of centralization and organization, we find that not only the independence but the resources of the worker grew less—the causes being on the one hand an excess supply of labour, and on the other the growing difficulty of the worker in earning any livelihood outside his own trade.[41]

When he speaks of the condition of workers, he looks at the list of grievances presented to Parliament and deems it sufficient to name the grievances without suggesting any precise estimate of their number or

[41] Mantoux, *The Industrial Revolution*, p. 71.

of the size of the population affected. The tailors and journeymen complained of insufficient wages, unemployment, seasonal work; rural apprentices, of competition, long hours, and poor working conditions. These conditions, however, are not worse than they were in the preceding century. These general data are rather vague and imprecise and can only leave an impression. The extreme of the qualitative presentation is best illustrated by the poem Mantoux quotes, which he defends as being of popular origin and hence characteristic of working conditions.

> Of all sorts of callings that in England be
> There is none that liveth so gallant as we;
> Our trading maintains us as brave as a knight,
> We live at our pleasure, and take our delight;
> We heapeth up riches and treasure great store
> Which we get by griping and grinding the poor.
>    And this is a way for to fill up our purse
>    Although we do get it with many a curse.
>
> Throughout the whole kingdom, in country and town,
> There is no danger of our trade going down,
> So long as the Comber can work with his comb,
> And also the Weaver weave with his lomb;
> The Tucker and Spinner that spins all the year,
> We will make them to earn their wages full dear.
>    And this is a way . . .
>
> And first for the Combers, we will bring them down,
> From eight groats a score unto half a crown;
> If at all they murmur and say 'tis too small,
> We bid them choose whether they will work at all:
> We'll make them believe that trading is bad;
> We care not a pin, though they are ne'er so sad.
>    And this is a way . . .
>
> We'll make the poor Weavers work at a low rate,
> We'll find fault where there's no fault, and so we will bate;
> If trading grows dead, we will presently show it,
> But if it grows good, they shall never know it;
> We'll tell them that cloth beyond sea will not go,
> We care not whether we keep clothing or no.
>    And this is a way . . .
>
> The next for the Spinners we shall ensue,
> We'll make them spin three pound instead of two;
> When they bring home their work unto us, they complain,

And say that their wages will not them maintain;
But if that an ounce of weight they do lack,
Then for to bate threepence we will not be slack.
    And this is a way . . .

But if it holds weight, then their wages they crave,
We have got no money, and what's that you'd have?
We have bread and bacon and butter that's good,
With oatmeal and salt that is wholesome for food;
We have soap and candles whereby to give light,
That you may work by them so long as you have sight.
    And this is a way . . .

When we go to market our workmen are glad;
But when we come home, then we do look sad:
We sit in the corner as if our hearts did ake;
We tell them 'tis not a penny we can take.
We plead poverty before we have need;
And thus we do coax them most bravely indeed.
    And this is a way . . .

But if to an alehouse they customers be,
Then presently with the ale wife we agree;
When we come to a reckoning, then we do crave
Twopence on a shilling, and that we will have.
By such cunning ways we our treasure do get,
For it is all fish that doth come to our net.
    And this a way, etc. . . .

And thus we do gain all our wealth and estate,
By many poor men that work early and late;
If it were not for those that do labour full hard,
We might go and hang ourselves without regard;
The Combers, the Weavers, the Tuckers also,
With the Spinners that work for wages full low.
    By these people's labour we fill up our purse,
    Although we do get it with many a curse.[42]

At the other extreme, Mantoux treats commercial expansion quantitatively and in detail, with diagrams to emphasize the change and suggest a trend between 1700 and 1800.[43] This vacillation between the quantitative and the qualitative, with more emphasis on the latter, may be explained by Mantoux's interest in explaining and by the nature of

[42] *Ibid.*, pp. 75–77.
[43] *Ibid.*, p. 102.

his topic, but it may be difficult to justify by any lack of data, judging from the extensive bibliography he refers to. The fact that explanation rather than measurement is his primary objective may be responsible for the differential emphasis, as fully illustrated in his chapter on factories. He not only discusses the changes, but also how they took place —he finds it necessary to explore the biographies of some pioneers— and why they happened. Therefore, he explores the relation between science and technology, the organizational aspects of the factories, and the social results of the change. All this he does largely in qualitative terms that provide impressions and possible explanations.

Turner's contribution is difficult to evaluate in this context because of the few data he uses, either quantitative or qualitative. Most of the information is in the form of opinion, assertion, or impressionistic conclusion. For example, he describes the frontier as a safety valve for the socially discontent, but attempts no estimates either of the discontent or the number of migrants. The same is true of his statements on warfare and the Indian threat to settlement. It is not the lack of data that restricts precision or documentation, since at least one of the essays was written recently enough that data should have been available.[44] In general, Turner is satisfied with qualitative measurements such as "important," "significant," or "influential" with no documentation. Therefore, although he combines the quantitative and qualitative, both are used with little emphasis on either, as shown in table 4.

The contribution of Cameron et al., like that of Clapham, is modern in the degree of emphasis on quantitative data, and it is equally concerned with qualitative information. This contribution has the advantage of dealing with quantifiable data, of treating a topic on which adequate monographic work has been done, and of benefitting from the debates going on in the field. Therefore, the authors manage to combine the "traditional" and the modern approaches without going to the extreme in either. Each of the case studies has parts that are narrative, mostly in qualitative terms, and other parts with figures, tables and diagrams. To illustrate the qualitative narrative: "The origins of country banking were diverse. Among the early bankers were men who had formerly been engaged—and frequently still were—in wholesale or retail trade, in manufacturing of both the domestic and factory types, in mining, and in tax collecting. The early lists also included

---

[44] Turner, *The Frontier*, pp. 244–246 for problems on which data can be found.

attorneys and an occasional land proprietor. The economic forces that called the country banks into existence as a specialized profession were equally diverse, but they may be grouped under three easily identifiable headings"; namely, the demand for remittance facilities, the increasing demand for bank services, and the deficiencies of coinage and the need for a circulating medium. This type of qualitative narrative can be found in all the case studies, although the chapter on Russia seems to tend in that direction more than the others. For example, "Russia was not yet ripe for the adoption of the system current in other countries, where, in addition to gold, first class securities were used as cover for note issues. The Russian government, in order to secure the necessary elasticity of the system, maintained gold reserves far in excess of legal requirements and refrained from fully exercising its rights to issue uncovered notes. The Russian ruble was thus more in the nature of a gold certificate than a banknote. The maintenance of this large gold reserve was a luxury for a country so deficient in capital. It was thought necessary, however, because Russia was a large-scale debtor. Russia had always had a balance of payments problem and was exposed to gold drains continually, not less during periods of economic and political crisis. The large gold reserves, especially the gold balances of the Russian Treasury and of the State Bank held abroad, helped to maintain the stability of the exchange rate." [45]

Needless to say, much of the content of these two statements could be quantified. Apparently, reference to secondary sources is deemed a sufficient documentation for the statements that give a general picture of the conditions described. One might suggest that this approach is indispensable. The important point, however, is to decide how far one can go in that direction without rendering the study mainly qualitative and generalistic. Cameron et al. have not allowed themselves to reach the margin. They have used enough quantitative data and direct documentation to prevent a tip of the scale. With forty-nine tables and sixteen charts and figures spread throughout the text, the authors have demonstrated the extent to which economic history can be quantitative and precise. Even if we ignore these tables, it is easy to demonstrate the quantitative aspects. For example, once legal obstacles were removed in 1832, the *Commandite* form of partnership became very common. "From 1826 to the end of 1837 only 157 *anonymes* obtained authorization, but more than 1,100 *commandites*, with a combined nominal

[45] Cameron et al., pp. 24, 214.

capital four times as large as that of the *anonymes*, registered with the Tribunal de Commerce of the Seine [Paris] alone. In the first seven months of 1838, at the height of the boom, 301 *commandites*, with aggregate capital of 800 million francs, registered in Paris. . . . In the two decades from 1840 to 1860 *Commandites par actions* were formed at an average rate of more than 200 per year, as against only 14 per year for *anonymes*." [46] Thus the authors document the statement on the change in company organization and demonstrate the complementarity between the quantitative and qualitative in writing economic history.

In general, then, these representative contributions suggest that both quantitative and qualitative data are necessary. Which of them should be emphasized depends on the topic. Limitations on data accessibility, however, frequently prevent the use of quantitative data and encourage dependence on the qualitative, which is less precise and easier to document in vague terms. As we shall see, the generalizations reached are influenced by which of these types of data are used.

## INTERDISCIPLINARY DATA

As shown in table 4, four contributions are highly interdisciplinary, three are moderately so, and one is only economic. It may be significant that the most recent contribution, by Cameron et al., is the most specialized or least interdisciplinary. Whether it conforms to a new trend or follows that approach only by chance is hard to say. In contrast, Marx combines economics, history, politics, and sociology and sometimes philosophy in order to discover the laws of motion of society. Given the dynamic nature of society, these aspects of behavior cannot be left out in trying to understand society, and Marx takes them into consideration when he deals with the motives of the capitalist, with social class, with the state and the Parliamentary process, with religion, and with economic and philosophic thought.

Political economy, which as an independent science, first sprang into being during the period of manufacture, views the social division of labour only from the standpoint of manufacture, and sees in it only the means of producing more commodities with a given quantity of labour, and, consequently, of cheapening commodities and hurrying on the accumulation of capital. In most striking contrast with this accentuation of quantity and exchange value, is the attitude of the writers of classical antiquity, who hold exclusively

[46] *Ibid.*, p. 112.

by quality and use-value. In consequence of the separation of the social branches of production, commodities are better made, the various bents and talents of men select a suitable field, and without some restraint no important results can be obtained anywhere. Hence, both product and producer are improved by division of labour. If the growth of the quantity produced is occasionally mentioned, this is only done with reference to the greater abundance of use-values. There is not a word alluding to exchange-value or to the cheapening of commodities. This aspect, from the standpoint of use-value alone, is taken as well by Plato, who treats division of labour as the foundation on which the division of society into classes is based, as by Zenophon, who with characteristic bourgeois instinct, approaches more nearly to the division of labor within the workshop. Plato's Republic, in so far as division of labour is treated in it, as the formative principle of the State, is merely the Athenian idealisation of the Egyptian system of castes, Egypt having served as the model of an industrial country to many of his contemporaries also, among others to Isocrates, and it continued to have this importance to the Greeks of the Roman Empire.[47]

This excerpt exemplifies well the interdisciplinary approach of Marx; history, sociology, and economic organization and thought are combined. The same approach is characteristic of his treatment of change in society, as shown in "Genesis of the Capitalist Farmer." "Now that we have considered the forcible creation of a class of outlawed proletarians, the bloody discipline that turned them into wage-labourers, the disgraceful action of the state which employed the police to accelerate the accumulation of capital by increasing the degree of exploitation of labour, the question remains: whence came the capitalists originally?" This is followed by a survey of the forces that created the land proprietors, including the economic processes, the tenure arrangements, the role of the state, and the structure of the community.[48] Thus, the change necessitated by economic forces was made possible by the tenure arrangements in society; and the implementation of these changes was made easier by the role played by the state and the inability of the peasants to resist. All four sets of conditions must be understood in order to explain whence came the capitalist farmer. Probably the interdisciplinary character of this contribution is best illustrated in the section on the Factory Acts, which begins, "Factory legislation, that first conscious and methodical reaction of society against the spontaneously developed form of the process of production, is, as we have seen, just as much the necessary product of modern industry as cotton

47 Marx, *Capital*, pp. 359–360.
48 *Ibid.*, pp. 766–768.

yarn, self-actors, and the electric telegraph. Before passing to the consideration of the extension of that legislation in England, we shall shortly notice certain clauses in the Factory Acts, and not relating to the hours of work." [49] The rest of the discussion goes into detail on the impact of the acts on sanitation, education, and welfare, as well as on labor organization, and how the expansion of the acts was due to changes in industry.

Like Marx, Weber deals with a phenomenon related to motivation and the impact of human behavior, but mainly that of the individual, not the group. To that extent, the discussion goes beyond the confines of any one discipline. The history of religion, attitudes toward work and business activity, the impact of education, and the impact of the group on the individual are touched upon in varying degrees of detail. Nevertheless, although Weber recognizes the interdependence of these disciplines in understanding capitalism, his discussion centers mainly around religion. Thus, he deals with religion and asceticism, law, and administration, but his treatment of the economic forces tends to be shallow. This may, of course, be due to his interest not in capitalism as an economic system but in the spirit of capitalism as a pattern of behavior or a source of motivation. In other words, the relevance of various disciplines varies according to the point under consideration. Weber, however, holds the economic, technological, and political factors almost constant, and concentrates on the religious aspects. The role of capital is dismissed after less than one page with the conclusion that where the spirit of capitalism "appears and is able to work itself out, it produces its own capital and monetary supplies as the means to its ends, but the reverse is not true." [50] It is in this sense that Weber's interdisciplinary use of data is less than the ideal.

Pirenne deals with total societies, and recognizes the interdependence of forces and disciplines. His table of contents shows that he deals with the economic, intellectual, political, cultural, and sociological aspects of society in the period he considers. All these aspects are treated from the standpoint of the unity or disintegration of the empire, and all are given almost equal weight. Pirenne's approach is closely related to his methodological views about the problems of historical analysis. Therefore, it might be possible to reduce the margin of error by combining evidence from various directions, including politics, law, religion,

[49] *Ibid.*, pp. 485–486; on the acts see also pp. 427–428, 489.
[50] Weber, *Protestant Ethic*, pp. 68–69.

sociology, and demography, as he does. This approach is followed in dealing with each of the periods relevant to the discussion. A good illustration is the concluding chapter which announces the beginning of the Middle Ages. After economic and social organization has been analyzed, the discussion shifts to political organization, and is followed by an analysis of the intellectual civilization of the period, completing the picture of revival after the disintegration caused by the Moslems. In a sense, this approach is unavoidable to the extent that Pirenne's topic deals with the total society rather than with a specific aspect of it. Trade was only a machine by which that total change was implemented. Pirenne explicitly declares his interdisciplinary approach to history and abides by it.

Heckscher's contribution deals with mercantilism, an all-embracing concept. Heckscher recognizes the interdependence between economic and noneconomic factors, and even though he describes his intention as the study of the economic aspect only, he deals with legislation, politics, local and regional administration, and international relations, at least in as much as these aspects relate to economic policy. Sometimes, however, these aspects are treated for their own sake. A good example is his discussion of the relations between the German territorial princes and the cities. Feudalism itself, with which Heckscher deals, is more a political than an economic phenomenon, unless we choose to specify a nontraditional meaning for that term. Heckscher apparently discusses the noneconomic aspects in order to clarify the environment within which mercantilist development took place. Another illustration is the detailed discussion of the relations between the central governments and the chartered companies.[51]

It is a little more difficult to classify Clapham's contribution as interdisciplinary or not because Clapham does not define his topic. He asserts that the history of a country must be studied in its wider perspective, but it is not clear what *economic development* means or what the broader perspective should be. He deals with politics, economic doctrine, legislation, labor organization, and welfare. Are these parts of economic development, or are they aspects of social history treated for their own sake? Often they seem connected with economic development, but not always. For example, river transport was as much political as it was economic because rivers know no political boundaries. Similarly, railroad expansion was as much political as it was economic;

[51] Heckscher, *Mercantilism*, pp. 134ff, 359.

in Belgium the decision to build was partly "for the glory of the young state," as, in fact, is the case today with newly developing countries. The policy on agriculture was always as much political and social as it was economic. This approach is illustrated in every single chapter dealing with the subject. For example, as Clapham puts it, "no discussion of German agriculture ever omitted the military aspect." Again "that opportunities for industrialization on the largest scale were limited by the course of political events in France, during the late nineteenth century, there can be no doubt." [52] Therefore, Clapham deals with these aspects in order to understand the industrial history. Missing, however, is a systematic exploration of the relation between the economic and the noneconomic, so that his interdisciplinary approach would acquire a logic and a rationale of its own. For this reason, Clapham's contribution has been classified as only moderately interdisciplinary.

Mantoux is equally aware of the interdisciplinary advantages and complications the historian faces. However, he is a little more analytical than Clapham and integrates noneconomic data with economic aspects more closely than Clapham does. He observes the simultaneous roles of the factory system, science, and democracy in shaping the intellectual and political evolution of society. An example of Mantoux's broad approach is his use of data on population, union organization, riots, legislation, and humanitarian activities. He illustrates this interdisciplinary interdependence by recalling certain dates in the lives of the founders of the factory system. "While Hargreaves and Highs were inventing spinning machinery and while Watt was mastering the hidden forces of steam, Jean Jacques Rousseau was David Hume's guest at Wootton Hall. Between the time when Arkwright settled in Nottingham and the time when he died, rich and titled, . . . the American and the French Revolutions broke out. A few months before Arkwright another pioneer died, full of years and good works: John Wesley, the apostle of Methodism." He goes on to show the impact of the factory system on manufacturers and employers. The relevance of government action is shown by the Act of 1802 in which Peel "laid special stress on the moral degradation of the young people employed in the factories." [53] These noneconomic aspects render the treatment imprecise,

[52] Clapham, *Economic Development of France and Germany*, pp. 109, 141, 221, 233.

[53] Mantoux, *The Industrial Revolution*, pp. 28, 464, 471.

but their inclusion shows Mantoux's interdisciplinary bent. However, to the extent that systematic data and analysis of these aspects are not evident, Mantoux should, like Clapham, be regarded as only moderately interdisciplinary in this contribution.

Turner's data are so meager that classifying them is almost meaningless. His analysis, however, is certainly interdisciplinary; he ties the military aspects of the frontier with the economic, social, and political forces that influenced frontier development. He does this with great consistency, both in presenting the fundamental premises and in commenting on the functions of the historian. For example, one of the areas of greatest interdependence is class conflict. Here Turner brings in the relevance of location, capital, land tenure, the distribution of power, and the ethnic and religious features of the population. These are then tied in with the system of government and attitudes toward it.[54] Finally, Turner insists on discussing the role of institutions in historical development. All this, however, is presented with such brevity that imputing meaning to his statements becomes almost unavoidable. Nevertheless, it is evident that Turner bases his analysis and frontier thesis on a highly interdisciplinary view of frontier life and settlement.

Finally, it has been suggested above that Cameron et al. are the least interdisciplinary in their approach. Put differently, their study of banking is the most specialized of the contributions. Therefore, they use mainly economic and financial data and only briefly touch on other aspects, such as the political and social environment. For example, they discuss attitudes toward paper money and other means of payment as these relate to tradition and to the development of banking and credit. They also discuss the legislative acts affecting banks and the role of government in that development. This is done in all the case studies, but that is the extent of their involvement in interdisciplinary analysis. There is little about the political, social, or intellectual environment during the take-off periods. In a sense these are held constant or irrelevant. Therefore, this contribution seems to be interdisciplinary only to a limited degree.

In conclusion, whereas all the contributors tend to use interdisciplinary data, they vary in the degree they use it according to whether their contribution is analytical or not, whether it deals with the total society or with a certain aspect of it, and whether the relation between the economic and noneconomic can be held relatively constant. The more

[54] Turner, *The Frontier*, pp. 2, 51, 59, 110, 334.

specialized the contribution and the shorter the developmental period covered, the less interdisciplinary the contribution tends to be.

## COMPREHENSIVE–SELECTIVE DATA

The biggest problem in historical and human research is probably the complexity and vastness of the material. There are so many factors and details that might be relevant, both in terms of time and in terms of complexity, that the researcher must decide how to simplify the analysis to make it manageable. One way, which is the most recent, is to narrow the area of study to an extent that comprehensive handling of the data becomes possible. The other, and more traditional approach is to select illustrations by which tendencies can be observed. Both approaches have drawbacks: the former can lead to results that are conclusive but narrow; the latter, to results that are vast but inconclusive and possibly biased in favor of supportive data. This latter approach seems common to the representative contributions, as shown in table 4.

To the extent that Marx's contribution deals with a phenomenon that cannot be pinpointed in terms of time and location, it is not possible to specify precisely the data relevance for those aspects. On the other hand, since the phenomenon affects the whole of society, all the aspects of society become relevant and therefore the data must be exhaustive. It may be impossible to handle all that data, so Marx resorts to selective illustrations of his observations, which he regards as sufficient to indicate tendencies. In fact, he admits his use of illustrations at various junctures of his study. For example, to illustrate the accumulation of capital, he deals with figures for the years 1853 and 1864 only. He presents data on housing, quarries, mines, ironworks, fisheries, gasworks, and railways only. Although these industries are significant, they are only a small number among those that could be evaluated. In dealing with agriculture, he illustrates his point with statistics on ten countries for the years 1851 and 1861. He analyzes incomes liable to taxation in England, Wales, and Scotland for the years 1864 and 1865 only. He gives illustrations of various points by considering different industries, localities, or years, but nowhere does he take all the relevant aspects in any one year or locality and consider them simultaneously.[55] Thus, the data are neither comprehensive enough, nor are they selected in a uniform or random way to permit contrary data to appear. Only supportive

[55] Marx, *Capital*, pp. 665–666, 466–467 for specific examples.

data are considered. It is true that comprehensive coverage might have been followed in the monographic inquiries prior to the presentation of the results, but there is no evidence or statement to that effect. Furthermore, it is not clear to what extent the illustrations were common or widespread, or how often, for instance, the courts reached a foregone conclusion, as Marx suggests they did, relative to the total number of conclusions reached. Therefore, it seems that Marx cannot be regarded as highly comprehensive in data use; hence the moderate rank assigned to his contribution.

The same comments apply to Weber's contribution. It is clear from his specification of the problem that the data cannot be exhaustive since there is no way of exhausting the material. It would seem necessary, therefore, to select those aspects or modes of behavior that exemplify the given stage of development or the phenomenon, and support the argument as data. That is what Weber seems to have done in selecting what he considers relevant or representative as his data. For example, to show the relation between asceticism and the spirit of capitalism, he asserts that "we can treat ascetic Protestantism as a single whole. But since that side of English Puritanism which was derived from Calvinism gives the most consistent religious basis for the idea of calling, we shall, following our previous method, place one of its representatives at the centre of the discussion." He selects Richard Baxter as one "above many other writers on Puritan ethics, both because of his eminently practical and realistic attitude, and, at the same time, because of the universal recognition accorded to his works." Not only is Weber selective in this approach, but he chooses criteria subjectively and in retrospect as if to add support to his thesis. To what extent was English Puritanism or Richard Baxter representative of the behavior illustrated is not indicated. Weber admits that his examples are only illustrations and that his objective is to establish tendencies or connections without attaching any empirical significance to the findings. Thus, it may be possible by these selective illustrations to "perhaps in a modest way form a contribution to the understanding of the manner in which ideas became effective forces in history." [56]

It should be noted, however, that once the example has been chosen, Weber deals with it in detail and almost exhaustively. Thus, English Puritanism and Richard Baxter are analyzed thoroughly. In this sense Weber's approach can be classified as moderately comprehensive, or

[56] Weber, *Protestant Ethic*, pp. 90, 155, 199.

moderately selective, Weber having combined his selectivity with a comprehensive treatment of the examples.

Pirenne's contribution is equally selective in that fragmentary data are used as bases for his conclusions. As has already been mentioned, a single case of slave trade is regarded as sufficient evidence of the continuation of trade and unity in the empire. For example, "great quantities of cereals were still moved from place to place. In 510 Theodoric sent quantities of corn to Provence on account of the ravages of war in that region. . . . The great estates, at this period, still yielded considerable revenues in money. In 593 Dinamius sent Gregory the Great 400 *solidi* from Provence; two years later the same Pope was awaiting the arrival of clothing and of Anglo-Saxon slaves, who were to be purchased in Provence with the revenues of his domains. Similarly in 557 Pope Pelagius was expecting supplies from Provence which were needed to relieve the distress of the Roman people. There was also a normal trade in corn. Despite his enormous resources, we find that Gregory the Great made purchases of grain. We find that in 537–538 a *pereginus acceptor* made important purchases in Istria; he must have been a corn-merchant." [57]

These statements fully illustrate the selective nature of the data. One or two activities of a pope are considered sufficient evidence, even though it is not shown that the cloth and Anglo-Saxon slaves were in fact purchased or that they had arrived. Continued trade in corn is assumed on the basis of one vague statement of purchase by a pope and another by an anonymous person who "must have been a corn-merchant." The dates are from the entire sixth century, but the movement of the select commodities relates to about a century before the advent of Islam and might in fact have little relevance to its spread. On the other hand, Pirenne in various instances implies a comprehensive treatment although the data are not presented. When tracing the availability of oriental commodities in the West, he notes that "mention of spices, like that of papyrus, disappears from the texts after 716." Looking at the list of supplies allowed for bishops when travelling, he asserts that there is "no mention of condiments," which came from the East.[58] In other words, in all the texts and in the bishops' universal list of supplies there is no mention of these oriental goods. Which texts and how many of them were surveyed is not indicated; it is not shown

[57] Pirenne, *Mohammed and Charlemagne*, pp. 77–78.
[58] *Ibid.*, pp. 170, 171.

either that the list was indeed universal or that the bishops abided by it.

Although the data might be lacking on most of these points, it may be more significant that Pirenne is interested in observing a trend for which these selective data might be adequate. Whether this justification is adequate or not, the fact remains that the author did not exhaust all the relevant data, and he concluded from insufficient information.

Heckscher is quite explicit in describing his data as selective, or noncomprehensive. To illustrate the struggle for unity, he selects the toll system as an example, but even within the context of the toll system he tends to select examples to illustrate more specific points. For instance, "economic policy in the Middle Ages offers sufficient examples of conservatism, but one of the best that I know is that the Florentines retained for 85 years, that is, from 1406 to 1491, the tolls against their own textile industry, set up by Pisa before its incorporation in the Florentine state." Heckscher assures us that we shall come across many other examples in later chapters. Only examples, not the degree or the frequency of conservatism, seem necessary data for the purpose at hand. Again, the seriousness of the policy of England toward the imposition of tolls is illustrated by "the fact that the inhabitants of a particular locality could ask for auditors to examine the accounts." Apparently the possibility of an audit is sufficient evidence regardless of the thoroughness or frequency of its occurrence. The same is implied in his discussing in some detail Brandenburg-Prussia as a representative of Germany on the assumption that "a few further examples from other territories will complete the picture." [59] In other words, Heckscher may be interested in a comprehensive coverage which is impossible and therefore resorts to selective illustrations of some degree of representativeness. Since, however, the degree of representativeness is not established and the selectivity is not systematic, there is little evidence that the bias inherent in incomplete data has been avoided. This is particularly evident in his tendency to draw illustrations and examples from data ranging over several centuries and a whole continent.

Selectivity may be unavoidable in the above contributions, but the same is not necessarily true of the period or areas covered in Clapham's contribution. Nevertheless, selectivity is evident, as he himself admits in various instances. For example, emancipation policy "fluctuated and only a full narrative could do justice to the finer points of the story. It must be sufficient here to indicate the course of events and the results

[59] Heckscher, *Mercantilism*, pp. 40, 47, 76.

of the edicts in outline, beginning with the east, where the main problems lay." Thus, the selectivity is dictated by the need for brevity and concentration of the problems, both of which lend themselves to arbitrary judgment. When dealing with the textile industry, Clapham observes that "the towns just mentioned do not nearly complete the list of French wool manufacturing centers, but they illustrate the widespread diffusion of the industry. Two more must be mentioned, even in the most summary account—Roubaix and Paris itself," apparently because they grew relatively fast. As to protective tariffs, "an example or two from the laws themselves and from the comments of interested parties will best illustrate the spirit which inspired them." Selectivity is also evident in the dates used to illustrate the trend of a period. For example, speaking of the currency systems after 1815, Clapham refers to the years 1817–1819, 1832, and the "period after 1850" in Switzerland and Belgium. Holland is mentioned for 1847, and Germany for the whole period but more specifically for 1838. These dates were selected either because they indicate the institutional changes or because of heavy coinage.[60] What happened in other years is not clear.

His selectivity is sometimes guided by the availability of data. In the chapter on rural France, 1848–1914, the following data are offered as illustrations: population in 1876, 1886, 1896, 1906, 1911; tenure groups in 1882 and 1892; farm distribution by size in 1862, 1892 and 1908; farm machinery in 1892, 1900, and 1908; wine making in 1900 and 1907, to represent the maximum, and 1898 and 1910 to represent the minimum in the respective intervals 1896–1905 and 1906–1913. These are just a few examples, but the point is already clear that selectivity is common in Clapham's contribution. This approach may be in conformity with Clapham's interest in partial analysis, as has been suggested above.

A similar mixture of comprehensiveness and selectivity is evident in Mantoux's contribution. In some cases he is satisfied with illustrations, as when he deals with the tendency to change the traditional patterns of production. Here he deals mainly with conditions in the textile industry. Then he takes "one more instance outside the textile industry, which has provided all the above examples." His new example covers the miners and colliers of Newcastle only. In contrast, when dealing with enclosure acts of Parliament, he surveys the period, in intervals, from the beginning of the reign of Queen Anne through 1810 with precision. "There were three Acts only in the twelve years of the reign

[60] Clapham, *Economic Development of France and Germany*, pp. 44, 67, 72, 124–125.

of Queen Anne; from 1714 to 1720, about one every year; . . . thirty-three Acts between 1720 and 1730, thirty-five between 1730 and 1740, thirty-eight between 1740 and 1750. From 1750 to 1760 we find one hundred and fifty-six such Acts; from 1760 to 1770 four hundred and twenty-four; from 1770 to 1780 six hundred and forty-two. Between 1780 and 1790 . . . the figure came down to two hundred and eighty-seven. But, between 1790 and 1800, it leapt up to five hundred and six, while between 1800 and 1810 the total reached was much higher: . . . during those ten years Parliament passed no fewer than nine hundred and six Acts." However, this comprehensiveness is not characteristic even of specific aspects within the same context as the Enclosure Acts. In part this is due to lack of data. For example, the responses to these acts were varied. "Formal protests were comparatively rare. Yet a few of them have reached us. Sometimes they attacked the very principle of the enclosure, . . . sometimes they denounced its operations as 'partial and unjust. . . . After 1760 such protests became more frequent and forceful. The suppressed anger of the villagers would break out suddenly. In some parishes, the announcement of the enclosure caused riots. Formal notices could not be posted on the church doors, because of the obstruction by riotous mobs who forcibly prevented the sticking up of bills. The constable in charge of those bills was confronted by threatening crowds, armed with cudgels and pitchforks; in a Suffolk village, on three successive Sundays, his notices were torn out of his hands, he was thrown into a ditch and stones were hurled at him." [61] These data show that some opposition existed, but not how frequent or widespread it was. These examples show once more that interest in tendencies, the need for brevity, and the lack of data are important in forcing selectivity and precluding comprehensiveness. Mantoux tries to reconstruct a general picture, not a detailed one. Selective data are sufficient outlines for such reconstruction.

In attempting to estimate the degree of comprehensiveness or selectivity in Turner's contribution, we again face difficulty because the data are too few to permit evaluation. What is available, however, suggests high selectivity and little comprehensiveness. Different examples are treated in the context of the different frontiers, and even those examples are not treated in detail or comprehensively, as will be seen in comparing his treatment of the various frontiers.[62]

[61] Mantoux, *The Industrial Revolution*, pp. 82, 141–142, 174–175.
[62] For illustration, see Turner, *The Frontier*, pp. 43, 44, 87, 95, 133, 143, 147, 172.

In direct contrast to Turner's contribution, that of Cameron et al. is quite comprehensive in dealing with the issues specified by the authors. The case studies are comprehensive in the sense that all accessible information relevant to banking in the take-off period is taken into consideration. In the absence of readily available data, they have attempted estimates, as has been already indicated. All types of financial institutions are analyzed. Data on credit, bank size, assets, and liabilities are given in the aggregate, thus becoming inclusive of all the financial institutions. In some respects, however, the treatment is selective and illustrative only. For example, illustrations are provided only for the direct participation and other behavioral activities of the banks in the development process. Apparently the lack of exhaustiveness is due to the technical difficulty of enumerating all cases of short-term and long-term credit or isolating direct participation from other banking and financial activities.[63] Hence, it seems necessary to resort to illustrations, even though they do not show the significance of that kind of behavior. How much investment capital, for example, resulted from the direct participation of banking institutions, or how much short-term and long-term credit was extended? In other words, although comprehensiveness in these respects may be technically difficult, its absence renders the results only indications of tendencies rather than measures of participation by the banks. Nevertheless, the data seem comprehensive, compared with all other contributions under consideration. This can be explained by the relatively narrow scope of the subject matter, in terms of both content and chronology, its objective nature, and the fact that data are relatively accessible. In addition, there is good reason to believe that the authors intended to present comprehensive data in the spirit of modern scientific research.

In conclusion, it appears that the majority of the contributions are relatively selective in their approach. Selectivity seems to be dictated by vastness of the research topic, lack of data, and the widespread interest in establishing rather than measuring trends. As we shall see, this selectivity has left an impact on the validity of the findings and the confidence in the proposed interpretations of economic history.

[63] Cameron et al., *Banking in the Early Stages*, pp. 52, 56–57, 76–77, 285.

# 6

# Methodological Choices

We have suggested that the method used is closely related to the data used and to the generalizations or conclusions reached. Although the method is only a tool, there are various tools and various ways of handling each tool. Three main approaches have been mentioned, descriptive, analytical, and synthetic. These approaches usually overlap in any given study, the line of demarcation between them being not clear or precise. It is possible, however, to specify one or the other of these approaches as the main feature of a study. An author may also have stated his purpose. In either case, this critique will be guided by these observations. It should be noted that a study may in actuality be high on more than one of these features, but it must be high on at least one of them, to be characterized as such.

## DESCRIPTION, ANALYSIS, OR SYNTHESIS

As table 4 shows, there is a low tendency toward description among the contributions under study. Only two are ranked high, two are ranked moderately so, and four are ranked low. It is interesting that all those ranked low on description are high on synthesis, but the converse is true only in one case. However, since all the contributions, with only one exception, are high on synthesis, we might suggest that the exception is due to an idiosyncrasy of the individual contributor. In this case it happens that Clapham abides by his own views of the study of history and the necessary division of labor among contributors. Some of these aspects will be explored in more detail, at least in those cases where descriptive history is moderate or high in ranking.

Marx's contribution is a composite of all three approaches. It seems that Marx did not hesitate to apply any methodological device that might serve his objectives. Whenever appropriate he described, analyzed, or synthesized in search of the laws of motion of society. The descriptive parts, however, are mainly to illustrate a proposition or emphasize a point. To demonstrate the impact of machinery and modern industry on workers, Marx suggests a "rapid survey of the course of the English cotton industry."

From 1770 to 1815 this trade was depressed or stagnant for 5 years only. During this period of 45 years the English manufacturers had a monopoly of machinery and of the markets of the world. From 1815 to 1821 depression; 1822 and 1823 prosperity; 1824 abolition of the laws against Trades' Unions, great extension of factories everywhere; 1825 crisis; 1826 great misery and riots among the factory operatives; 1827 slight improvement; 1828 great increase in power-looms, and in exports; 1829 exports, especially to India, surpass all former years; 1830 glutted markets, great distress; 1831 to 1833 continued depression, the monopoly of the trade with India and China withdrawn from the East India Company; 1834 great increase of factories and machinery, shortness of hands. The new poor law furthers the migration of agricultural labourers into the factory districts. The country districts swept of children. White slave trade; 1835 great prosperity, contemporaneous starvation of the handloom weavers; 1836 great prosperity; 1837 and 1838 depression and crisis; 1839 revival; 1840 great depression, riots, calling out of the military; 1841 and 1842 frightful suffering among the factory operatives; 1842 the manufacturers lock the hands out of the factories in order to enforce the repeal of the Corn Laws. The operatives stream in thousands into the towns of Lancashire and Yorkshire, are driven back by the military, and their leaders brought to trial at Lancaster; 1843 great misery; 1844 revival; 1845 great prosperity; 1846 continued improvement at first, then reaction. Repeal of the Corn Laws; 1847 crisis, general reduction of wages by 10 and more per cent in honour of the "big loaf;" 1848 continued depression; Manchester under military protection; 1849 revival; 1850 prosperity; 1851 falling prices, low wages, frequent strikes; 1852 improvement begins, strikes continue, the manufacturers threaten to import foreign hands; 1853 increasing exports. Strike for 8 months, and great misery at Preston; 1854 prosperity, glutted markets; 1855 news of failures stream in from the United States, Canada, and the Eastern markets; 1856 great prosperity; 1857 crisis; 1858 improvement; 1859 great prosperity, increase in factories; 1860 Zenith of the English cotton trade, the Indian, Australian, and other markets so glutted with goods that even in 1863 they had not absorbed the whole lot; the French Treaty of Commerce, enormous growth of factories and machinery; 1861 prosperity continues for a time, reaction, the American Civil War, cotton famine; 1862 to 1863 complete collapse.[1]

Detailed description continues through four more pages, with a brief analytical comment here and there. In many cases, Marx reproduces descriptive material from other sources, such as the Reports of Inspectors or other officials, for the purpose of illustration. In no place is it apparent that Marx describes in order to answer the question What hap-

[1] Marx, *Capital*, pp. 457–458.

pened? Rather, he illustrates and analyzes as steps toward his main, synthetic objective. Therefore, while descriptive material is included, it is selected and arranged for a different objective; hence the classification of his method as moderately descriptive.

Weber and Pirenne follow the same approach, but they give a much briefer descriptive picture than Marx does. Because of the need for condensation and possibly for lack of sufficient data, they use description only to a low degree.

Heckscher explicitly classifies some of his material as descriptive. "To convey an impression of the extent to which the history of the toll system can be used as a general illustration of mercantilist policy directed against feudal disintegration, the description outlined in the previous chapter must be extended to include the development of internal economic administration in other spheres. But it is quite sufficient to confine such a description to the principal points." [2] The following excerpt will give an idea of his "cursory" description of coinage and the confusion surrounding it.

The royal coinage, however, also suffered from dualism, since two different units of reckoning were used, *tournois* and *parisis*, deriving their names respectively from Tours and Paris. The *parisis* unit was equivalent to one and a quarter *tournois*. It is noteworthy that the provincial unit and not that of the capital that carried the day, which was an unusual occurrence, and an additional proof that coins of smaller value drive out those of greater value . . . In Germany, coinage conditions resembled toll conditions and, if anything, were even worse. The right to issue coinage was an almost unchallenged privilege of the Empire, but already in the early Middle Ages, it had become illusory since rights were farmed out and imperial money was at the same time prohibited. There followed the farming out of the right to strike coins and after the 11th century, the similar farming out of other rights connected with coinage, the right to determine the content of coins, the right to dispose of coinage at will, such as the right to re-mortgage or re-dispose of acquired coinage privileges. The eagerness of the more important princes to obtain coinage rights was as unbounded as their desire for tolls. The only condition limiting the privileges was the fact that, like the tolls, they were confined to particular places, but this limitation disappeared by degrees after the beginning of the 14th century.[3]

Heckscher's contribution contains many long passages that are similarly descriptive. Nevertheless, he ranks as moderately descriptive for two

[2] Heckscher, *Mercantilism*, pp. 110, 120–121.
[3] *Ibid.*, pp. 120–121.

reasons. First, he describes only those aspects relevant to the problem at hand; in that sense he does not give a full picture of the topic he deals with, except as it sheds light on the specific problem. Second, his interest is explicitly to construct a theory of mercantilism through synthesis, to which purpose the main efforts are geared. In other words, synthesis rather than description is the main feature of his contribution.

In contrast, Clapham's contribution is mainly a survey of economic change, with little analytical or synthetic emphasis. As such, it is primarily descriptive of the conditions at various points in time so that differences can be observed and change noted. His description is sometimes detailed, depending on how important he considers a topic to be. This is not to say that Clapham gives only facts. On the contrary, opinions and impressions are frequent, but only when there are some historical facts to back them. To take an example at random, "With the late seventies had begun that world-wide fall in prices which continued, broadly speaking, until the end of the nineteenth century. Many causes were at work, but the main causes, in the agricultural sphere, were the railway, the marine engine and the telegraph, working internationally. And the article most affected in the early days was wheat. Before 1860 France had been on the average self-sufficing in wheat. Between 1861 and 1880 she had an exportable surplus in five years, and had to import in the remaining fifteen. The bad harvests of 1878–9 which she shared with England had necessitated heavy imports, or what seemed heavy to Frenchmen, unaccustomed to get their bread from abroad."[4] Then he goes on to give details about imports.

Another example will illustrate further. "The Revolution of 1848 found the position thus. There were thirty to forty companies in existence, dealing with various sections of the national programme. Many of them were under obligation to do the whole work themselves, the state retaining merely a right to buy back the lines. . . . But the government was not strong enough even to make a beginning. The only piece of railway legislation of the years 1848–52 was the concession to a company of the line from Paris to Rennes. The state gave the company what was coming to be recognized as the most useful form of assistance, a guarantee of interest.[5] In other words, though the major characteristic of his contribution is in the nature of "these are the facts," here and there the author tries to explain or raise the question as to

[4] Clapham, *The Economic Development of France and Germany*, p. 180.
[5] *Ibid.*, p. 146.

what they mean. On this basis the contribution has been classified as highly descriptive.

The contribution of Cameron et al., other than the introduction, has two main parts, the case studies and the conclusions. The case studies are highly descriptive, whereas the synthesis comes in the concluding parts. In this sense the contribution has been classified as high on both. The case studies describe the banking institutions in full, and this is regarded as a major objective of these chapters, thus contrasting on both criteria with the contributions of Marx and Heckscher. The authors describe their contribution as analytic.[6] Nevertheless, narration is encountered to various degrees in every case study. The Russian case is, in fact, quite descriptive, compared with the other case studies. A few examples at random will illustrate.

Branches not included, Scotland had 18 note-issuing institutions at the beginning of the nineteenth century; three in Edinburgh, two each in Glasgow, Aberdeen, Dundee, Stirling, and Paisley; and one each in Perth, Greenock, Falkirk, Ayr, and Leith. In addition at least 11 private (nonissuing) banks catered to the banking needs of the country. The period of Bank Restriction witnessed the proliferation of new banks in Scotland as in England; by 1810 there were more than 40 independent banks, a number which was maintained with negligible fluctuation for the next ten years. One reason for the rapid increase was dissatisfaction with the increasing conservatism of the old established banks. During the Napoleonic Wars the chartered banks invested heavily in government securities . . . thus reducing their capacity to lend to local industry and commerce.[7]

This section continues with a discussion of what conditions prevailed and, more briefly, why they did. Here is another example from a treatment of state savings banks in Russia.

Although legislation introducing savings banks goes back to 1841, there were only two such banks in 1862. Until the 1880's development was very slow. The expansion of the savings banks owes much to the drive initiated by finance minister N. K. Bunge. In 1881 he raised the interest rate on deposits to 4 per cent. In 1884 the State Bank was authorized to open savings banks in each agency of the State Bank without waiting for the initiative of urban or rural councils. Bunge also prepared the plan for the introduction of Post Office savings banks, whereby the rural population would be reached. These were introduced in 1889, and they led to a vast increase in savings, which continued even after interest was reduced to 3.6 percent. Table VII.13 shows the evolution of savings in the state savings banks.[8]

[6] Cameron et al., *Banking in the Early Stages*, p. 1.
[7] *Ibid.*, p. 71.
[8] *Ibid.*, p. 208.

Thus the changing conditions are described in conjunction with institutional changes that might have permitted those changes in savings to take place. The rest of the section continues in the same vein but with less analysis and more statements of fact than shown above. In part, this approach is unavoidable because the case studies set the stage for the synthesis. Therefore, all the relevant facts have to be stated. Once this is done, the case studies include their own concluding syntheses of the material. Hence, in terms of purpose as well as comprehensiveness, the classification for description is high.

As can be seen from the above, the majority of the contributions do not involve extensive description. The conditions they deal with are either described elsewhere or the authors simply do not regard that part of history as their objective. In the latter case they confine their description to clarification of those aspects relevant to the objective. On the other hand, a few seem to specialize in narrative or descriptive economic history. The majority are concerned with synthesis, but also with analytical or interpretative history, as is shown in table 4.

## THE CONCEPTUAL SCHEME

We have proposed in table 3 that regardless of the type of generalization anticipated, all studies ideally would place a high degree of emphasis on a conceptual scheme. The conceptual scheme can vary in content between one study and another, but a complete scheme is essential. A system of concepts, a set of relevant institutions, or a system of behavior relations would constitute a conceptual scheme. A complete set of one or more of these qualifies for a high rank of 3, if the set is presented as a unit or a body. If the elements are there but not in systematic form, it will be classified as moderate. Finally, a few definitions or disconnected relations would qualify only for a low rank of 1. A problem that will arise is how to treat implicit assumptions or relations. In this context it has been decided to classify only the explicit statements, although the implicit assumptions will be pointed out or suggested.

As table 4 shows, only two contributions are equipped with a conceptual scheme that qualifies for rank 3; two lack any systematic or conceptual framework and can qualify only for rank 1; the remaining four have a moderately compact or complete conceptual framework.

Marx's contribution is one of the high-ranking contributions. In his attempt to pursue a scientific social investigation, Marx devotes the first three, long chapters to an exposition of the theory he presented in detail in an earlier work. He defines his concepts and proposes a system of relations governing economic behavior; the meaning of *commodity*, the principle of exchange, and the concept of *value* are explored in detail; the processes of production and distribution are carefully stated. Marx differentiates constant and variable values, by use of examples, and analyzes the meaning and significance of *surplus value*. On the logic of these concepts, he proceeds to explore the processes of capitalist accumulation and reproduction as logical sequences to production and distribution. The model used by Marx is well contained and complete and, if applicable, would allow predicting the behavior of the economic system and the pattern of its evolution toward socialism and communism. Marx's conceptual scheme is important methodologically not only because it facilitates and systematizes his later contribution, but also because of at least two important methodological innovations. First, Marx explores and applies the concept of *process*, which is a forerunner of dynamic economic and social theory. Second, his model is an aggregate or macromodel that precedes macroeconomics by almost three-quarters of a century. To that extent Marx's contribution must be classified as high on the use of a conceptual scheme.

Weber's contribution is a little looser with respect to a conceptual scheme, but still it contains a general and fairly comprehensive framework. Weber's objective is to find the relation between an idea and an action, or between the Protestant ethic and the spirit of capitalism. Because his study was almost unique among its kind, there was no ready-made system of concepts or relations to guide it; therefore, he chooses to specify the intended meanings of the relevant concepts. For instance, "a capitalistic economic action . . . [is] one which rests on the expectation of profit by the utilization of opportunities for exchange, that is on (formally) peaceful chances of profit." Acquisition is rational if the "corresponding action is adjusted to calculations in terms of capital" such that receipts and payments are compared.[9] Western capitalism implies a continuous calculating behavior; rationality is a pattern, rather than an isolated endeavor. It is also characterized by rational bookkeeping and the separation of business from household. These features are closely related to the availability of free labor, another precondition of capitalism.

Weber goes beyond specifying the meaning of these concepts. He postulates certain relations. For example, every attempt to explain

[9] Weber, *The Protestant Ethic*, pp. 17, 18.

occidental rationalism must, "recognizing the fundamental importance of the economic factor, above all take account of the economic conditions. But at the same time the opposite correlation must not be left out of consideration. For though the development of economic rationalism is partly dependent on rational technique and law, it is at the same time determined by the ability and disposition of men to adopt certain types of practical rational conduct. When these types have been obstructed by spiritual obstacles, the development of rational economic conduct has also met serious inner resistance." The spirit of capitalism in this context is an "ethically coloured maxim for the conduct of life." It is acquisition not for utilitarian reasons, as pictured by Benjamin Franklin, but as an expression of a value system, as pictured by Jacob Fugger.[10]

Another conceptual or behavioral relation postulated is that a certain behavior may become internalized such that the pattern of behavior will continue even after the origins from which it derived have vanished. For example, it is proposed that capitalist behavior in the West, once established, would no longer need the support of religious values; it would persist for its own sake.[11] Weber's most difficult conceptual problem is probably to identify capitalism, capitalist behavior, and the religious ethic. No pure type of any of these phenomena can be identified, so Weber resolves the problem by adopting, for analytical purposes, the ideal-type approach. An ideal type is an abstraction artificially constructed for methodological convenience. Ideal types of the capitalist entrepreneur or of the spirit of capitalism are not average behavior patterns. They are forms of logical and consistent constructs created for the purpose of a specific study. That is, they are models of behavior used as standards of measurement and comparison. As such, the conceptual framework used by Weber is fairly clear and complete, although it permits reinterpretation as lacking in objectivity. This may be due to the nature of the phenomena he deals with, in which case no reflection on the framework as a whole should be implied.

In contrast to both of these contributions, Pirenne's lacks all form of a conceptual framework. He gives few definitions, if any. He speaks of a *nation*, but it is not clear what he means.[12] He defines *economic unity* by certain criteria, already mentioned, but he does not explore the logic of that unity. He assumes that these two concepts are clear to the reader.

10 *Ibid.*, pp. 26–27, 51–52.
11 *Ibid.*, p. 72.
12 Pirenne, *Mohammed and Charlemagne*, pp. 23–24.

In that sense, there is little use of a conceptual framework. However, we can infer certain premises from his analysis. For example, he conceives of economic unity as a function of trade. Economic relations appear to be dependent on two forces: demand for the product and political influence. Rome, being the center of population and of political power, determined the flow of trade and hence was the center of an economic unity. It is not clear what degree of political influence or volume of trade is needed to maintain unity.

At least at one point it seems as if Pirenne accepts social evolution as a premise. He only hints at this when he states that "in the midst of these incessant and victorious wars . . . the Empire was adapting itself to the deep-seated process of evolution which was transforming society and manners." It is not clear, however, whether *evolution* means progress or only change and adaptation. Another socio-political relation implied as a premise is that a minority can effectively change the character of the majority if it chooses to dominate.[13] However, there is no further explanation of the origin of this premise, and Pirenne writes without preparing the reader conceptually. Apparently, his interest lies in the empirical findings only as facts to be interpreted inductively after they have been observed. That is what he does, as we shall see below.

We have noted Heckscher's modernity in approaching historical research. Therefore, we should expect his contribution to contain a complete conceptual scheme, but one is not fully realized. Heckscher provides a conceptual framework for analysis in the form of concepts and definitions, certain theoretical relations, and assertions he plans to illustrate. The assertions are in part *a priori* postulates and in part an anticipation of the empirical findings. For example, he asserts on *a priori* grounds a certain relation between economic and political phenomena, from which he derives the premise that "the state stood at the centre of mercantilist endeavours as they developed historically: the state was both the subject and the object of mercantilist economic policy." Having illustrated this relation with a few examples, Heckscher describes mercantilism as an agent of *unification*, a system of power, a system of protection, a monetary system, and a conception of society.[14] This generalized model of mercantilism is presented as a hypothesis, or what Heckscher calls "the argument." It is not explicitly stated as a hypothesis, nor is it clear how the model was derived or how it can be tested. Apparently the illustrations function as a test of the model.

13 *Ibid.*, pp. 37, 69.
14 Heckscher, *Mercantilism*, pp. 21, 22–30.

Heckscher proposes certain concepts which he defines or specifies in order to render his argument meaningful. For example, he defines *feudal disintegration* as the disintegration of the state. Another conceptual clarification is implied in the statement that "the difference between medieval and modern conditions lies, to a large extent, in the fact that wants and demands have altered their direction, in other words, it lies in a sphere that evades any attempt at quantitative measurement of purpose." To clarify further, we are told that the modern system had "the overcoming of medieval particularism as its first postulate." [15] Both assertions are neither obvious nor conclusions from the study, but parts of a postulated conceptual framework.

Sometimes Heckscher's definition is a description of the empirical situation. For instance, the distinction bewteen manufacture and handicraft is considered difficult. Nevertheless, the manufactures are always placed on some special footing. "Either by technique or by organization, either as technical units or as business undertakings, they represented associations of a larger number of forces than the ordinary small workshops. As opposed to handicrafts, they were large-scale undertakings, even in the very frequent cases where they were not really large industrial plants." [16] Although the discussion continues for several pages, the distinction remains ambiguous and in many ways impressionistic. It is true that the real world did not distinguish clearly between one type of production and the other, but methodological clarity demands more specificity for judging the relevance of data and for keeping the problems in perspective.

Similar difficulties arise where Heckscher introduces *rural industry* into his discussion. He recognizes the ambiguity of the term, for "if it is taken to mean the whole area which did not belong to the towns organized in gilds, that is if it is taken to include the suburbs and the towns without gilds, this kind of industry has already been dealt with previously. But the conditions in those industries which were combined with agriculture, above all the widely ramified textile industry, were not all the same. Rural industry must now chiefly be considered as of this latter kind." [17] The reader is expected to know what *rural industry* means.

Probably the most important, but least clear concept is the term *medieval*. In various instances Heckscher describes an approach or a

---

[15] *Ibid.*, pp. 39, 42, 43.
[16] *Ibid.*, p. 188.
[17] *Ibid.*, p. 204.

behavior pattern as medieval. Yet, it is not explicitly stated what *medieval* is supposed to mean, other than that it is not *modern*, which is equally ambiguous. In dealing with wage assessments, Heckscher concludes that "here too the approach was medieval." [18] Although *medieval* is a time specification, it seems to also imply certain behavior patterns and standards.[19] Both the patterns and the standards are not clear. For example, "a large proportion and, perhaps, the majority of the institutions that have generally passed for medieval are really not medieval at all, or rather they are medieval only in the sense that the ideas on which they were based date from the Middle Ages. Their actual historical evolution belongs to a much later period—in part, even to the 18th century." [20] Yet, neither the medieval period, the medieval ideas, nor the Middle Ages are specific enough to be objectively identifiable. Therefore, although there is a conceptual framework, because of the lack of specificity and the remaining ambiguities this contribution has been classified as moderate in presenting a conceptual scheme.

In contrast to all the contributions discussed so far, Clapham's contribution ranks low for the conceptual framework criterion. In part, the problem lies in the absence of any statement of the objectives or method of the study. What *economic development* means or how to measure it is not clear. Some conceptual relations can be gleaned from the text, but these are not presented as a system of relations or as the framework to be followed. For example, Clapham speaks of "all the economic forces," but nowhere does he identify these forces or the weights to be attached to each of them with respect to development. He uses the concept of *class* but does not define it; actually he does not use it in a consistent manner. Sometimes it is an occupational group; in others it is a tenure group or a political group. In another context he speaks of the *compact village*. He also speaks of an *average* Western village, but none of these structures is defined, nor is it clear how one differs from the others.[21]

The framework he uses tends to change with the subject matter. "For comparison with Belgium and England, the development of engineering

[18] *Ibid.*, pp. 133, 229.
[19] *Ibid.*, pp. 22, 48.
[20] *Ibid.*, p. 133.
[21] Clapham, *Economic Development of France and Germany*, 18–19, 31, 119, 190.

and the extent to which machinery was used are more significant than the condition of the primary iron industry," which would be appropriate in comparison with other countries. Which of these is a better indicator of the development of metallurgy, or why, is not specified. As far as analytical relations are concerned, they are equally vague and far apart. For example, "France was in all these matters [commercial organization] several generations ahead of Germany, thanks to her much more complete urbanization." [22] Why urbanization should lead to better commercial organization is not shown; actually many contemporary examples would contradict this assessment. Clapham is convinced that cooperation and education are good for agricultural development, but the relation remains vague. The author simply illustrates the changes in both areas.[23]

Clapham is not unaware of the need for definition, as he himself admits in dealing with agricultural syndicates, for which he adopts the legal definition for lack of a better one.[24] One particular conceptual framework which recurs more than once is a stage approach to the development. Although Clapham does not specify the stages, he alludes to the theoretical framework. For example, "the revolutionary movements of 1848 mark a definite stage in German agrarian history." Or, "some trades even passed in a single generation through the three stages —independent handicraft, outwork, and the factory system—an evolution which . . . had taken several centuries in earlier ages." Again, "stages in the development of produce, mineral and metal exchanges are not easily traced, because records are scarce." [25] The first usage of the term *stage* could mean just a benchmark, but later usages clearly indicate an evolutionary process. Whether or not Clapham holds to a stage theory is not stated, but one might surmise as much from his pronouncements. Given the absence of a body of concepts or of clear definitions, this contribution is low for the conceptual framework criterion.

Mantoux's contribution is rich in concepts and relations that describe dynamic behavior in the economy, although these concepts are not set out as a body or with full clarity. In a sense the study is guided by a model that is a mixture of Marxist and neoclassical economics, although

---

[22] *Ibid.*, pp. 61, 119, 159, 183.
[23] *Ibid.*, p. 183.
[24] *Ibid.*, pp. 186, 199, 278.
[25] *Ibid.*, pp. 194, 301, 372.

neither is specified by the author. Three main characteristics can be observed regarding economic change. First, it is treated as relating to a system of interdependent components; second, change is gradual and evolutionary; and third, it goes through stages, which may be roughly defined in terms of the dominant feature of each stage. The three aspects of the framework relate to the form, or pattern, of change in society. Mantoux is equally concerned with the process of change. Therefore, he sets in fair detail a series of statements or assertions that indicate the changes to be expected within his framework. In a way, the explanation of change becomes dependent on understanding the system as a whole. More specifically, the explanation of change becomes a search for the beginning of a trend rather than for its origin. Once the beginning has been pinpointed, regardless of the causes, change will follow through the various stages up to the stage under consideration. This determinism is implied also in the assertions that govern the process of change. Mantoux, however, points out that change may not be due to "natural evolution," by which he means an internal process of change without external influence. Large-scale industry, for example, grew up prior to the Industrial Revolution not by natural evolution, but by government support and therefore was not self-sustaining.

Two fundamental facts, closely interwoven, transforming one another, infinitely varied in their consequences and always the same in principle, govern this evolution: the exchange of commodities and the division of labour. As old as the desires and the work of mankind, they pursue their way together through the changes in all civilizations, which they accompany or direct. Every extension or multiplication of exchanges, by throwing open more channels to production, gives rise to an ever more elaborate and effective division of labour, a more and more narrow distribution of functions between producing areas, between trades and between different parts of the same trade. Conversely, division of labour, aided by improvement, which is its most active manifestation, implies a cooperation between all these mutually interdependent specialized activities, which becomes ever more extensive and in which the whole world ultimately takes part.[26]

He describes this relation further.

The periods which are marked in the history of economics correspond to the more or less clearly defined stages of this double development. From this point of view the use of machinery itself, important as are its consequences, is only a secondary phenomenon. Before it became one of the most powerful

[26] Mantoux, *The Industrial Revolution*, p. 29.

causes in influencing modern societies it began by being the resultant, and as it were the expression of these two phenomena, at one of the decisive moments in their evolution.[27]

These are only examples of his assertions or statements regarding evolution and the stages of economic development. Actually, evolution and the stage approach are generalized to various sectors of the economy, such as the development of industrial classes, labor unions, and factories and technology. All these are said to evolve gradually in correspondence with exchange and the division of labor.[28]

This is a general model of change, but the details are spelled out only in the various statements that fill the introductory chapter and that preface many of the other chapters of the study. To take a few examples: "As soon as the means of production no longer belong to the producer and a class of men is formed who buy labour from another class, an opposition of interests must become manifest." "Behind this use of human labour and of mechanical force, capital is at work, swept forward by its own law—the law of profit—which urges it ceaselessly to produce, in order ceaselessly to grow." "Export stimulates existing industries, import leads to the creation of new ones." "All these interconnected facts, big periodic fairs, travelling merchants, primitive simplicity in methods of transport, are due to one thing: insufficient means of communications." "Internal freedom is the one thing modern industry cannot do without. As soon as that is taken away industry ceases to move, and movement is its basic law: continual change, irresistibly carried forward by technical progress, and continual expansion." [29]

This array of statements explaining the process of change forms what may be regarded as Mantoux's model for the study of the Industrial Revolution. To the extent these statements could be generalized, the model would apply to the study of any movement of industrial and economic change. It is not relevant at this point where these relations came from. The reason for classifying this contribution as only moderately conceptualized is that these statements do not form a body or a compact model, and the definitions are not always explicitly stated.

Turner's conceptual framework is brief and simple. He begins with certain assertions or premises. For example, "behind institutions, behind

[27] *Ibid.*, p. 41.
[28] *Ibid.*, pp. 68, 89, 246, 279.
[29] *Ibid.*, pp. 26, 74, 104, 112, 261.

constitutional forms and modifications, lie the vital forces that call these organs into life and shape them to meet changing conditions." [30] The forces in this case are the frontier and the conditions surrounding it—danger, free land, and dependence for capital. Another premise is that political actions are determined by economic and social forces; hence the economic significance of the frontier and its impact on the development of American democracy. The most important conceptual construct is the frontier itself, or the West, which is more a moving frontier characterized by relations than it is a physical entity. This conceptual construct is devised as a convenience in that it permits flexibility and generalization.

Whereas these concepts and relations are explicitly stated, others remain implicit. For example, Turner's evolutionist bent is not stated in explicit terms, although it is used in interpreting certain facts as if it were derived from them.[31] Is it true, for example, that social development followed everywhere from buffalo trails to railroads, and from trading posts to commercial settlements? Certain experiences may have followed this pattern, but not necessarily all of them. The evolutionary bent as a premise is implicit and remains so. Another implicit assumption is indicated in the conclusion that "the advance of the frontier decreased our dependence on England." [32] In this statement Turner must be attributing a certain role to communication, size of population, and distance, or some other factors. In part, the problem is due to the brevity of the essays. Although a conceptual framework exists, it is neither complete nor compact; hence the classification as moderate for this criterion.

The contribution of Cameron et al. has been classified as only moderate even though it is guided by a conceptual framework, or what the authors call "Preliminary Definitions and Theoretical Considerations." Having defined *economic growth, early stages of industrialization,* and *financial sector,* they present a series of statements of what they consider the functions of the banking institutions in economic development and industrialization. "Financial institutions serve as intermediaries between savers and investors; . . . [they] may supply part or all of the circulating media or means of payment. Although this function is not inherent

[30] Turner, *The Frontier,* p. 21.
[31] *Ibid.,* pp. 14–15.
[32] *Ibid.,* p. 23.

in the definition of financial institutions, they may supply initiative and enterprise, as well as finance, for the creation, transformation, and expansion of industrial and other ventures." [33] The authors debate some of these issues, including the question of whether banks generally finance innovation by granting loans. They suggest that while bankers' criteria for granting loans vary, "two are likely to be prominent in all times and places: (1) a reasonable prospect that the loan will be paid; . . . and (2) a reasonable expectation that the loan will be part of or contribute to a continuing profitable relation between the banker and the customer." [34]

However, these theoretical assumptions and considerations are parts of a larger framework that remains implicit, such as economic mobility and rationality, competition, and free enterprise. Otherwise, why should banks be able to allocate capital efficiently or have an active role as the authors assume they do? Another and more significant problem relates to the definitions used in the introduction. For example: "Economic growth is defined here as a sustained increase in output per person; economic development is defined as economic growth accompanied by a substantial change in the economy. Specifically, economic development involves an increase in the size of the secondary sector of the economy and a corresponding decrease in the relative importance of the primary sector. By 'early stages of industrialization' we mean that transitional period in which manufacturing industries, normally the largest component of the secondary sector, adopt new, more capital-intensive techniques of production and grow rapidly relative to agriculture."

"In what follows the term 'financial sector' will frequently appear with its synonym, the 'financial system.' Technically the set of financial institutions is a subsector of the tertiary, or service-producing, sector of the economy." [35] These definitions are very vague. An increase or decrease can range from a minute value to infinity in one direction or another. This change applies to per capita income, the structural composition of the economy, and the degree of capital intensity. The flexibility in the range of what is an increase or a decrease may be unavoidable because of the difficulty of precise measurement. However,

[33] Cameron et al., *Banking in the Early Stages*, pp. 6–8.
[34] *Ibid.*, p. 13.
[35] *Ibid.*, p. 6.

it is possible to specify certain limits to render a definition more useful for communication, comparison, and analysis, as they have done in measuring the density of financial institutions.

Therefore, given the fact that certain relations are left implicit and that some of the concepts are defined in very general terms, this contribution has been classified as moderate for the criterion of conceptual scheme.

A number of observations can be made from this survey of representative studies. First, it is clear that the majority of the contributors have formulated conceptual schemes to aid the investigation and presentation of their material, although a few have kept their conceptual framework implicit. Second, there is little evidence that emphasis on a conceptual scheme is related to topic, or to whether an investigation is narrow or broad in scope. It is probably safer to suggest that the personal interest of the investigator is the most important determinant of whether a conceptual scheme is formulated or not. In fact, there is little evidence that the contributors in general have associated a conceptual scheme with scientific method or objectivity. Third, in view of the last statement, it is possible to understand why only in exceptional cases are conceptual relations stated in complete and clear form. Certainly Marx's approach seems to be far ahead of the economic history and other social sciences of his time. Finally, although the conceptual schemes are generally vague or incomplete, it seems that the contributors are aware of more relations than they have put down in writing.

## SYSTEMS ANALYSIS

In a sense the conceptual scheme is closely related to the systems approach, as was discussed above. The mere assumption of an economic or social system implies a model or a conceptual framework, but the converse is not true. As shown in table 4, only one contribution classified as high for the systems approach is also high for the conceptual scheme, four of the five classified as moderate are also moderate for the conceptual scheme; and one is low for both; only two contributions are not consistent for the two criteria. We have classified as high for the systems approach any contribution that has a statement of intention to that effect and has implemented it, or that deals with its unit of study as an aggregate whole with the interdependences between the parts and the whole clearly shown. Where either the interdependence is vague or the statement of intention is incomplete, we have classified the contribution as moderate. Where neither a statement is made nor the interdependencies shown clearly, the ranking is low.

Much of the material relevant to this section has already been presented. Therefore, only a brief statement will be made to explain the classification shown in table 4. As has been already suggested, Marx applies an aggregate model and deals with society as a system in which economic and noneconomic factors interact and all the economic sectors converge to make up the economy. These interdependencies are stated fairly clearly and are kept in view throughout the study as necessary in the search for the laws of motion of society. Thus, even when he is dealing with a sector or subsystem, the total society is considered to be undergoing change, as would happen in an organic whole because of the action or inaction of one of its component parts. This is also shown by the attention Marx gives to the noneconomic forces—such as the state, Parliament, or the class structure—in analyzing capitalist production. Therefore, we have classified his approach as high in using a systems approach.

In contrast, Weber has a high ranking for conceptual scheme but a low one for systems analysis. Weber is more concerned with individual behavior. Rationality, asceticism, and calling are all related to the individual; there is no mention of a system or a capitalist economy. Interdependencies are mentioned but there is no statement of the relation between the various aspects of the economy, nor the relation between individual behavior and the rest of society. The closest he comes to a systems approach is to consider Protestantism as a system, and Protestants as a unified whole. This, however, would be stretching the point a little too far, since in religious matters the individual remains the sole decision maker as far as his own behavior is concerned. Given the absence of any evidence of a systems approach, this contribution has been classified as low.

Pirenne is more implicit than explicit in applying a systems approach, but enough evidence exists to suggest his interest in this conceptual approach. For example, he deals with the empire as an economic unity; he also treats it as a united political system, even though socially and culturally the provinces were autonomous. This treatment leaves out the definition of a system and a statement of the relations that tie it together, although the position of Rome and the political power of the emperor are emphasized as unifying factors. Economically, the Mediterranean formed the unifying element of the system. Thus, the system is held together in general terms such that certain important modifications could take place without disrupting the functioning of the system. For example, at various times in the period under consideration, the emperor or the king loses all power but remains a titular head. Yet, the system remains intact. Apparently, even the disruption caused by the Moslem invasion changed the direction of trade, but did not disrupt the system. Two alternative interpretations of this approach are possible. The first is that the systems concept does not apply and these comments are therefore irrelevant. The second, which is more probable, is that the system was capable of adjusting and readjusting so that even radical changes could take place without causing total or permanent disruption. In other words, if the system broke down, another system would be created to fill the gap, and might have various similarities with the former system. This flexible approach implies an evolutionary conception of the system. However, such an approach would be of little use unless both the components of the system and the ties that hold it together are specified. In view of the absence of any such specification, the classification could not be high. However, because of the explicit treatment of the empire as a unity, it has been classified as moderate for this criterion.

Heckscher's interest in the systems approach is equally implicit. On one hand, Heckscher does not explain economic development or developments, and whether they relate to the economy or to a given sector; he deals with individual industries, towns, or sectors of economies, but in no place does he show the connection between the part and the whole. On the other hand, he deals with unification and disintegration, both of which imply an aggregate system. He also treats various aspects as leading to the same goal, namely unification. Protection, money, power, and the conception of society all converge toward unification, which is the objective of mercantilism. In other words, all these factors are related to the state of the society and economy through the medium of economic policy. Although Heckscher uses the term *system* in a number of instances, he does not state his intention of using a systems approach.[36] Nevertheless, the explicit statements regarding disintegration and unification and the persistent treatment of these concepts as the focus of his analysis seem adequate evidence to rank this contribution as moderately involved in a systems approach.

[36] Heckscher, *Mercantilism*, pp. 46, 73, 79, 92, 146.

Clapham's treatment is less easily classified because much is left unsaid. His inclination to use an evolutionary or stage approach could imply a system, but there is no specific reference to such an association. Clapham deals with national economies, and one can regard these as economic systems, but the idea of a system does not come up, nor is there any attempt to consider interdependencies between the components, in contrast to his reference to the "interdependence of nations" which might imply a systems approach.[37] Similarly, the "rational economic organization of society" might imply a system with interdependencies, but no explicit statement is made to that effect. In part, this may be due to Clapham's orientation toward partial economic analysis, but it cannot be totally so, because even in partial analysis, a unit, say a firm, can be treated as a system. In essence, his descriptive tendency explains the absence of a systems framework, which is more relevant for purposes of explanation.

These comments about Clapham's contribution are well illustrated in Mantoux's work. Mantoux tries to explain change within a situation in which various socio-economic and political aspects are interconnected. There is no mention of the economy as a system, but the relations that tie the components together are clearly shown. The factory system, which characterizes the economy, covers the relations between the various components, such as capital, labor, technology, organization, and communication. The roles of technology and communication in the division of labor are highly emphasized as factors causing change. The role of institutions and legislation is another determinant in the economy. Mantoux deals with the dynamics of change both within and of the economy as a whole. It is in this sense as much as in the substance of the relations that he is comparable with Marx in approaching economic change. He deals with the factory system as a whole, with the Industrial Revolution, and with England, each of which is in some way a system. Furthermore, he deals with evolution of the total, as well as of the parts. In all these aspects, Mantoux seems to address himself to a conglomeration of components that act on and react to each other according to certain theoretical principles and laws. Nevertheless, because no explicit statement is made in this regard, Mantoux's contribution has been classified as moderate for use of the systems approach.

The same features are apparent in Turner's contribution. The frontier is a system in which economic and noneconomic factors interact.

[37] Clapham, *Economic Development of France and Germany*, pp. 136–138.

Change characterizes the frontier, which itself forms part of a larger system, the American society. Thus, the frontier is both a system and a subsystem. Turner deals with it in the former framework, although he does not ignore the interaction between the subsystem and the system, as for example when he discusses the frontier as the safety-valve for the discontented, or its impact in reducing American dependence on England. All this, however, is too brief and sketchy to be a systems approach to the study of the frontier. There is no explicit statement of the relations or interdependencies, nor is the treatment systematic. However, because he considers the interdependencies, we have regarded this treatment as moderate for the systems approach.

Cameron et al. do not speak of an economic system, but they treat each of the economies they study as a unit. They also speak of the economy at given stages of development, which is possible only if the economy is treated in the aggregate. Banking, which is the subject of the study, is both a subsystem and a system. More accurately, they speak of the financial system, which is a part of the larger whole. The relation between the part and the whole is treated briefly, but there is very little about the relation between the various other parts that can affect or be affected by the financial institutions. Just to take one example, what is the relation between technology and banking, or between literacy, population, or urbanization and banking? These aspects can all be expressed in the concepts of demand for and supply of financial and banking services, but the relations are not stated. Furthermore, in terms of the systems approach, the noneconomic or financial institutions are hardly brought out in the discussion. The distribution of land and land tenure are cases in point. Were these institutions and their evolution considered, the impact of banking might be seen differently. The financial institutions might be seen as passive elements that facilitate change but do not cause it, contrary to what the authors suggest. For instance, land tenancy has increased during the last century in most countries—other than Japan, which the authors use as an example—regardless of banking policies. The relevant factors seem to be private ownership, population pressure, and an indifferent government policy, regardless of whether "quasi-bankers" existed or not. Even in the U. S. where population pressure on the land has been relatively low, technological change and private ownership have caused an increase in the rates of tenant farming. If the systems concept were used explicitly, it would have necessitated reconsideration of the role of banking in these developments.

Apparently there is a tendency in the representative studies toward looking at the whole as a body of interconnected parts, but treatment of these parts as a system is frequently more implicit than explicit. Furthermore, lack of specification is compounded by the assumption, rather than statement, of a system of relations connecting these parts and holding the system together. As a result, there is a tendency to give a partial, and often an insufficient explanation of change in an economy or in a larger system. Although it might be necessary to isolate the various components so as to reduce complexity, there is an inherent danger in such an approach because it can leave important factors out of the picture, as has been the case in most of the sample contributions.

## DEDUCTION AND INDUCTION

One of the most complicated areas of this critique is to estimate the degree to which deduction and induction are applied. The complexity arises in part from the absence of a statement on this issue in most research, and from the difficulty of separating deduction and induction from each other. In a sense, we have associated deduction with the use of theory and hypotheses, and induction with generalization from the empirical facts. We have also suggested that the study of history depends more on induction than on deduction. Nevertheless, the sample contributions have been classified according to the degree each of these approaches has been used, allowing for the general impression that most research in the social sciences uses both to varying degrees.

As table 4 shows, there is a strong tendency to use induction, although deduction is used to a moderate degree in three of the case studies. In contrast, induction is used to a high degree in six instances, and moderately so in the two remaining instances. Those cases in which induction is used moderately tend to be the cases that are more concerned with general ideas or that lean greatly toward description and involve little analysis.

Marx's contribution is a good illustration of an effort to combine deduction and induction. On one hand, Marx begins with a model of capitalist production, distribution, and exchange. On the other, he illustrates the relations of that model from the historical experience of

England. The former part can be regarded as deduction; the latter, induction. This oversimplification is almost inevitable, because it is not possible to find out the degree to which the model is derived from the empirical analysis or from intuition. Marx formulated his theory prior to carrying out his extended empirical investigations. Obviously he studied the history of various societies and observed change in England and other European countries. But there is no evidence that these studies were systematic enough to derive a theory therefrom. Furthermore, some of the relations he states in the model could not have been derived empirically and, therefore, must have been derived from more general premises and then taken as points of departure. For example, the law of value according to which the exchange value of a commodity is determined by the amount of socially necessary labor embodied in it must have been derived from the premise that labor is the only source of value. In this case we know that the law of value did not originate with Marx and, therefore, could not have been derived from his empirical investigations. Thus, the general premise that labor is the only source of value cannot be an empirically derived law, but a postulate. From this definitional postulate may be derived all the processes embodied in his theory, including the variations in the rate of surplus value and the rates of profit and exploitation. Some scholars would deny this interpretation and assert that Marx's theory does not depend on the theory of value, because surplus value is an empirical fact, but this is independent of the source of the theory itself.

Another premise that seems to be empirically premature implies full knowledge of bourgeois society even before that society came fully into existence. For example, "the categories of bourgeoisie economy consist of such like forms. They are forms of thought expressing with social validity the conditions and relations of a definite, historically determined mode of production, viz., the production of commodities." [38] Such a generalization can be derived only from the general premise that commodity fetishism is peculiar to the capitalist mode of production, which becomes true by definition. Put differently, Marx's theory of economic change could have been derived from the definitional concepts he starts with, regardless of the empirical data he later accumulates and uses to illustrate the theory. The fact that he makes empirical observations tends only to bring his model closer to reality than if he kept it an abstract theory. Undoubtedly Marx succeeds in combining deduction

[38] Marx, *Capital*, p. 47.

with inductive interpretation and thus renders his theory historically more useful. That he depends on deduction can be seen from his generalizations regarding advanced stages of capitalism and later of socialism, both of which did not exist empirically before his time. In a sense, Marx is quite modern in proposing his theory as a hypothesis and proceeding to "verify" it empirically. The only problem is that he proceeds to illustrate the content of the hypothesis rather than to test it, as has been suggested in our discussion of selectivity in data accumulation. A few examples will show how the conclusions are derived.

Marx adopts the laws of value and exchange with some modifications from his predecessors. However, once these relationships are accepted as given, certain results follow. For example: "We have seen how money is changed into capital; how through capital surplus-value is made, and from surplus-value more capital. But the accumulation of capital pre-supposes surplus-value; surplus-value presupposes capitalistic production; capitalistic production pre-supposes the pre-existence of considerable masses of capital and of labour-power in the hands of producers of commodities. The whole movement, therefore, seems to turn in a vicious circle, out of which we can only get by supposing a primitive accumulation (previous accumulation of Adam Smith) preceding capitalistic accumulation; an accumulation not the result of the capitalistic mode of production, but its starting point."

Accordingly Marx proceeds to illustrate the existence of primitive accumulation rather than observing it first and then explaining its impact and processes. For another example, "Since the demand for labour is determined not by the amount of capital as a whole, but by its variable constituent alone, that demand falls progressively with the increase of the total capital, and at an accelerated rate, as this magnitude increases." This generalization is true by definition, and it is not shown to be empirically true or accepted as true. The following is a seemingly more empirical conclusion: "The enormous power, inherent in the factory system, of expanding by jumps, and the dependence of that system on the markets of the world, necessarily beget feverish production, followed by over-filling of the markets, whereupon contraction of the markets brings on crippling of production. The life of modern industry becomes a series of periods of moderate activity, prosperity, over-production, crisis and stagnation. The uncertainty and instability to which machinery subjects the employment, and consequently the conditions of existence, of the operatives become normal, owing to these periodic changes of the industrial cycle. Except in the periods of prosperity, there rages between the capitalists the most furious combat for the share of each in the markets. This share is directly proportional to the cheapness of the product." [39] This conclusion is a result of the model rather than a generalization from the observation of actual international competition, although Marx tries to support his conclusion with an extensive survey of the fluctuations during the whole preceding century. It is not evident, however, that these fluctuations are results of the capitalist mode of production, unless the earlier premises are taken as given. This explains expressions like "inherent" and "necessarily," which render the conclusion deterministic, regardless of the empirical conditions to be observed. Despite these reservations, Marx's emphasis on empiricism and induction render justifiable the classification of his contribution as high for induction.

Weber's contribution is more completely dependent on empirical observations and less related to theory and deductively derived principles of behavior. Even the definitions are supposed to be generalizations from the historical observations, as has already been pointed out. It is true that once the concepts—such as rationality, asceticism and calling —have been defined, certain patterns of behavior might be anticipated. However, Weber proceeds to survey the behavior of those groups who were converted to Protestantism or indoctrinated in the new Calvinism. He does not regard their behavioral patterns as predetermined unless they have been observed to be rational, ascetic, and convinced of the calling. Even then, he tends to interpret the observed behavior, because the results do not necessarily follow, nor are they clearly consistent with the premises postulated. Only observation and interpretation can help in illustrating the hypothesized relation between the idea and business behavior. However, the problem with Weber's induction is that he does not have sufficient or well-controlled data to justify his conclusions. He pays little attention to sequence between cause and effect. He also leaves out factors other than religion which might have contributed significantly to the development of capitalism. Once he has shown that a certain "correlation" exists between Protestantism and the spirit of capitalism, he regards his mission accomplished. In other words, while his approach is highly inductive, his conclusions are preconceptions more than inferential generalizations from historical observation.

For example, Weber points to the "smaller participation of Catholics

[39] *Ibid.*, pp. 736, 643, 455.

in the modern business life of Germany" as opposed to the tendency of minority groups in other countries. However, neither the smaller participation nor the tendency follow from observed facts. The evidence consists of a footnote reference to "passages" from the works of Sir William Petty. Weber notes the "numerous" monks and businessmen among the proselytes in France at the time of the spread of the Reformation. This is based on the opinion of another authority; namely, the observations of Sir William Petty concerning the Netherlands, and of Gothein regarding the "Calvinistic diaspora" as the seed-bed of capitalistic economy.[40]

In all these cases, although the references may be sufficient documentation, the data given are too meager to support any inference but that certain authorities *believe* Protestants to be more active in business than Catholics. The problem of inference is even more complicated in Weber's treatment of ideas. How to establish, for example, the existence or significance of an idea?

So far we have considered only Calvinism, and have thus assumed the doctrine of predestination as the dogmatic background of the Puritan morality in the sense of methodically rationalized ethical conduct. This could be done because the influence of that dogma in fact extended far beyond the single religious group which held in all respects strictly to Calvinistic principles, the Presbyterians. Not only the Independent Savoy Declaration of 1658, but also the Baptist Confession of Hanserd Knolly of 1689 contained it, and it had a place within Methodism. Although John Wesley, the great organizing genius of the movement, was a believer in the universality of Grace, one of the great agitators of the first generation of Methodists and their most consistent thinker, Whitefield, was an adherent of the doctrine. The same was true of the circle around Lady Huntingdon, which for a time had considerable influence.[41]

This passage illustrates how Weber infers from certain observations. It is not clear how representative these believers were, or how significant the attitude of John Wesley was. Nevertheless, Weber concludes that the dogma of predestination was the basis of Puritan morality. In other words, whether he uses a method of difference or of agreement, a certain degree of impressionism creeps in and renders his inference somewhat subjective. Nevertheless, empiricism remains the basis of these inferences, and this justifies classifying his contribution as high for induction.

[40] Weber, *Protestant Ethic*, pp. 39, fn. 11, 43, 189.
[41] *Ibid.*, p. 125.

The same observations apply to Pirenne's contribution, although it is more systematic than Weber's as far as the controlled treatment of data is concerned. Pirenne's theme is fully empirical, and any supporting premises are only implied rather than explicitly stated. The author observes, compares, and concludes from the observed facts. The closest he comes to deduction is to use the method of elimination of the alternative hypothesis, in the sense that if the opposite is false, the original hypothesis cannot be rejected. Otherwise, his conclusions are induced from the observations. The only problem with Pirenne's induction is that he depends on examples rather than on systematic samples or representative data. He seems to generalize from meager data, mostly by impressionism rather than by any statistical analysis, and without consistency in following a theory, such as probability theory or the law of large numbers. A few examples will illustrate. Pirenne concludes that the barbarian invasion left "Romania" intact, even though "at the beginning of the 6th century there was not an inch of soil in the West still subject to the Emperor. At first sight the catastrophe seems enormous, . . . but if we examine it more closely it seems less important. For the Emperor still had a legal existence. He had abdicated nothing of his sovereignty. . . . No one ventured to assume the title of Emperor. . . . The Empire subsisted, in law, as a sort of mystical presence; in fact—and this is much more important—it was 'Romania' that survived." [42] The fact that no invader assumed the title of emperor seems to be the only evidence. He may not have abdicated any of his sovereignty, but was he able to enforce his rule? More directly relevant examples can be found in Pirenne's presentation of economic and social conditions. He observes that tenure arrangements remained the same: there was no redistribution of the soil, and no new methods of cultivation; Roman colonists remained tied to the soil, and big estates with slaves remained unchanged. Land taxes were retained, there was a normal trade in corn and clothing, and the class system also continued as before. These are important indicators, but they are presented as great generalities and more in the form of assertions. No attempt is made to show exactly what percentage of the estates survived, or what percentage of the invaded land was seized, nor is there any evidence that trade was not affected. The evidence might be adequate to suggest a certain degree of continuity, but not that the invasion had no impact. Traders from the East, Syrians and Jews, were still active, but this does

[42] Pirenne, *Mohammed and Charlemagne*, pp. 32–33.

not indicate their number nor that the scope of their activity was not diminished.[43] Pirenne finds evidence on imported commodities in levies by the Church or in menus. However, no estimate of the change is attempted or even possible, since the evidence suggests only the existence or absence of a commodity from these records.

Pirenne is more explicit in evaluating the impact of the Moslem than the barbarian invasion. He observes the total disappearance of commodities and activities, not only their decline. For example, he concludes that navigation in the Mediterranean from the middle of the seventh century became impossible because of war with the Moslems. Piracy put an end to trade. Papyrus and spices disappeared since no mention of them in the records is to be found. Pirenne notes the scarcity of information, but he nevertheless finds it permissible to "assert" that "by the end of the 7th century and the beginning of the 8th century [spices] had disappeared from the normal diet. They did not reappear until after the 12th century when the Mediterranean was reopened to commerce." At the same time gold, which had disappeared, resumed its appearance. Similarly, the suppression of trade drove the professional merchants into the interior.[44] These are assertions of what can be regarded as only probable, not as empirical evidence from which inductive inference can be made.

Pirenne's method of concluding from assertions becomes especially suspect when his assertions are themselves supported only by general assertions that also lack empirical evidence. For example, he asserts that a minority can transform a majority if it chooses to dominate; however, the barbarians did not wish to dominate whereas the Moslems did; the barbarians would not interfere with trade, but the Moslems prohibited trade with the enemy. These assertions imply full knowledge of the psychology and intentions of the invading groups. They also imply a passive psychology on the part of the citizens of the empire. These are general impressions that can be posed as hypotheses, but cannot be admitted as evidence or as accepted premises. In his own words, "The German became Romanized as soon as he entered 'Romania.' The Roman, on the contrary, became Arabized as soon as he was conquered by Islam. It is true that well into the Middle Ages certain small communities of Copts, Nestorians and, above all, Jews, survived in the midst of the Musulman world. Nevertheless, the whole environment

[43] *Ibid.*, pp. 77–78.
[44] *Ibid.*, pp. 172, 173.

was profoundly transformed. There was a clean cut: a complete break with the past. . . . When it was converted to Christianity the Empire, so to speak, underwent a change of soul; when it was converted to Islam both its soul and body were transformed. The change was as great in civil as in religious society." [45] The situation might have been as described, but the evidence is not there. Pirenne, for instance, fails to reconcile his interpretation with Islam's tolerance of Christianity as long as taxes were paid. He provides no evidence on the degree of conversion, or the fact that Christians continued to be widespread in the eastern parts of the empire which became physically dominated by the Moslems. Therefore, although the study may be genuinely empirical, the inferences are largely impressionistic interpretations, rather than scientific inductive conclusions.

Heckscher's contribution, like that of Marx, is interesting as an attempt to combine theory with fact and deduction with induction in arriving at conclusions. Strictly speaking, the study is inductive in the sense of generalizing from the smaller observations to the phenomenon in general. However, the observations are guided and explained, at least in part, by more general and fairly accepted theories or premises. For example, to the extent feudal disintegration was an obstacle in the way of modern developments, and to the extent mercantilism was an agent of unification, mercantilism was a mechanism for promoting modern developments. Similarly, if a system of power was necessary for unification, and mercantilism promoted unification, then mercantilism must have included a system of power. To give credence to his inferences, Heckscher proceeds to illustrate these inferences by examples. Deductive inference, however, is used in arriving at less general conclusions from more general principles. For example, "a country such as England, with its remarkably long coast line in proportion to its land area, had, for this reason, far greater possibilities of achieving political union than continental states, and of these none was worse than Germany." [46] This conclusion is possible only on the premise that communication is necessary for political unity and that long coasts offer better communication than land area. One might actually wonder whether unity was not promoted more by the isolationism characteristic of an island, by the danger inherent in the exposure of a long coast, by political alertness or political apathy, or by certain economic conditions peculiar to the

45 *Ibid.*, p. 152.
46 Heckscher, *Mercantilism*, p. 36.

English territory. It is true that only "greater possibilities" are stipulated, but there is no reason to regard even this limited premise as true except as an assumption.

Sometimes Heckscher applies deduction as if to avoid concluding from inadequate data. For example, "the obvious conclusion follows that if in the Middle Ages goods were forced to use the land routes, where they by no means escaped taxation, the effect of the river tolls must have been terrific." Apparently it is not certain how big the effects were, and they can be inferred only if the significance of land routes can be determined, which is not apparent either. He sometimes uses economic theory to analyze certain behavioral patterns even though they are not purely economic. For instance, "the reason for the complaisance on the part of the more powerful is, undoubtedly, that all the princes recognized that it was in their common interest to respect their own sovereignty, and they preferred to suffer great inconveniences rather than take any action which could be interpreted as an attack on the very order which guaranteed their existence." This conclusion is derived more from an assumption of rationality than from empirical evidence. The princes are assumed to be rational, self-interested, and therefore anxious to minimize costs; the alternative to their observed behavior would have been elimination of the order of which they were a part. The assumption of rationality is used in another way. Mobility of masters is explained, at least in part, on the premise that "when an organization, both on historical grounds and by reason of its inherent tendencies, is inextricably bound up with the business interests of strictly exclusive districts, any expansion or growth of the organization is bound to make migration between different parts of the country more and not less difficult." [47] If this premise is correct, the conclusion follows because both the organization and the individual would be interested more in the benefits of the immediate environment than in those of remote areas. The question that needs to be answered, however, is whether the premise would still hold if the benefits outside the immediate area were greater than those offered in one's environment.

Heckscher sometimes infers certain conclusions without specifying the premises from which they are derived. For example, "if the toll had fulfilled any particular function in economic policy, its continuance or renewal would have been only natural; but no mercantilist aims could be furthered by it." Yet, he states in the previous sentence that the

[47] *Ibid.*, pp. 61, 66–67, 148.

toll was revived on the Rhone "without ever disappearing again." On one hand, institutions had to be functional to remain in existence. On the other, the toll on the Rhone continued to exist even though it served no function to mercantilist policy. His reliance on theory continues to be somewhat obscure. For example, the standardization of coinage was easier than in other areas because "there were certain universal and specific factors, easily explained by monetary theory, which often cooperated to support the unifying efforts." [48] Neither the monetary theory nor the universal factors are explored except for a passing reference to Gresham's law. He does not explain why these theories and factors worked in one place or time and not in another.

Another vague reference to theory is the statement that "without manifesting any kind of 'capitalist' touch, any profession can set a price on itself and thereby become expensive, simply by becoming a monopoly." All this is to say that monopoly makes entry difficult, which is true by definition, regardless of the capitalist touch it may demonstrate. As far as unification, a monopoly serving the whole country might be quite effective, rather than be opposed to the unification efforts of mercantilism.[49]

An interesting use of theory is implied in his comparing English with continental companies. The companies in England are supposed to have been created in response to the market, whereas those in France catered only to the royalty. Therefore, the former were able to take advantage of innovations while the latter were not. Heckscher, in this context, is using competitive theory as a premise that the market economy is more conducive to change and innovation than one catering to royalty.[50] This might have been true in actuality, but the theory behind this premise is not stated nor are its implications generally accepted. It is not certain that modern developments are more easily promoted by the market than by other forces. At least in retrospect one can point to examples where development proceeded as rapidly regardless of the competitive market forces.

These various examples illustrate two basic points. First, Heckscher makes use of economic theory and of deductive reasoning whenever he sees an opportunity to do so. Second, he does not explicitly state the

[48] *Ibid.*, pp. 101, 118.
[49] *Ibid.*, pp. 175, 201–202.
[50] *Ibid.*, p. 221.

theory or the premises he uses. This in part is a basic criticism of traditional history, as will be seen later.

This reference to deduction and theory should not hide the fact that Heckscher's contribution is primarily inductive. Heckscher observes instances of what he calls "mercantilistic economic policy" as well as certain illustrations of these policies, and from these he generalizes to the phenomenon as an abstraction. His inductive inference is based on the comparison of both similar and dissimilar experiences. The phenomenon common to all the cases compared, though appearing at different times, is thus associated with those factors observed to be common to all the cases in the stage of mercantilist development. However, not all his inductive inference is based on comparison, nor does all comparison lead to inference. For example, Colbert did very little "after 1664 in the provinces outside the *cinq grosses fermes*, which again proves that he never intended a general unification." [51] To justify this interpretation inductively would require an estimate of the probability that all those who were able and had the intention to unify would in fact do so. Otherwise, the interpretation remains impressionistic.

Induction, according to Heckscher, can lead to both narrow and broad generalizations, including the formulation of theory. For instance, "in spite of its narrowness and its tendency to diminish rather than increase the supply of goods, the consumers' standpoint . . . has supplied the science of economic policy with one of the foundations of its theory. . . . It has drawn attention to the satisfaction of human wants as the final aim of economic activity." The implication is that from empirical observations a theory can be derived, just as Heckscher himself builds a general theory of mercantilism from historical observations. Similarly, the effects of "inbreeding" are derived from observations of the textile industry. However, even though a case could be built by intuition to reach the same conclusions, Heckscher would rather derive them from history.[52]

Before concluding this section, it should be noted that Heckscher's extensive use of inductive inference suffers from a lack of formalism and precision. There is no systematic control of the data or the derivation. Most of his material appears as illustration of the theory ex-

[51] *Ibid.*, p. 104.
[52] *Ibid.*, pp. 128, 176.

pounded in his first chapter, as has been observed of other contributions.

Clapham's contribution demonstrates the limitations of descriptive history. He uses little reference to economic theory and little inference from the facts after they have been recorded. Reference to theory, where it exists, tends to be more implied than explicit. For example, "happily for Prussia, her simple economic life had rendered overborrowing, or the complete debauching of the currency by inflation, difficult during the wars." Whether or not this statement is based on theory is not clear, especially since Clapham adds that overborrowing was not possible because there was no one to borrow from, and not because the economy was simple. A theory of development is perhaps implied by the statement, "All the forces tending towards industrialism and urbanization had struck Germany at once. . . . Crowding fast on one another in two generations, came the railways; the abolition of the last remains of medieval economic restriction after 1848; the expansion of the Zollverein; the creation of a modern financial and banking system; the great steel inventions; the swift, cheap, glorious and exhilarating achievement of national union; and the period of electricity, overseas expansion and world policy." If this is a theory, it lacks elaboration and detail, both of which are not to be found in the text. These changes themselves are parts of the development process and, as such, their occurrence needs explanation. Finally, a glimpse of the quantity theory of money can be discerned, but the analysis is mainly factual and has little theoretical content.[53]

These limitations are equally characteristic of inductive inference in the study. Clapham describes and estimates changes, but he does not go through the necessary steps into inference and generalization. This is clear from his treatment of statistics. In most cases he is content with showing that there was change, and sometimes how it came about, but rarely does he say why it did when it did. For example, he provides statistical data on the labor force and the tenure groups only to show that their composition was relatively constant. Other data show that the machines "had not even conquered the larger French holdings in 1892." He gives statistics on imports, gold discovered or coined, cooperation and syndicates, but in none of these cases does he attempt to formulate or discover relations that might lead to broader generalizations. Inference remains outside the scope of his contribution. His clas-

53 Clapham, *Economic Development of France and Germany*, pp. 122, 279–280.

sification as moderate for induction is based on his great emphasis of historical facts and observations and the role they play in facilitating inference.

We have seen in the discussion of conceptual scheme that Mantoux presents a whole series of law-like statements which form a model of industrial and economc change. It is not clear, however, whether these statements are meant as general principles or are conclusions derived inductively from the study. Remembering Mantoux's assertion that laws must be discovered by inductive research, one should expect these principles to be inductive inferences. Yet, the material presented and the manner in which it is used do not support this interpretation. Furthermore, if they were derived from the study, which is limited to one experience of industrial revolution, they cannot be used to explain that same experience because as premises they must be based on other and more general experiences than the one they are supposed to explain. While some of the statements are integral parts of economic theory, the majority seem to be conclusions or impressions derived from the study itself, but which the author illustrates empirically. In other words, the principles governing the process of change can be considered elements in a model inductively derived from the study of the Industrial Revolution in England but which remain to be tested by other empirical experiences. This interpretation would seem to be consistent with Mantoux's methodology as discussed above.

That his statements would fit better as inductive hypotheses or impressions can be seen in another way. Both the nature of his material and his selectivity generate only impressions or hunches, but do not suffice for the formulation of laws or theories. Furthermore, there is no evidence that Mantoux has systematically applied inductive inference either by difference or by agreement. Needless to say, to do so would have been impossible given the inadequacy and variability of the data and the difficulty of measurement. On the other hand, his insistence on historical observation and on the necessity to build laws from such experiences renders his contribution high for the inductive criterion, but leaves it low for deductive inference.

Turner's approach is certainly inductive in the sense that he would not formulate a theory and then proceed to illustrate or verify it. He states his intention to study history and derive therefrom a theory that explains the phenomenon. However, there is little evidence of systematic inductive inference in his contribution. Turner presents illustrations rather than a systematic empirical study from which to derive conclusions. His study of the various frontiers suggests that he has a basis for inference, but even when all his essays are put together as one study, they do not adequately form such a basis. On one hand, he observes mainly the common features and ignores the differences. On the other, he does not attach any significance or weight to the frequency of the common features, as we shall see when dealing with his comparative approach. The study has been classified as only moderate for induction mainly because of the paucity of information, despite his explicit statement regarding the source of generalizations.

The best example of inductive inference among the contributions under study is the one by Cameron et al. The authors keep economic theory in view and precede their study with certain theoretical considerations, as has been pointed out. However, the bulk of their conclusions are inferences from the empirical data they gather, classify, and compare. The conclusions are based on an analytic process that also takes advantage of probability theory and the law of large numbers, although this is more implied than explicitly stated. In that sense, one may conclude that deduction and induction overlap greatly in the study, as can be seen from the way in which some of the conclusions have been reached. At several points it seems as if the data were illustrations of theoretical premises postulated at the beginning; the data are not analyzed so that causal relations can be shown, nor are contrary observations taken into consideration. Neither induction by elimination nor by enumeration is systematically carried out. What seems to be the common procedure is something as follows: Since so many A's behaved in form X, then behavior X must have been common, regardless of how many A's did not behave in form X, or how many non-A's behaved in form X. This procedure seems to be followed in both the country studies and the comparative analysis from which the generalizations are derived. In fact, frequently a form of behavior is stipulated and then illustrated by certain examples as evidence. The evidence given might be true, but not all the relevant evidence is given. A few examples will illustrate this.

In discussing short-term credit in England, it is proposed on the basis of a few examples and a footnote that "the traditional theory of commercial banking requires modification to fit the facts of English country banking during the Industrial Revolution." However, the data presented on the country banks do not suffice to show what the operations of these banks were. Furthermore, a theory does not have to be modified because the experience of one country happens to contradict it. If the functions of the English country banks were shown to be characteristic of the other countries as well, then it might be necessary to modify the theory, or even to reject it. Similar doubt is cast on orthodox economic theory of long-term credit on the basis of one experience which, for all practical purposes, can be considered a special case.[54]

Another conclusion is reached regarding official behavior in England and the response of the private sector. "At almost every point at which banking and monetary policy might have been used constructively to promote economic growth, the authorities either made the wrong decision or took no action at all. . . . Paradoxically, however, the very obstacles placed in the way of a rational banking and monetary system stimulated the private sector to introduce the financial innovation necessary for realization of the full benefits of the technical innovations in industry." [55] This statement comes in the conclusion of one country study; it is far from supported by adequate evidence. It is not shown how many times in the span of the ninety-four years under study wrong decisions were made or no decisions at all were made. Actually it might be adequate to note as contrary evidence that the law was purposely kept loose enough to permit individual initiative and innovation. It is also not shown how frequently innovations followed obstacles or how frequently they failed to follow or were independent. Induction as a scientific method requires enumeration of the supporting events or elimination of the contrary events for measuring the strength or probability of the relation inferred. One might argue that the author's interpretation is based on the premise that the private sector is more efficient than the public sector and that government intervention is always worse than nonintervention. If this premise has in fact been invoked, the above conclusion cannot be regarded as an empirical finding, but as an illustration of the premise.

Another dubious piece of evidence is supposed to lead to the conclusion that the Scottish economy was backward. The evidence consists of the apparent lack of gold, the existence of foreign coins, and of the rarity of gold coins. Furthermore, the evidence consists in part of Adam Smith's opinion that in Scotland "silver very seldom appears except in the change of a twenty shillings banknote, and gold still

[54] Cameron et al., *Banking in the Early Stages*, p. 54.
[55] *Ibid.*, pp. 58–59.

seldomer," and Robert Owen's testimony that "even gate-keepers on
public turnpikes were entirely unacquainted with gold coins." This
sounds like rhetoric, unless one begins with the premise that gold and
silver are characteristic of a developed economy. Furthermore, the opinion of Adam Smith and the testimony of Robert Owen may be relevant,
but they are inadequate as evidence or as a basis for influence. Why,
for example, should gatekeepers see gold coins, regardless of the degree
of development, unless we are told that the turnpike fee was equivalent
to a certain denomination of gold coins? In another statement, the fact
that "the Scottish banks could function with such slender reserves was
due to widespread public acceptance of their notes, along with frac-
tional coinage, as the most desirable if not the only legal form of
money." [56] Yet, no other evidence is given to show public acceptance.
This is somehow inferred and used as a premise for a conclusion regarding the behavior of banks. If this is inductive inference, the data
are not there to support it.

Inference from inadequate evidence is sometimes backed up by reference to other studies. For example, "comparison with English and
Scottish data reveals that the complaints of French business were justified: bank facilities were too few, and bank resources pitifully inadequate. At the end of its 'take-off' period the French economy had
approximately the same bank density as Scotland had had in the middle
of the eighteenth century." [57] Yet, France developed and passed through
the take-off stage in seventy years, compared with ninety-four years for
Scotland. This suggests that bank density might not be a good indicator
of bank contribution to development. It might also suggest that the
evidence is neither adequate nor relevant to evaluate the contribution
of French banks. This conclusion might be supported by the observation that French businessmen responded to difficulties in the same way
as did the Scottish, regardless of official policy and of banking facilities.

One other example from the French country study will be helpful.
It is suggested that the lack of easy short-term credit is the reason small
business remains small, side by side with large scale efficient enterprises.[58] If this were a major reason, one might wonder why the large
enterprise did not swallow up the small. A more thorough inductive
investigation might show that the reason for this "schizophrenic de-

[56] *Ibid.*, pp. 65, 92.
[57] *Ibid.*, p. 110.
[58] *Ibid.*, p. 115.

velopment" lies in other areas than finance, or possibly economics in general.

These illustrations of insufficient data for inductive inference are enough to suggest the problems in this contribution. Either because of the lack of data or because of a deeper implicit knowledge of the history of banking, the authors have tended to reach conclusions in a summary fashion. Most of the conclusions, however, are carefully documented, and all the conclusions are presented as tentative because of data limitations and other reasons. The inductive nature of the study is quite clear. It is also clear that a serious attempt has been made to make use of theory in the study of history.

This brief survey of inference in the contributions under study suggests four observations. First, there is a limited tendency to use theory or deductive analysis. Even when such attempts are made, theory is used only to support certain observations rather than to test the theory or to build on it. The exception is Marx's contribution, which emphasizes theory as an objective of the analysis. Second, the tendency is much stronger toward the use of empirical or inductive inference. However, such inference fails to satisfy scientific rules of inference, either because the data are inadequate or because the data are not used formally and systematically. Third, there is a tendency to leave ideas and premises implicit rather than to state them explicitly. This often leaves much room for impressionistic and loose interpretations. Finally, there is a strong tendency to use empirical data to illustrate apparently preconceived conclusions.

## STATISTICAL INFERENCE AND ECONOMETRICS

Looking at table 4 suggests that the question of statistical inference and econometrics is almost irrelevant to the contributions under consideration. Strictly speaking, if we think of statistical inference as the application of theories of statistics, and of econometrics as the measurement of economic variables, neither is common to these contributions. The closest to either are the contributions of Marx and Cameron et al. Marx uses quantitative data, as has been mentioned, but he goes a little further by computing percentages that might suggest the significance of a given observation. For example, to show the trend toward concentration between 1853 and 1864, Marx computes the annual rates of increase of income for seven economic sectors. He also tries to show the degree to which income increments came from profits in annual rates.[59] That, however, is the extent to which he uses statistical analysis. There is no attempt to show how any two variables are related or the significance of such a relation. This is understandable in Marx's case because of when he wrote. However, no such attempt is made in any of the other contributions, regardless of the period in which they were undertaken, including the most recent, that of Cameron et al. In one place the authors observe "an intimate correlation between the tardy development of the banking structure and the equally slow progress of industrialization in France." [60] No correlation coefficients are given, nor is it shown what *intimate* means. In fact, it seems that the bulk of information, both quantitative and qualitative, in most of the contributions was little analyzed beyond computing percentages or yearly rates of change.

The picture is equally dim regarding the use of econometrics. Only Cameron et al. make any attempt to measure variables when statistics are not readily available. For example, quantitative estimates are made to fill gaps in information on the stock of money, means of payment, national income, and velocity of circulation in England and Wales for selective years between 1688 and 1913. The estimates are made with the aid of theory, but only as rough approximations. Conclusions are then derived from these estimates.[61] To that extent, the authors have in a way participated in the new trend of research in economic history. No econometric models are formulated, nor are extensive analyses or estimates attempted. Nevertheless, compared with the other contributions, that of Cameron et al. is a little more cognizant of the new techniques.

However, a common approach to measurement is the use of vague ordinal expressions that are highly subjective and render verification difficult. For example, Mantoux uses expressions such as "greatly felt," "predominant," "several," "interesting," "a great many," "more significant," and "very frequent," but these expressions are never given any precise meaning. Heckscher uses similar expressions, such as "interesting as a matter of curiosity," "not altogether insignificant," "most powerful," and "most purposeful." Even Clapham, who tends to be more quantitative and precise than the others, uses expressions such as "considerably modified," "true villages," "harmful working," "large

59 Marx, *Capital*, pp. 665–666.
60 Cameron et al., *Banking in the Early Stages*, p. 111.
61 *Ibid.*, pp. 42–47.

farmers," and "judicious." Whether these expressions can be avoided or not is beside the point. It is relevant, however, that such expressions prevent clear communication between scholars and preclude the verification of findings.

## COMPARATIVE METHOD

One of the most common features of the contributions under study is the use of comparison. Invariably, the contributors resort to comparison as if to compensate for the difficulty of direct observation or experimentation. At the same time it seems equally characteristic that comparative method is only moderately used both in terms of extent and perfection.

Strictly speaking, Marx's contribution is not a comparative study, but he does resort to comparison when he deems it useful to do so. For example, he draws on the history of the Slavonic and Asiatic societies to show that labor used to be common labor of which the product was not a commodity, in contrast to labor in capitalist England. He compares England with the Danubian principalities to show the variation in the degree of greed for surplus labor. He frequently compares the conditions of agricultural laborers in England with those in Scotland and Ireland. A more systematic comparison of the impact of machinery in Scotland and Ireland is carried out for three subperiods between 1858 and 1868. However, the most systematic comparison is his discussion "General Law of Capitalist Accumulation," in which villages, various countries, and England and Ireland are compared.[62] Comparison is used also to show that depopulation, concentration of capital, and deterioration of the workers' condition took place during the period he predicts it should.

Yet, despite these attempts, it is safe to suggest that his comparison is not systematic. It is not carried out according to specified criteria either in terms of background, processes of change, or the theoretical grounds for comparison. It is selective, and comparative data are used only when they seem to support a given theory. Contradictory examples or evidence have been automatically eliminated. There is no mechanism by which these comparisons could show that the same results were or were not due to different reasons. In other words, everything other than the point in question is held constant, even though they might not have

[62] Marx, *Capital*, pp. 49 fn., 219, 252–284, 324, 435, 695–696, 707–735.

been. For these reasons, the use of comparison in Marx's contribution can be regarded at best as moderate.

Weber takes capitalist development as given, and tries to establish only that the missing preconditions for capitalist development in other societies were created in the West by Protestantism, that they were created prior to that development, and that the Protestant ethic had enough impact to influence the development of society in general. He tries to do this by resorting to comparison. Thus he compares Protestants with non-Protestants and various sects of Protestants with each other. The former comparison is intended to establish the premise that Protestantism did create the necessary conditions which were lacking in other religions; the latter comparison suggests the logical sequence between the spirit of capitalism and the phenomenon itself.

The comparison between Protestantism and other religions is carried out primarily by means of observations of the behavior of different religious groups in different countries. These are observations from the literature, but they lack any precise estimation of the actual differences. He admits that the comparison with non-Christian religions is inadequate because of the lack of information about oriental religions. Neverthelesss, the alleged differences are interpreted to show that Protestantism created the spirit of capitalism lacking in other religions. The comparison with Catholicism is a little more precise, but equally impressionistic. Even when the facts seem inconsistent with the hypothesis, the same results are derived anyway. For example, when Catholic circles are observed to have adapted themselves to acquisition, Weber concludes that "the feeling was never overcome, that activity directed to acquisition for its own sake was at bottom a *pudendum* which was to be tolerated only because of the unalterable necessities of life in this world." [63] This unsystematic comparison, in terms of relevance, sequence, and criteria of evaluation, renders the conclusions highly impressionistic.

Weber's comparison of Protestant sects tends to show the changes that took place within Protestantism and how these changes penetrated the various theological circles and established the doctrine of worldly asceticism in each of them. He analyzes the dogmatic teachings of the sects and the controversies among theologians, although he insists that it is not the formal teaching that counts, but the underlying psychological effects which eventually led to capitalistic behavior. The analysis,

[63] Weber, *Protestant Ethic*, pp. 30, 43, 73.

however, is in the form of a history of each of these sects, rather than a comparison of their teachings in a systematic manner.

It should be noted that Weber's comparison poses a contradiction. Unless a certain uniformity of behavior is assumed under similar circumstances, comparison is useless. Yet, if all historical situations are unique and if all behavior is unique and individualistic, as Weber holds, no regularity can be assumed, and comparison cannot be used. Weber uses comparison as a substitute for experimentation, but he does not resolve the inherent contradiction between his premises and the method he uses. Therefore, despite Weber's explicit interest in comparison, the lack of formalism, and the apparent contradiction in the logic of the methodology he applies, we have classified his contribution as moderate for comparative method.

Pirenne's contribution offers a good example of comparative method, even though no formal model is set up and some of the variables compared are observed in great generalities. Nevertheless, having explained his main hypothesis, Pirenne proceeds to compare the conditions of the empire in four main periods: prior to the barbarian invasions; after the barbarian invasions but before the Moslem invasion; after the Moslem invasion; and after Moslem decline and the beginning of revival in the West. The comparison is carried out in terms of the political, social, cultural, and economic conditions in each of these periods, at least in terms of what Pirenne considers to be relevant variables. Having established change in the conditions, such as the composition and direction of trade, he connects the change with the influences affecting the empire, which are narrowed down to the Moslem invasion. The process by which this influence and the results are connected is explored fairly carefully; he examines the differences in religion, attitudes toward power, independence, and domination, and the role of trade and the Mediterranean in the unity of the empire.

Although the method is correctly applied in principle, Pirenne leaves the door open for criticism by failing to regulate the chronology of comparison in order to establish a correct sequence between cause and effect. He also fails to establish critical values of change to show whether significant change actually occurred. These, however, are weaknesses in detail that may be unavoidable, given the chronological and temporal scope of the study. Another problem is the selectivity in the comparative data, as has been suggested above. Despite these criticisms, Pirenne's contribution rates high on the use of comparative method.

Heckscher is equally explicit concerning comparison. Having decided to investigate the unifying role of mercantilism by studying its policy toward tolls, he suggests that "it is very instructive to draw a comparison between the toll systems in England, France and Germany. More than in any other sphere, England here represented a type clearly distinguishable from that of the other countries, while, on the other hand, conditions in France and Germany were largely similar at the beginning of the Middle Ages. Differences in the later development of both countries can, therefore, to some extent, supply a standard for comparing the effectiveness of mercantilism; in the one case under the most favourable, and in the other under the least favourable, political conditions." Thus, Heckscher states his position regarding comparison and contrast as methods of studying mercantilism. He points out only three countries, whereas in actuality he deals with many others, sometimes systematically and at other times only casually. For example, the rise of the turnpike system was more characteristic of English internal trade than of any other continental country. Heckscher's comparative method includes both comparison and contrast. For example, he deals with Germany as a case of contrast with England, as seen by an English observer.[64]

Heckscher goes into more detail by comparing different internal regions with each other, such as the Rhine and the Elbe. And, having contrasted England with Germany, he deals with France as an example of an intermediate situation as far as feudal organization and toll distribution are concerned. Another aspect is intertemporal comparison, which shows the changes in each country brought about by mercantilist policy. Thus, by observing the conditions in one country relative to those in another he tries to demonstrate the differences. For example, "the description of the French toll disintegration and its outcome can give some idea of how far the development in Germany was due to the narrow policy of the smaller states and how far to general impotence in the face of the feudal system." [65]

Another subject of comparison is the attempt to unify weights and measures in each of the countries under consideration, and within each of these countries. The same approach is also applied to the regulation of industry. In all cases, however, Heckscher is quite generalistic. He does not specify a formal system of comparison or critical limits to es-

[64] Heckscher, *Mercantilism*, pp. 46, 49, 56ff.
[65] *Ibid.*, pp. 68ff, 78, 108.

METHODOLOGICAL CHOICES                        195

timate the significance of similarities and differences, as was the case in
Pirenne's contribution. For one thing, the comparison fluctuates in
composition; once it is France and England, next it is France and Germany, or Germany and Sweden. It is not a systematic comparison between a given number of instances in which the conditions, the processes, or the results are compared and contrasted. The comparison is
usually a survey of policies in a given period toward a given industry
but without specification of the conditions held constant and without
consideration of all the alternatives or all the results. The author simply
notes what seems to him to be relevant to support his theme without
sufficient scrutiny to establish the grounds for inference. Consequently,
the results are not inferential conclusions, but impressions that can
hardly be verified or tested. For example, if Germany was divided into
several separate political entities, what rationale exists to compare
France as one political entity with the composite Germany and not with
each of the separate German political entities? If the latter approach
were applied, inference from the comparison might be different. Which
approach should be used is not in question; what requires justification
is the choice made, regardless of the content.[66]

When comparing Dutch and English companies, the differences and
similarities are noted individually, but no attempt is made to bring
all the features and results together and to then reach conclusions.
Some of the observations may be interdependent; some may be irrelevant or neutral; and some may be explicable in more appropriate terms
than when each feature is treated separately.[67] In other words, comparison of the various cases as whole units, say in tabular form, in order
to see all the factors simultaneously is not attempted. Yet without simultaneous observation, it is hard to evaluate similarities and differences,
to enumerate either, or to eliminate the irrelevant explanations. Nevertheless, Heckscher's attempt at comparison is explicit, comprehensive,
and quite fruitful. For this reason, it has been classified high for comparison.

Comparison is probably the most characteristic feature of Clapham's
contribution. As if to compensate for the lack of exact measures and
standards, Clapham resorts to comparison to convey the extent of
change in the economies of France and Germany. He compares one
industry with another, one country with another, and conditions in

[66] *Ibid.*, pp. 108–109.
[67] *Ibid.*, pp. 357–361.

one period with those of another. However, although he emphasizes the
differences and contrasts, he does not go into the possible reasons for
these variations. Actually it would be hard to explain these differences on the basis of his comparisons because of the way they are conducted. His comparisons tend to support certain impressions descrip-
tively, rather than deal with specific and precise results that could form a
basis for inference. For example, "the open-field region of the north,
like the open-field districts of England, was a land of true villages rather
than hamlets." The position of the *censiers* in France is compared with
that of the copyholders in England. This approach to comparison continues, "The French farmer class did however contain a small section
comparable with those capitalist tenant farmers . . . in England." In
dealing with German agriculture, Clapham compares one district with
another in order to point out the major agricultural characteristics of
the country as a whole. Similarly, he vaguely compares the slow emancipation in Germany with the faster process in France. In comparing
population growth, Clapham is more precise and advises the reader to
"consider the French figures and facts from 1801 to 1851, bearing in
mind what was happening in contemporary England." The figures for
England, however, are sketchy. Where statistics are available, as mentioned earlier, the comparison is more systematic and comprehensive,
but equally descriptive. For example, improvements in communication
are described for the years 1850, 1870, 1890, and 1910 for Belgium,
France, Germany, Italy, Spain, Holland, Switzerland, and the United
Kingdom. However, no analysis of these comparative data is attempted
beyond showing the different rates of change. The same approach is
applied to change in steam power and generation of electricity, which
are described during the period from 1840 to 1913 in decennial intervals.[68] Given the lack of comparative analysis and the non-uniform or
consistent application of comparative method, this contribution has
been classified as only moderate for the criterion of comparison.

Mantoux is equally concerned with comparison, equally loose in applying it, but a little more analytical than Clapham. He compares the
preindustrial with the postindustrial, one industry with another, and
sometimes England with other European countries. That is why he
starts with a chapter on the old type industry, in which he sets up a
standard for comparison and for estimating the degree of change due

[68] Clapham, *Economic Development of France and Germany*, pp. 9, 13–14, 16,
30ff, 37, 53, 240, 339.

to industrialization. His approach is best illustrated in his comparison of the woollen and cotton industries before and after the Industrial Revolution. Similarly, he compares the conditions of the workers in the two periods.[69] However, all these comparisons are loose and can only lead to impressions. Nowhere does Mantoux set up a system of comparison or attempt to estimate actual change. As a result, his comparisons can at best suggest that there was change in England and that the change was felt. He infers further that since change occurred at the time of the revolution, it should automatically be associated with the revolution. This is why his contribution has been regarded as moderate on comparison, like that of Clapham.

Strictly speaking, Turner does not have any comparison in his study because he deals with various frontiers in separate essays. However, attempts have been made to evaluate his use of comparison even though he makes no explicit statement of his intentions. In comparing his treatment of six different frontiers, it appears that most of his results are supported by observations for three or less of the six frontiers. Many observations are almost unique to a given frontier. Even though these same observations might be valid for other frontiers, Turner does not use the comparative approach as he might have been able to do. For example, the role of the frontier in explaining class conflict between settlers and absentee owners is discussed only in the context of the Massachusetts Bay. The same is true of his treatment of land-grant policy and its relation to the trades.[70] The significance of the frontier for individualism is discussed in the context of two frontiers only, the Old West and the Mississippi Valley. Even the pattern of change in the development sequence is discussed for only four of the six frontiers; for one of these the pattern is not shown to be consistent and for another it is only asserted rather than discussed or supported by evidence. Therefore, despite the fact that Turner deals with various frontiers, there is little evidence that he applies comparative method before generalizing—at least not in the confines of this contribution.

The contribution of Cameron et al. is comparative in word and in action, the authors explicitly stating their interest in comparison and following a uniform system of presenting the data in each of the case studies. In the concluding chapter the observations from the various

[69] Mantoux, *The Industrial Revolution*, pp. 30, 33; for other examples of comparison, see pp. 72, 86, 105, 108–109, 146, 197, 297, 361, 362, 389, 399, 429.
[70] Turner, *The Frontier*, pp. 51–59, 62.

case studies are brought together and analyzed. One general comment
that should be made right at the start is that the authors do not take
full advantage of the data they have compiled in the case studies. More
serious, however, is the fact that they frequently reach conclusions without fully considering all the relevant data. For example, they conclude
that the banking system can contribute to development, especially in
mobilizing capital. However, they do not show how frequently such a
contribution was made and how often it was not made. Given the
framework of the study, an estimate of the frequency might be impossible because all the countries under study did develop anyway. It
even seems that in the cases in which bank contribution was rather
limited, development through take-off was more rapid than in cases
in which bank contribution was considered fairly extensive. In comparing bank assets as a percentage of national wealth, only three of the case
studies are considered, with the addition of the United States, even
though no detailed study of the latter is presented.[71] Apparently, the
experience in the United States offers support to a given idea or impression and is therefore included.

A more significant conclusion is that the contribution of the banks
was highest where competition was most free. In a way this is tautological because the authors' definition of a contribution implies freedom of action. In the absence of freedom a contribution must be limited. The question might be raised whether under relatively restrictive
conditions development did or did not take place. The comparison does
not take all the cases into consideration, nor does it provide adequate
evidence to support that conclusion.[72] One might argue that the conclusion is presupposed and only supportive evidence is presented. Yet,
it would be instructive to know what happened in France, Russia, and
England. How could restriction have delayed development when development was actually faster in the restrictive than in the less restrictive
countries?

The problem with their comparison is that cases of contrast are not
taken into consideration to show the differences between countries that
developed and those that did not. Another problem is that no critical
limits are established to indicate what constitutes contribution, growth,
or restriction. Hence, it is easy to conclude that a contribution or the

[71] Cameron et al., pp. 292, 307.
[72] *Ibid.*, p. 313.

lack of it was characteristic. Were such precautions taken, the banking institutions might appear as passive agents only in the sense of supporting development once it is underway. It might also appear that regulated banking need not be less of a contributor than free banking, and that the substitutes for free banking contribute more to development than the unregulated institutions. The rate of development of an economy may be a good indicator of the contribution of banking; if the rate is higher in conjunction with banks than in their absence, it might be possible to conclude that their contribution is positive. Finally, it might be highly useful to define the take-off stage in terms of rate of growth, per capita income, rates of investment, or other such indicators by which comparison can be more precise and dependable for drawing conclusions. Another missing variable is the development background or the stage of development of the countries studied. The contribution or efficiency of the banking system cannot be evaluated in terms of an absolute optimum.[73] In an empirical investigation it might be appropriate to gauge the contribution against the development background. For example, to expand at an annual rate of 2 percent in a handicapped situation may be a higher contribution than expanding at 3 percent annually when the handicap does not exist. The contribution of the relevant agency may be much more significant in the former than in the latter, even though the rate of growth is higher in the latter. In other words, the meaning of efficiency can only be relative, and not absolute.

These criticisms have been raised because Cameron et al. have explicitly committed themselves to comparative method. The failures cannot be blamed on the lack of data, the difficulty of measurement, or the vagueness of the method. It is possible that the authors have reasons for choosing this more limited and standard approach, but these reasons are not given. Nevertheless, the contribution must be classified as high for application of comparative method.

In conclusion, it appears that the contributors have generally tended toward comparison, either explicitly or implicitly. However, there is a tendency to apply comparison with little formalism or systematization. In particular, cases of contrast do not seem to enter into the analysis. There is also little attempt to specify the framework of comparison or to control the objects or the criteria. Consequently, the advantages of

[73] *Ibid.*, pp. 308–309.

comparative method are not fully realized, and the objectivity that can be derived from the formal application of comparison tends to be slighted. Therefore, although it may be emphasized that the contributors have resorted to comparative method, there is room for more formal, rigorous application to reap the benefits of that method.

# 7

# Types of Generalization

Having surveyed the nature of the data and the methodological choices of each of the representative contributions, we shall now survey the types of generalization or conclusions they reach. Our concern is mainly with the breadth of these generalizations and their predictive power, or the degree to which they contribute to the formation of theories of change or development. Five possible types of generalization have been singled out, on the assumption that certain data-method combinations lead to certain types of generalization. As table 4 shows, few of the contributions can be characterized by any single type of generalization. Therefore, we shall be concerned primarily with finding what kinds of generalization each contributor reaches, and with trying to explain whether the type or types reached by each contributor are justified by his data and method. It may be possible to arrive at some tentative conclusions regarding the tendency of those contributors in formulating generalizations. Accordingly we shall deal with the results of each as one whole, rather than by type of generalization as in table 4. No attempt will be made to present all the findings of each contribution, because the emphasis is on type of generalization and therefore only examples will be given. Finally, an attempt will be made to estimate the degree to which the findings are conclusive and verifiable, as shown in table 4.

The contribution of Marx combines at least three types of generalization of varying degrees of intensity. He deals with specific problems in England, with capitalist development in England, and with laws of change in general. The last of these topics provides the basis for classifying his generalization as cosmic. These are the laws of motion of society Marx was searching for. We have already mentioned his law of accumulation from primitive stages through capitalist development. We have also pointed out his highly predictive treatment of business fluctuations. A similarly predictive law relates to the impact of machinery on value and labor substitution.[1] His more limited generalizations regarding concentration in agriculture and manufacturing have also been pointed out. Concentration in these areas, however, is actually part of the general tendency of concentration in capitalism.

[1] Marx, *Capital*, pp. 443–444.

Most of the laws we have mentioned are predictive to a certain extent and go far beyond the experience of England. They form parts of his theory, which can be regarded as cosmic in that it is general and deterministic. However, even his empirically derived conclusions tend to be comprehensive and predictive. For example, "the mode of production in which the product takes the form of a commodity, or is produced directly for exchange, is the most general and most embryonic form of bourgeois production." [2] Apparently Marx applies the principle that all bourgeois production follows the same pattern, and since commodity production characterized English capitalism in its embryonic stage, it must therefore characterize all capitalist systems of production. Marx, in this case, expresses his acceptance of an evolutionary philosophy as well as a principle of universality, at least within the framework of the capitalist mode of production, which would render his conclusion highly predictive and even deterministic.

Another conclusion which appears as a law is the following: "The history of the regulation of the working day in certain branches of production, and the struggle still going on in others in regard to this regulation, prove conclusively that the isolated labourer, the labourer as 'free' vendor of his labour-power, when capitalist production has once attained a certain stage, succumbs without any power of resistance. The creation of a normal working day is, therefore, the product of a protracted civil war, more or less dissembled, between the capitalist class and the working class." [3] Yet the data and the method used by Marx do not prove this law conclusively as he suggests. It is not clear in fact at what stage of capitalist production the civil war begins. There are further conclusions and examples, but it is already evident that some of these conclusions are relevant to a much wider area than England, whereas others relate to developments within English capitalism only. The main question is to what extent these generalizations are conclusive, or valid, and to what extent they are verifiable. Answers to these questions would show the degree to which the findings follow from the data and applied methods.

It may be suggested that although Marx emphasized empirical analysis and collected large amounts of data, he was a prisoner of his own genius and philosophical inclinations. Once he had formulated his conceptual scheme, it must have been impossible for him to use the data

2 *Ibid.*, p. 54.
3 *Ibid.*, pp. 284–285.

carefully and objectively. He must have found justification for concluding from insufficient data. Furthermore, his acceptance of evolu-
tionism and the dialectic method made it necessary for him to interpret
data within that framework regardless of whether adequate data was
available or not. The inadequacy of his data, it should be noted, does
not change the character of his conclusions, nor does it nullify their
relevance; it only reduces their predictive power and conclusiveness. On
the other hand, the unsystematic handling of data and method renders
verifiability difficult. Marx's contribution presents a dilemma in these
respects. As general tendencies of the pattern of capitalist economic development, his observations might be observable, in part, if not *in toto*.
However, to observe tendencies is not sufficient for prediction, nor does
it give conclusive results. Verification requires precision and well-defined
criteria, both of which are lacking. Furthermore, given the fact that
Marx studied a period now long past, verification proper might be out
of the question. The only thing possible might be to estimate the
validity and relevance of his data and determine whether additional data
would support his conclusions. This is the problem of historical and
social research in general. A few examples of the difficulty of verifying
Marx's conclusions will be helpful.

Accumulation, concentration, and a falling rate of profit are fundamental processes in Marx's theory. All these are empirical concepts and
should be verifiable as tendencies both with respect to the period covered by Marx and in general, at least in as much as they are parts of the
general evolution of capitalism and the breakdown of that system. Yet,
there is no clear statement of the criteria of a breakdown. Nor is there
a clear definition of the class conflict or of class consciousness or the
degree of consciousness necessary before breakdown becomes a reality.
In fact, Marx's interpretation of this process leads to circular reasoning:
the breakdown comes when class conflict has reached dangerous proportions, and such a conflict will have become dangerous when the
breakdown has become apparent. Thus, lacking well-defined limits for
the degree of concentration, for the fall in the rate of profit, or for the
time period necessary for the change, it is impossible to conclude whether
his prediction has been validated. One can always argue that the predicted change is still on the way.

Looking at the problem another way, it seems difficult to test the
validity of his conclusions, given the dynamic nature of external influences. For example, class conflicts may be consciously contained

within acceptable limits far short of revolution or breakdown. The workers may continue to use the strike, bargaining, or lobbying for legislation to improve their lot, but within the framework of capitalist production. In both cases, the nature of the conflict undergoes change through policy measures. Would this contradict Marx's predictions, or would it support them in the sense that had such reform policies not been introduced, the breakdown might have been realized and the prediction come true? Obviously an answer would have to be speculative, and verification would remain impossible.

A predictive conclusion that has aroused much interest and controversy is the tendency for the increasing misery of the proletariat as capitalism advances. The controversy has centered around the meaning of *misery* and the institutional environment to which it applies. It has been debated whether Marx meant absolute or relative misery and how one can define the income of the working class, or the proletariat, or who its members are. In the absence of a clear definition of the relevant criteria it has been difficult to verify Marx's conclusions.

To a certain extent, these problems have been due to the methods used by Marx. Whereas some of his generalizations are true by definition, his empirical findings are impressionistic observations more than scientific inferences. He did not estimate the degree to which these results might have been due to change, assuming they were true observations. He generalized from inadequate information and from information not well organized. At the same time, Marx did not isolate his environment from outside influences in order to show the extent to which these occurrences were due to the internal processes he was studying. Of course, Marx could not have taken any of these methodological precautions because he was writing long ago and because of the uniqueness of English capitalist development during his time. Therefore, assuming his observations were accurate, and there is no reason to doubt their accuracy, his generalizations can at best be regarded as hypotheses rather than valid conclusions. The only way they may seem valid is to place them within the framework of his evolutionary dialectic analysis, which would render them deterministic and almost true by definition. Needless to say, many scholars of Marxism would reject this interpretation and emphasize his empiricism, but the available evidence would not support them as empirical findings.

Strictly speaking, Weber's generalizations fall more in the area of limited or trend generalizations than prediction. As Weber sees his own conclusions, they are interpretations of a unique phenomenon: the relation between the Protestant ethic and the spirit of capitalism. They establish the conclusion that Protestantism led to a new ethic and a new morality reflected in asceticism, rationality, and the calling. Another group of interpretative conclusions are those that establish the features of modern Western capitalism, or the spirit of capitalism. However, the use of comparative method would suggest comparative-predictive results tying the spirit of capitalism to the ethics generated by Protestantism. These comparative-predictive results might even be universally applicable to the phenomenon of capitalism in the West or to capitalist development in general. In that sense it should be possible to predict on the basis of these generalizations in the sense of "if . . . then." But such an interpretation of the results may be contrary to Weber's views of his own results and of methodology in the social sciences. Although this interpretation cannot be imposed on the results, the mere fact that it might apply suggests a contradiction between Weber the methodologist and Weber the historian; the former denies the possibility of generalization while the latter derives generalizations as logical conclusions from his analysis. Weber's generalizations, however, are not fully derivable from his data. For instance, he does not consider all the relevant common characteristics and differences other than religion that might have influenced the development of capitalism. The predictive value of his conclusions is thus reduced to the realm of possible influence, with no assessment of the significance of that influence being possible. These problems or complications can be seen more clearly when one tries to assess the degree of conclusiveness of the results or to test their validity.

Verification and assessment of the validity of the results are almost impossible. Weber does not state his conclusions as definitive statements and he therefore precludes any possible assessment of the accuracy or validity of his findings. Yet, in more than one place he makes statements that suggest definitive observations. For example, "as a rule, it has been neither dare-devil and unscrupulous speculators, economic adventurers such as we meet at all periods of economic history, nor simply great financiers who have carried through this change. . . . On the contrary, they were men who had grown up in the hard school of life, calculating and daring at the same time, above all temperate and reliable, shrewd and completely devoted to their business, with strictly bourgeois opinions and principles." This statement leaves no room for exceptions, nor for uncertainty as to who these people are. But for an outside observer, there is no way of identifying these people and checking whether they conform to Weber's description. A similar conclusion that renders verification difficult is that the "origin of this type of life [the ascetic] also extends in certain roots, like so many aspects of the spirit of capitalism, back into the Middle Ages. But it was in the ethic of ascetic Protestantism that it first found a consistent ethical foundation." In recapitulating, Weber concludes that Protestant asceticism "acted powerfully against the spontaneous enjoyment of possessions; it restricted consumption, especially luxuries. On the other hand, it had the psychological effect of freeing the acquisition of goods from the inhibitions of traditionalistic ethics. It broke the bonds of the impulse of acquisition in that it not only legalized it, but (in the sense discusssed) looked upon it as directly willed by God." [4] There are too many ambiguities in this statement to allow verification. Furthermore, the conclusion is based on indirect observations made from the literature, but which do not exhaust the relevant literature, and they do not analyze the actual behavior that followed from these teachings.

Finally, another problem of verification relates to the central relation between the spirit of capitalism and the Protestant ethic; Weber's observations may be mere coincidences or they may be true by definition. For instance, "one of the fundamental elements of the spirit of modern capitalism, and not only of that but of all modern culture: rational conduct on the basis of the idea of the calling, was born—that is what this discussion has sought to demonstrate—from the spirit of Christian asceticism. One has only to reread the passage from Franklin . . . in order to see that the essential elements of the attitude which was there called the spirit of capitalism are the same as what we have just shown to be the content of the Puritan worldly asceticism." [5] But the fact that the two doctrines are similar does not prove Weber's conclusion, because an observation cannot be used to prove its own validity. It is also possible that the coincidence is due to the fact that the spirit of capitalism has been defined in terms of Protestant ethic rather than as a generalization of the observed behavior of capitalists in various religions or environments. To verify the relation between the ethic and the behavior it is necessary to observe the same ethic or spirit among all Protestants, whether capitalists or not, and to show that all capitalists were

[4] Weber, *Protestant Ethic*, pp. 69, 169–170.
[5] *Ibid.*, p. 180.

Protestants. In other words, even though it may be possible to verify Weber's documentation from the literature, it does not follow that the relations inferred from these observations are true or verified. All this leads to the conclusion that Weber's interpretations suffer from subjective influences and that his conclusions are broader than would be justified by the data and the methods used.

Pirenne's generalizations are primarily interpretative of a trend limited to a certain phenomenon. No predictive power is implied by the author, although one might stretch the point beyond the author's own expectations and interpret the results more broadly. For example, Pirenne concludes that despite the barbarian invasions there was continuity in the essential features of the empire. Islam, in contrast, caused a break with the past. The break was due mainly to the closing of the Mediterranean to navigation and trade. As a response Europe turned northward away from the Mediterranean. These conclusions are rather specific. However, the implications can be viewed in a wider perspective. It can be inferred that trade can sustain or break the social and economic equilibrium of a system; that an external factor might be sufficient to disrupt that system; and that in response to certain changes, an economic or social system tends to seek outlets to restore a viable equilibrium. These interpretations could lead to a generalization that socioeconomic systems tend toward evolutionary, stable organization. These are important generalizations if they can be attributed to Pirenne. We shall, however, refrain from this line of argument in order to avoid misinterpretation of the author. Of more immediate relevance is the degree of conclusiveness and verifiability of his findings.

As has already been suggested, Pirenne's findings cannot be conclusive. The evidence is neither complete nor adequately observable. This point implies a contradiction. On one hand, Pirenne admits that historical data are never complete, which means that the findings can never be conclusive. On the other, he presents his findings as if they were true beyond doubt. This puzzle may be explained by the fact that Pirenne emphasizes his conclusions in order to arouse interest in testing them. This interpretation may seem generous, but it is hard to believe that Pirenne would consider his findings conclusive, having admitted more than once that adequate or scientific data were not readily available. Verifiability, however, is a different matter. Generally, findings can be verified by obtaining adequate data and by evaluating the degree to which the conclusions can be inferred from these data. It is true that much of Pirenne's evidence is impressionistic, but in essence it is empirical and can be observed and evaluated. His main problem is that he concludes from too little evidence. He also fails to establish critical values as to what constitutes continuity and change. Tendencies can be observed without establishing such limits, and this is what Pirenne seems to do. For example, it should be possible to find out whether the barbarians were assimilated in the empire or not; whether their allegiance was complete; and whether Latin continued to be the predominant language and trade continued. It might be difficult, however, to establish the psychology and intentions of the barbarians and the Moslems and their attitude toward the empire. But these points can be disregarded to the extent to which data on actual behavior is obtainable. Similarly, it should be possible to verify the degree to which the Arabs prohibited trade, dominated the Mediterranean, or to which commodities from the Orient disappeared. Such evidence should be possible to establish in the right sequence, because a logical sequence of events determines the relevance and accuracy of the conclusions. In a sense, even statistical analysis can be used for verification, assuming adequate data can be obtained. The only problem of verification relates to interpretation of the findings. Even if continuity or a break were established beyond doubt, it remains necessary to establish a causal relation between these invasions and the phenomenon in question. The relatively long period and the large environment covered by Pirenne may render such a casual relation difficult to discover. Selectivity and subjective interpretations may also be difficult to avoid, as has been characteristic of research in most of the other contributions.

Heckscher's results are hard to evaluate for two reasons. First, it is not clear whether these results are derived from the observations or whether they are hypotheses to be tested by those observations. If the former, one might accept them as hypotheses still in need of verification, in which case this critique would concentrate on the relevance of the observations and their adequacy for confirming the hypotheses. Second, the conclusions are of various degrees of relevance to the phenomenon under consideration, almost to the extent of making some of them irrelevant. Some of the conclusions can also be applied to a much wider scope than the one under study—to be almost cosmic in relevance. Others are quite limited or even unique in their applicability. However, most of the generalizations are of the limited type, followed in frequency of occurrence by the trend type. For example, Heckscher concludes that his observations refute the argument that history is economically determined, which hardly follows from the observations. Another broad generalization is that "the history of the Middle Ages certainly proves that people can live in much more restricted units of society, held together and tied to a larger cultural circle by means of one chiefly spiritual bond. Not only is such a life physically possible, but, in it, human problems can be truly perceived which in larger social structures must more or less necessarily be sacrificed." [6] This is a generalization regarding human nature, social organization, and the relation between the spiritual and physical environments. How the generalization was derived is not totally clear, except that since some people existed in restricted communities, such existence must be possible.

Less general but more relevant conclusions are derived from Heckscher's comparison and serve as predictive generalizations. One of these is that modern economic or capitalist development cannot depend on the production of luxuries. Luxuries are insignificant to capitalist development.[7] This generalization is based on a comparison of England with the Continent, especially France. It is made possible by accepting a limited comparison as a basis, and by using imprecise terms such as *insignificant* and *luxuries* without specifying either the degree of insignificance or the nature of the luxuries. Would the conclusions be true if the luxuries were exportable items?

Another such generalization is that a strong central authority that helps to unify the economy and shows interest in agriculture is basic to development. These conditions prevailed in England, in contrast to their absence on the continent.[8] Heckscher emphasizes the impact of these factors, especially the free mobility of economic resources. Thus, his conclusion can be rewritten to say that mobility is basic to development whether it is guaranteed by the state or by some other agent. Heckscher, however, is quite realistic in noting that mobility can hardly be realized without unification, which requires action by a strong central authority.

The more common generalizations apply to Europe, within a given period or a given country only. A trend of disruption was common in Europe of the later Middle Ages where the countries were not unified or where power was transferred from the state to "spiritual and temporal vassals." The exceptions to this rule were England, Burgundy, and Ara-

[6] Heckscher, *Mercantilism*, pp. 34, 42.
[7] *Ibid.*, p. 222.
[8] *Ibid.*, p. 225.

gon. Or, "in the Middle Ages the greatest obstacles to trade were the tolls," and consequently "medieval trade was much more restricted than was warranted by purely technical difficulties." Although these conclusions can be turned into predictive generalizations, they are presented here only to describe a trend that prevailed over a given period. The same may be said of the conclusion that "the attempt to create gilds in rural areas [did] fail almost completely, but the inefficiency of the innumerable regulations diminished in proportion to the distance from the towns which had gild organization." [9] This conclusion might be predictive if Heckscher had not restricted it explicitly to the eighteenth century, apparently because of the inadequacy of data.

The following is a more directly relevant observation. "The general impression of the achievements of mercantilism in the field of industrial regulation, and perhaps even more of domestic trade, is that it did not lead to much in the direction of greater internal unification, nor did it give an impetus to the positive forces which caused the great economic upheaval of the 18th and 19th centuries." This generalization can be regarded as predictive to the extent that evaluation of measures similar to those represented by mercantilism is possible. However, Heckscher gives it such an impressionistic character that it can hardly be considered predictive. One more illustration of the trend type of generalization is that "the unification in economic matters at the beginning of the 19th century was thus more than usually conspicuous by its absence. Before 1815 little could be done." [10] Again the conclusion describes a trend that, if correct, supports Heckscher's theory of mercantilism as an agent of unification without which modern development would be impossible. To what extent Heckscher means these conclusions to be descriptive or predictive is not clear.

The largest number of generalizations falls in the area of limited generalizations, which relate to a given country or to a relatively short period, and which constitute data for the broader generalizations. A few examples will illustrate. "The century after Colbert's death until the French Revolution . . . brought no important advance in the work of unification." "The intervention of the French state which was the most powerful, most typical and most purposeful achievement of mercantilism did not pave the way for that development which set its mark on the economic life of the last 150 years." "English legislation did allow

[9] *Ibid.*, pp. 38, 45, 210.
[10] *Ibid.*, pp. 326, 462.

more and not less particularism to creep in than the continental legislation, that is, to the extent that English gilds were allowed to retain their local exclusiveness." [11]

Similar conclusions abound in Heckscher's study. They can be found on at least thirty-four other pages. It is significant, however, that although these generalizations may be empirically derived, many of them lack adequate data and depend greatly on impressions. In that sense, they can only be tentative, but they are verifiable if the data can be obtained. Nevertheless, one limitation on verifiability is the ambiguity implied in expressions such as "more," "less," "significant," and other imprecise terms which Heckscher uses frequently, as has been suggested previously.

Clapham's conclusions are of different categories; some are mere summaries of facts, others suggest a trend of change in a limited geographical area or industry, and still others imply more sweeping generalizations that hardly follow from the data. For example, before 1815 in France, "silk had the most elaborate and capitalistic industrial organization"; "it was in the linen manufacture that really primitive conditions were most prevalent." For another example, "That Prussian tariff of 1818, immeasurably the wisest and most scientific tariff then existing among the great powers, sprang from the application of trained reason to the very peculiar fiscal position in which Prussia found herself after 1815." A somewhat different type of conclusion is "Summarizing the railway work of the Second Empire, it may be said that in its early years (1852–60) the 1842 programme of trunk lines was completed, almost as originally planned, together with a considerable number of subsidiary lines; that in its later years the trunk lines were modernized and further additions made to the subsidiaries; so that the French railway map of 1870 contained most of the main features of the map as it was in the twentieth century." This conclusion is limited to the program, the period, and the country, and is primarily a summary of facts. Even when data are available in a more precise and comprehensive fashion, the conclusions are still of limited applicability. For example, statistics on cotton consumption are summarized "easily": "stagnation from 1876 to 1890 and steady growth for the next twenty-four years." [12] No attempt at further analysis is made.

[11] *Ibid.*, pp. 106, 192, 234.
[12] Clapham, *Economic Development of France and Germany*, pp. 64, 97, 149, 247.

Clapham, however, reaches broader conclusions. For instance, "with the late seventies had begun that world-wide fall in prices which continued, broadly speaking, until the end of the nineteenth century . . . and the article most affected in the early days was wheat." Another such conclusion is that "division of the common grazing ground and waste was closely associated, as in the English inclosure movement, with the rearrangement of the common arable fields." Of somewhat different scope is the conclusion reached in evaluating France's commercial policy. Clapham finds that policy encouraging in some respects and a handicap in others, but he adds, "A nation which aims at self-sufficiency, as she did, broadly speaking, must not expect to be a great ocean carrier. History seems to show that people who carry much for others have always been obliged to carry much for themselves." [13] Whether the evaluation of the French policy followed from this premise or was actually derived from empirical data is not clear, nor do the facts themselves show how they lend support to that premise.

A similarly broad conclusion is reached regarding the development of communication. "All the going to and fro, the buying and selling, insuring and speculating, loading and unloading, . . . in short all the commerce in its widest sense, absorbed a growing proportion of the population in every country." This observation is almost true by definition. However, Clapham connects it with a more general observation when he adds that "as a rule, each fresh means of communication, though at first seemed to threaten its predecessors with extinction, after a time added to their vigour and to the number of those who lived by them." [14] This conclusion is based on data of the German occupational structure in the years 1882, 1895, and 1907 only.

Probably the most relevant conclusions of the study are those that come in the Epilogue and are a mixture of speculation and summary observation. Here Clapham addresses himself to the welfare of the common man, the class relations, and the growing interdependence of nations. The results, however, are summaries of earlier observations and do not carry the reader any further in understanding history, predicting tendencies, or planning change. They do, nevertheless, give an idea of what happened in the century following the Napoleonic era.

Clapham presents his conclusions as true descriptions of the developments in the nineteenth century. He supports them with data whenever

[13] *Ibid.,* pp. 180, 201, 245, 364.
[14] *Ibid.,* p. 364.

possible. In that sense, and to the extent that he sticks closely to economic and institutional aspects, his findings may be verifiable. A problem arises, however, when we recall the ambiguous expressions and terms he uses to describe some of these developments and the selectivity characteristic of his data. For this reason, it may be justified to regard his findings as only tentative, as he would probably consider them to be.

Mantoux's conclusions have already been described as being more like assertions than inferences from his observations, which were not extensive enough to permit such broad generalizations as he has come up with. For example, "the centralization of modern industries is bound up with certain facts by which alone it can be explained," such as division of labor, specialization of functions, intensified output, and capital accumulation.[15] However, it is not shown that these phenomena themselves were not consequences of centralization or that they have been observed clearly in the history of England. No sequence of events is determined to support the conclusion.

Another conclusion of broad implications is that "with this great new event, the invention of the steam engine, the final and most decisive stage of the industrial revolution opened. By liberating it from its last shackles, steam enabled the immense and rapid development of large scale industry to take place. For the use of steam was not, like that of water, dependent on geographical position and local resources. Wherever coal could be bought at a reasonable price a steam engine could be erected." However, a few sentences later, the author states that the new industries were built in the older industrial districts which existed prior to the introduction of steam. A similarly loose, but broad conclusion is that "Wherever it could develop under favorable conditions, the factory system brought about the rise of these mighty centers of population whose monstrous growth is still going on under our own eyes." [16] However, the relation between industrialization and population growth is not explored further, even though it is not an obvious relation; many population centers grew up without a factory system, and many factories grew up without creating monstrous population centers.

Nevertheless, most of Mantoux's conclusions are empirical in nature and possible to test empirically, given the availability of data. Many of them are also more limited than those already mentioned. For instance, "in the metal as in the textile industry, most of the inventions on which

[15] Mantoux, *The Industrial Revolution*, pp. 56–57.
[16] *Ibid.*, pp. 337, 355.

modern technique is based were the result not of abstract speculation but of practical necessity." "With the factory system a new class, a new social type came into being." "In spite of its recent origin, of the dissimilar elements which had gone to its making and of the unequal moral value of its members, the manufacturing class soon became conscious of its own existence." [17] These generalizations, however, are too vague to mean much unless they are left in this oversimplified fashion, which in turn renders them of little use in understanding or predicting the process of change.

Probably the most important conclusions are those Mantoux himself classifies as conclusions. These consist of dating the Industrial Revolution and specifying its technological, economic, and social characteristics. In particular, the factory system appears as the most important process in the revolution. These conclusions are significant and useful as tendencies and generalities, but they are of limited value for predictive purposes. As has already been pointed out, they are not derived totaly from the data and are presented in such a form that verification might be impossible. For example, what level of factory system is necessary before the impact on population can be observed? Is the relation between these two processes constant, or is it determinate in any way? These questions are not answered, but they hold the key both to verification and to rendering the conclusions predictive in nature.

Turner's generalizations are quite sweeping. They fall mainly in the trend and predictive categories. The main problem with these generalizations is that there is little data to support them, nor are they true by deductive reasoning. They seem to be more like hunches or hypotheses for further study and testing, as in fact Turner would want them to be.

The question that needs to be answered is the extent to which they can be verified and how broadly they can be applied. Neither question can be answered in a straightforward way. Turner does not seem to have been concerned with verifiability. Not only has he left out much of the supporting and relevant data, but he has also made statements in a manner vague enough to preclude verification. Read, for example, Turner's observation that "the new settlements, by a process of natural selection, would afford opportunity to the least contented, whether because of grievances, or ambitions, to establish themselves. This tended to produce a Western flavor in the towns on the frontier. But it was not until the original ideals of the land system began to change, that the op-

[17] *Ibid.*, pp. 311, 338, 367.

portunity to make new settlements for such reasons became common. As the economic and political ideal replaced the religious and social ideal, in the conditions under which new towns could be established, this became more possible." Although an illustration of what is meant is given, the statement remains vague; what is "Western flavor"? What are the "ideals of the land system" and whose ideals are meant in the statement? Furthermore, the change occurs sometime in the "latter part of the seventeenth century and during the eighteenth." Anything might be observed in such a relatively long period, given the time span of frontier settlement. The rhetoric is repeated in another statement in the same essay. "That the movement of expansion had been chiefly from south to north, along the river valleys, should not conceal from us the fact that it was in essential characteristics a Western movement, especially in the social traits that were developing. Even the men who lived in the long line of settlements on the Maine coast, under frontier conditions, and remote from the older centers of New England, developed traits and a democratic spirit that relate them closely to the Westerners, in spite of the fact that Maine is 'down east' by preeminence." [18] Nothing in these statements indicates what "Western" means or how to evaluate their accuracy. This, of course, does not mean that the observations are not correct. It only suggests that interpretation and reinterpretation are unavoidable. Furthermore, general statements that lack precision in meaning make it difficult to use the conclusions in interpreting other experiences or in trying to predict similar events. How would other frontiers affect social and political relations? Or should we regard these conclusions as relevant only to the American frontier in a given period? Despite their vagueness, Turner's conclusions have much wider relevance than the American frontier and, therefore, deserve to be more precise and more verifiable.

The conclusions of Cameron et al. range in variety from those relating mainly to banking to those dealing with a given country or with development in general. The synthesis of the case studies is broad enough to fit into a general theory of banking and development. A few examples will illustrate. The historical evidence coincides with the theoretical reasoning "that the banking system can play a positive 'growth-inducing' role as well as responding passively to the demand for financial services." However, "the potential role of the financial system is greater in cases of derivative or imitative industrialization." Banks contribute

[18] Turner, *The Frontier*, pp. 76–77, 79.

mostly in mobilizing capital, and failure in that respect can hinder development. A more limited finding is that "banks were subjected to greater restriction and regulation than other forms of business enterprise." "The right or privilege of note issue is one of the most effective means both of eliciting a rapid growth in the number of banks and of habituating the public to the utilization of financial intermediaries." The authors also find a relation between density of banks and of population. The tendency to concentration in banking usually came near the end of the "take-off" stage and was aided by the rise of joint stock. Finally, it seems that competition in banking has been associated with better bank performance.[19]

We have left out the unique and interpretative generalizations and presented only those regarded by the authors as universally applicable. These are mainly comparative-predictive generalizations. They fall short of the cosmic type because they leave out of the comparison various economic systems in which banking and finance may play a role, such as socialist and even feudal economies. These broad generalizations, however, are not laws. They are more like hypotheses that need further testing and verification. The authors recognize the data limitations, the need for simplification, and the difficulty of arriving at final conclusions in any historical and social study. Therefore, they admit that their conclusions are tentative and frequently precede them with cautious expressions such as "seems" or "suggests." The question, however, is whether these generalizations can be verified. On the face of it, the study reaches verifiable conclusions. It deals with empirical data and often in quantitative terms. Yet, given the lack of statistical analysis, the absence of precise definitions and critical values for the relevant evaluative concepts, it seems hardly possible to expect full verification. The authors have made impressionistic judgments and have inferred on the strength of theoretical concepts, but without having adequate supportive data. Therefore, their conclusions have not been precise enough to be tested except as broad tendencies. One problem of verification deserves special attention; namely, the case in which the conclusion seems almost tautological. For example, free competition seems to facilitate efficient bank performance. The optimal bank growth rate seems to be the natural growth rate under free competition.[20] This conclusion seems to be circular. Efficient performance has been identified with per-

19 Cameron et al., *Banking in the Early Stages*, p. 291.
20 *Ibid.*, p. 313.

formance under free competition; therefore, the performance under free competition must be optimal.

In conclusion, it seems common among the contributors to aim at broad generalizations, often to the extent of going beyond the confines of their explicitly stated objectives. It seems also that all contributors derive a combination of generalization types rather than aim at any one type. Even Clapham, who stays on the side of limited generalization, ends his study by wandering far and wide in assessing the impact of economic change on welfare and social being.

On the other hand, there is insufficient effort to reach conclusive and verifiable conclusions. Although the majority of the contributors recognize and admit the tentative nature of their findings, they do little to put these findings in a form precise enough to permit testing and verification. These comments will be elaborated in the next chapter.

# PART THREE

## The Conflict and
## Its Resolution

# 8

# Traditional History
# in Retrospect

The preceding critical survey of the predominant features of representative contributions to economic history focused on some of the strengths and weaknesses of what has been criticized as traditional economic history. This criticism has been an indirect result of the missionary activities of the "new economic historians" who, in order to promote a new history, have condemned what came before them. We shall deal with some of the achievements of the new history in the next chapter. At this point, however, it is appropriate to synthesize the observations of the last chapter by trying to answer three questions. What are the most common features of traditional history? To what extent are these features consistent with scientific method, and how justified are the criticisms directed by the new historians? And what steps would be necessary to close the gap between the traditional and the new historians?

As far as can be ascertained, no attempt has been made to clarify the meaning of *traditional history*, except in the context of discussing the new history. Apparently, the concept is interpreted as relative to what is less traditional. Thus, traditional economic history today is non-econometric history, or the history that is not part of the new history. However, the difference from the new history is not chronological, but relates to the methodological substance of the two types of history. Although the new economic historians have not carefully analyzed traditional history or stated what they mean by that concept, they have specified the innovations that differentiate them from traditional historians. These innovations include: (1) a more extensive use of economic theory in the analysis of historical data; (2) the use of econometric tools and statistical theory; (3) abidance by the rules of scientific method; (4) precise specification of the model, hypothesis, and criteria relevant to the research; and (5) explicit use of the counterfactual hypothesis as a basis for confirmation.*

* Bibliographies of the new economic history can be found in Douglas North. "The State of Economic History," *American Economic Review* 55 (May 1965):

Although these innovations are set out in "more or less" terms, it may be possible to assess the degree to which these methodological features are lacking in traditional economic history. It may also be possible to evaluate the effects of such a lack on the results, at least as evidenced by the representative contributions. To begin with, it seems that traditional historians have been greatly concerned with problems of methodology in economic history and in the social sciences in general. They have, to varying degrees, dealt with basic questions relevant to scientific method. Even though they have proposed no definitive solutions, their comments have been quite enlightening. They have emphasized the role of empirical evidence, and the need for facts and the right perspective. Traditional historians have recognized the role of abstraction and the need for concepts, and have stressed—somewhat cautiously—the usefulness of theory. Apparently, they have associated theory with oversimplification, unwarranted precision, and an unrealistic perspective. They have been sensitive to the question of relevance and to the danger of mistaking the potential for the actual or the symptom for the cause. Although less commonly so, there has been some interest in the counterfactual approach and an awareness of the difficulty of experimentation and of exhausting the relevant data.

Apparently it has been difficult for traditional historians to practice what they preach. For example, in the majority of the sample cases the problem of relevance is not resolved. The topic, or objective, and the unit of study remain vague. The criteria of relevance are not specified. Consequently, the contributors have tended to follow their intuition in gathering and interpreting data and in answering their self-styled questions. In those cases in which the problem of relevance is reduced, the topic of study seems to be narrow in both subject matter and in length of the period covered. For example, the historians dealing mainly with economic variables are more successful in specifying the unit of study and in resolving the problem of data relevance than are those dealing with interdisciplinary questions. Similarly, the shorter the period covered, the easier it has been to resolve the relevance problem.

Although these traditional historians emphasize facts and observations, in practice they commonly resort to indirect or secondary data; such as the impact of institutions, human attitudes, or ethics on eco-

86–91; R. W. Fogel, "The Specification Problem in Economic History," *Journal of Economic History* 27 (September 1967): 283–308; and R. L. Andreano, ed., *The New Economic History* (New York: John Wiley and Sons, 1970).

nomic change. However, both their primary and secondary data tend to be historical; hypothetical data are used only rarely. Guesswork is practiced in certain instances, but these historians invariably tend toward historical data, even when applying the counterfactual method. Their interest in historical facts has many implications, whether data are lacking or abundant. When data are lacking, they have judged it reasonable to conclude from inadequate data; when abundant, to be selective because exhaustion of the material would be impossible. Furthermore, interest in historical data has led these historians to resort to qualitative data whenever quantitative data are not readily available, because they assume that qualitative data are more easily accessible and that hypothetical estimates should be avoided.

This interpretation is consistent with the apparent tendency of traditional historians to stick to historical data, to be qualitative, and also to be selective in data use. To this complex of features can be added the general inclination of traditional historians to go beyond economic data and apply an interdisciplinary approach to their topics of investigation. Interdisciplinary investigations have in turn made it necessary to be both qualitative and selective, because of the complexity of analyzing extensive data. However, given the rationale for an interdisciplinary approach and the tendency of traditional historians to apply it, it seems unavoidable to be selective and qualitative. Interest in historical data, therefore, seems to support selectivity and qualitativeness only incidentally. Nevertheless, these features have left an impact on the methods of analysis and on the results of research, as will be seen below.

Traditional historians have tended much more toward analytic and synthetic history than toward descriptive history. Apparently, the conditions they deal with are either described elsewhere or they simply do not regard recording and describing as their major objective. When they do describe, it is mainly to clarify points relevant to their objective. Those who specialize in descriptive history are a minority.

Contrary to certain observations, traditional historians have been greatly interested in what may be called a model, or framework for analysis. The majority, at least as suggested by the above contributions, have tried to formulate a conceptual scheme, either explicitly or implicitly. In fact, this general tendency seems to be independent of the topic of investigation or its scope. Apparently, the most important factor is the personal interest of the investigator, for it does not seem that the formulation of a conceptual scheme is related to any commitment to scientific method or to any methodological refinement. This probably explains why in the majority of the representative cases the model or conceptual scheme remains vague, disjointed, and often incomplete. Frequently, parts of the model are left implicit and the relations unspecified, contrary to the requirements of scientific analysis. This is well illustrated by the ambiguous systems approach applied by most of the contributors. In general the contributors tend to treat their unit as an aggregate or a body of interconnected parts. However, the treatment is more frequently implicit than explicit. They tend to assume certain functional or structural relations, but they do not state them explicitly. As a result, they often give only partial or insufficient explanations of the changes characterizing the system under consideration. Some investigations might require the isolation of certain parts from the rest of the system, but to do so without specifying the anticipated effects on that part, and on the system as a whole, can easily distort the results.

One of the most complicated questions treated in this critique is the degree to which theory has been used by traditional economic historians and whether they have tended toward deduction or induction. The survey of the sample contributions suggests that traditional historians tend to use theory and deduction only in a limited way. When they attempt to do so, theory is used only to support certain observations, rather than to test a hypothesis or build on that theory. In general, historians have been much more interested in empirical or inductive inference. Yet, their use of inductive inference is less rigorous or systematic than is required by scientific method. Inference frequently is made from inadequate data or from informal and unsystematic interpretation of the data. The lack of rigor and formalism is compounded by a tendency to keep the ideas guiding analysis implicit rather than to state them explicitly. Thus, much room remains for impressionism and loose interpretation. In part, this tendency leads to and augments the illustrative use of data. Empiricism is often turned into the illustration of preconceived ideas and conclusions, and induction is turned into impressionistic and subjective generalization.

This loose approach to empiricism explains the absence of statistical or econometric analysis of data. Although econometrics as a field is too recent to have been used by traditional historians, the same is not true of statistics and formalism. Nevertheless, traditional historians have tended to ignore statistical theory and the careful analysis of data, even when such data were available in quantitative or quantifiable terms.

Only in exceptional cases are attempts made to measure and estimate economic values as would the new historians, but these attempts are too few to change the general character of traditional history.

Probably the most common tendency of traditional history is the use of comparison in order to derive generalizations. Being aware of the difficulty of observation and experimentation, traditional historians have resorted to comparison as a substitute. However, this highly appropriate substitute is applied with little formalism or rigor. In particular, there is a tendency to emphasize similarities and to ignore differences or cases of contrast. The framework for comparison usually remains vague; the criteria are not defined, and no common standard is established to guide the comparison. In fact, the cases compared changed in composition during the period of comparison. The selection of cases and variables for comparison seems to play an important role in distorting the application of comparative method and thus in biasing the results. Usually, only those cases and observations that would support the researcher's ideas or hypotheses are used in comparison, contrary to scientific induction, which takes all relevant observations into consideration.

Given these critical observations, it is to be expected that the results are general, imprecise, and difficult to verify. The generalizations of the contributions studied range from the unique to the cosmic, but the majority are either trend or comparative predictive generalizations. An attempt has been made in this critique to discover any possible relations between the kinds of data and methodology used and the generalizations derived. No tendencies can be safely noted in that respect. However, a few observations summarize the findings. In general, the narrower the scope of investigation and the more precise the data, the more limited is the generalization. On the other hand, the broader and more interdisciplinary approaches tend to result in broader generalizations. Nevertheless, it seems that historians have been inclined to generalize broadly from insufficient data. Often a single observation is found adequate to generalize to the whole class of events to which the observed event belongs. Furthermore, the generalizations tend to be vague and imprecise so that their verification is difficult. Although the authors, in the majority of cases, describe their results as tentative, they do not state their conclusions precisely enough to permit the testing or evaluation of their validity. Consequently, these results remain hunches still to be reformulated as hypotheses for testing. These observations would hold regardless of whether economic theory were used or not, and whether induction or deduction were applied. The weaknesses seem to be more a result of nonformalism, imprecision, and vagueness. The results are frequently more general than the data would warrant because of the ambitiousness of the objectives, or because of the investigator's personal conviction. Seven of the eight contributions display a tendency to go beyond the confines of the data at hand.

On the positive side, we should note that traditional historians have been sensitive to the interdependence between economic and noneconomic aspects of human behavior. They have recognized the role of institutions in economic change, and have also displayed an unmistakable conviction that laws of behavior can be discovered. In other words, they have recognized the significance of history to the present and to the future. Therefore, they have aimed at complex explanations of social and economic change. This explains the interdisciplinary approach, the use of comparative method, and the tendency toward fairly broad generalizations.

These observations suggest that the charges of the new economic historians are justified to a large extent. Traditional historians have made little use of theory, of statistics, and of the method of hypothesis. They have also failed to specify the model and criteria they used. Consequently, they have derived vague and broad generalizations that cannot . be subjected to testing and confirmation. On the other hand, it might be suggested that most of the weaknesses are due to the lack of formalism and systematic treatment of the data, and not to the neglect of theory or the counterfactual approach. What is needed is a higher degree of formalism, more precision, and an explicit specification of the problem, the method, and the conclusion. It is not necessary to resort to deductive method. Induction, if applied carefully, would bring the field more closely toward scientific method. The extent to which formalism and precision can be applied, given the broad scope of research in history, is another matter and cannot be treated on an *a priori* basis, although there is no reason a broad study cannot be formal and precise. In conclusion, it seems there is much room for improving the scientific quality of research in economic history without compromising its substance or changing its perspective. The new economic history may be one approach to deal with the dilemma. Innovations in other social sciences may suggest other approaches. Therefore, we shall explore the innovations in both of these areas as part of the search for solutions to the problems facing economic historians.

# 9

# The New Economic History

The problems associated with traditional economic history are largely problems of the social sciences in general. They derive from the complexity of human behavior, its changeability, and the difficulty of observation, exprimentation, and measurement. Historians face the additional problem of dealing with events long past, only some of which are recorded, but this is merely a complication of the basic problems. Economic historians and other social scientists face the same problems of precision, confirmation, and the predictability of their generalizations. This chapter will explore the achievements of the new economic historians; the next chapter will survey some of the methodological innovations of the other social sciences and their impact on economic history.

Studies in the tradition of the new economic history have certain features in common. Almost all of them tend to be revisions of earlier studies, and are aimed at correcting errors of traditional research. Almost all set up models of competitive economic behavior in which rationality and mobility of factors of production are assumed, realistically or not, to prevail. Finally, they all deal with small sectors of an economy, although the authors seem to hesitate very little in generalizing from the small to the large or to an economy as a whole.

It would be impractical to try to review all, or even most, of the relevant studies within the confines of this essay. Many of the points that should be raised have been dealt with in the literature already. However, to illustrate some of the problems of the new economic history from the standpoint of this critique, two studies will be evaluated, the first because it represents the methodology of a major spokesman of the new history, and the second because it illustrates the impact of the new tradition on recent graduates.

## AMERICAN RAILROADS RECONSIDERED

In his study of the railroads, *Railroads and American Economic Growth: Essays in Econometric History*, Robert Fogel tries to reevaluate the contribution of railroads to the economic growth of the United States. His objective is to correct "errors" and to abolish "myths" surrounding the role of railroads in American history during the nineteenth century.

One of the alleged myths current in the literature is that railroads were not only important but "indispensable" for the growth of the economy during the nineteenth century. As Fogel puts it, "if the axiom of indispensability merely asserted that railroads were an efficient form of producing transportation services, there would be no reason to question it. . . . The crucial aspect of the axiom is not what it says about the railroad; it is what it says about all things other than the railroad. The crucial aspect is the implicit assertion that the economy of the nineteenth century lacked an effective alternative to the railroad and was incapable of producing one." Therefore, to determine whether railroads were indispensable or not, it is necessary, according to Fogel, to establish whether alternative means of transportation were available, or if "the incremental contribution of railroads over the next best alternative directly or indirectly accounted for a large part of the output of the American economy during the nineteenth century." It is not enough to demonstrate that railroads caused a boom psychology or that they contributed to the construction of certain important manufactures such as coal and iron. Rather, it is necessary to show either that these sectors of the economy would have remained unaffected by the absence of railroads or that the railroad contributions were substantial. It is necessary to consider not only what alternatives existed, but also what could have been created as substitutes for the railroads. Waterways might have been built, cars might have been advanced more rapidly than they were, or the pattern of settlement might have been different. Fogel suggests that the evidence usually presented does not support the axiom of indispensabilty because it fails to "establish a causal relationship between the railroad and either the regional reorganization of trade, or the change in the structure of output, or the rise in per capita income, or the various other strategic changes that characterized the American economy of the 19th century." It does not even establish the proposition that railroads were essential for growth, let alone were indispensable. Therefore, given the new tools of analysis, Fogel proceeds to investigate the validity of the axiom of indispensability by estimating the impact of railroads on agriculture, interregional and intraregional, on the iron industry, and on the structure of the economy in the light of

Rostow's "take-off" thesis. Finally, he draws certain implications from his study regarding the application of theory and econometrics to the study of economic history.

Investigation of the incremental contribution of railroads depends basically on the concept of "social saving," which is defined as the difference, in any one year, between the actual cost of shipping by railroad and the cost of shipping exactly the same collection of goods between exactly the same set of points by other means. The cost of shipping agricultural goods includes transportation costs to primary and secondary markets. Shipping from primary to secondary markets constitutes interregional distribution. Intraregional distribution includes shipping "from farms to primary markets and from secondary markets to the points immediately surrounding them." The main hypothesis Fogel investigates is that "Railroad connections between the primary and secondary markets of the nation were a necessary condition for the system of agricultural production and distribution that characterized the American economy of the last half of the nineteenth century. Moreover, the absence of such railroad connections would have forced a regional pattern of agricultural production that would have significantly restricted the development of the American economy."

As for the "take-off" thesis and the impact of railroads on industry, Fogel tries to estimate the contribution of railroads to the growth of coal, iron, machinery, transportation equipment, and lumber on the assumption that most of what was purchased by the railroads came from these industries.

The estimate of social saving resulting from the transportation of agricultural products by rail is based on four commodities, wheat, corn, beef, and pork, which accounted for "42 percent of income originating in agriculture."

In using social-saving estimates for testing the hypothesis, Fogel stipulates that "if the calculation shows the saving to be zero, then obviously the absence of the interregional railroad would not have altered the existing productive pattern. On the other hand, if the social saving turns out to be very large, say on the order of magnitude of national income, it would be equally obvious that in the absence of the interregional railroad, all production of surpluses in the Midwest would have ceased."

The social saving is calculated for one year, 1890, on the assumption that the efficiency of the railroads was higher in that year than in the previous four decades and that the social saving estimates would there-

fore have an upward bias, if any. The cost differential is calculated between rail transportation and "feasible," though nonexistent, transportation by water. In the absence of adequate data, least-cost estimates
are said to be made by linear programming for the given markets and
distances. One model used to estimate the least cost of transportation
places no constraint on the form of transportation; a second model used
to estimate the least cost excludes railroads. The difference between the
two estimates reflects the absence of railroads and constitutes the social
saving. "What is the nature of this estimate? The desideratum is the
'true' social saving—the difference between the actual 1890 level of national income and the level of national income that would have prevailed if the economy had made the most efficient possible adjustment
to the absence of the interregional railroad." However, the estimated
difference probably exceeds the true social saving because adjustment
to the absence of railroads might not have resulted in the most efficient,
or least-cost use of transportation; hence the possibility of an upward
bias. The cost factor takes into consideration direct payments and indirect cost components. The primary and secondary markets, and the
data on actual costs, volumes, and distances are obtained from official
and private sources. These data are frequently used as a basis for
estimating unavailable data to fill gaps. Similar methods are applied to
the analysis of the intraregional distribution of twenty-seven agricultural products. In the latter case, two estimates of the social saving
are derived. The first estimate, $\propto$, is similar to that derived for interregional distribution. However, in intraregional distribution, Fogel
regards it as appropriate to make use of data on land values to remove some of the upward bias of the estimates. He proposes that
"without the railroads, the high cost of wagon transportation would
have limited commercial agricultural production to ranges of land lying
within some unknown distance of navigable waterways." If the boundaries of this region of feasible commercial agriculture were known, the
social saving could be broken into two parts: "(1) The difference between the cost of shipping agricultural commodities from farms lying
within the feasible region to primary markets with the railroad and the
cost of shipping from the same region without the railroad; (2) The
loss in national product due to the decrease in the supply of agricultural
land." The social saving thus derived would be the second estimate, $\beta$.
The two problems to overcome in this respect are how to determine
the feasible region and how to estimate the loss of national income due

to a decrease in the supply of land. Economic theory on rent and land value provides a way out of these difficulties.

The results of these investigations can be summarized as follows. The social saving resulting from the use of railroads in interregional distribution amounted to $73 million, after indirect charges are accounted for. The first approximation of direct cost differences gives negative results, showing railroad transportation costs to have been higher by $38 million over the next alternative, waterways. However, considering neglected cargo losses of $6 million, transshipping costs of $16 million, additional inventory costs of $48 million due to loss of time in water shipping, supplementary wagon haulage of $23 million, and neglected-capital costs of $18 million, railroads were cheaper than waterways by $73 million. The social saving in interregional agriculture that can be attributed to railroads was thus very small, or just 0.6 percent of the gross national product. The intraregional social saving was larger, but still small relative to GNP, as estimates $\alpha$ and $\beta$ show. The $\alpha$ estimate is $337.2 million, or 2.8 percent of GNP, and the $\beta$ estimate is $248.1 million, or 2.1 percent of GNP.

Fogel then analyzes the feasibility of extending waterways. Looking at the problem technologically, geographically, and economically, it appears that the extension of waterways, if there were no railroads, would have been feasible. Furthermore, taking account of projected waterways reduces the $\alpha$ estimate to 1.8 percent and the $\beta$ estimate to 1.5 percent of GNP.

An extension of the analysis to all commodities would obviously give a larger social savings. Although no such estimates are currently feasible, an approximation is suggested by multiplying the combined inter- and intraregional social savings by four. The results are 7.1 percent for the $\alpha$ estimate and 6.3 percent for the $\beta$ estimate. Fogel concludes that these results do not support the axiom of indispensability, even though they do not necessarily show that railroads were unimportant. Fogel suggests that the ultimate judgment must await estimates of social savings on nonagricultural items and for research on "the likelihood that the existing scientific and technological knowledge would have allowed society to find more effective substitutes for the railroads than were examined in this volume." Finally, considering the derived effects of railroads, this probability cannot be "resurrected on socio-political grounds without stronger evidence than is now available." The current arguments for derived effects are not adequate. For example, it must be established that railroads uniquely influenced population growth. The empirical findings do not sufficiently support the contention that population growth is a function of the level of per capita income, on which contention the impact of railroads on population must be based. Furthermore, the limited impact of railroads on the supply of land would have little effect on the location of economic activity. It is not sufficient to argue without further evidence that railroads affected the sociopolitical structure to the extent of being indispensable for economic growth.

Fogel's discussion of the take-off thesis consists in a survey of the economic activities of the nineteenth century, especially of the manufacturing industries. Reevaluation of the data, according to Fogel, suggests that rapid growth was continuous, and not concentrated between 1843 and 1860 as Rostow suggested, nor was it related "directly to the requirements for building and, especially, maintaining the railway system."

Finally, Fogel deals with the impact of railroads on the iron industry. As a hypothesis, he paraphrases statements, without documentation, to the effect "that the proportion of the output of iron purchased by railroads was of such a magnitude that the absence of these purchases would have significantly diminished the demand for iron and retarded the growth of the industry." He then proposes that the available information has not been carefully examined. Therefore, he proceeds to examine these data by constructing four indices: "the share of the output of the iron industry represented by rails; the determination of pig iron production; the determination of the amount of iron consumed in the manufacture of rails; and the determination of total domestic crude iron production and consumption." Fogel applies a model that gives estimates within a range of one to eight percent of reported data on rail replacement, on the ratio of new to total rails in 1856, and on the predicted average weight of rails on main tracks at the end of 1869. The results show that replacement demand became important in the early 1840s, but that by 1860, scrap iron had become gradually more significant in replacement demand, accounting for about 60 percent of the replacement iron. Hence, the "net addition to pig iron production required for rails between 1840 and 1860 amounted to less than 5 percent of the output of blast furnaces." Even if all rail demand for iron is aggregated, it amounts to an average of only 17 percent of the total iron production between 1840 and 1860, rising to 25 percent in the last six years of that period. Considering these results, "the strongest statement that can be made in support of Rostow's thesis is that the demand for railroad iron played an increasingly important role during the fifties in maintaining the *previous* level of production when the demand for other items sagged. Otherwise, one could just as well argue that nails rather than rails triggered the 1845–49 leap in iron production. Indeed in 1849 the domestic production of nails probably exceeded that of rails by over 100 percent."

In his conclusion, Fogel draws broad implications for the theory of growth. For example, "no single innovation was vital for economic growth during the 19th century." Another is that "economic growth was a consequence of the knowledge acquired in the course of the scientific revolution of the seventeenth, eighteenth and nineteenth centuries. . . . The effectiveness of the new innovations was facilitated by political, geographic and social rearrangements," regardless of the railroads, as was also the case in England. It is not justifiable to look for leading sectors to explain growth which, according to Fogel, is a consequence of "a body of knowledge accumulated over all preceding centuries," through a "broad supply of opportunity." Particular conditions might have changed the pattern, but not the substance. "The fact that the condition of cheap transportation was satisfied by one innovation rather than another determined, not whether growth would take place, but which of many possible growth paths would be followed."

Fogel's study is remarkable as an innovative effort in using new tools in the study of economic history. It is systematic and precise to the extent possible, given the nature of the data and the type of questions it deals with. One of its main features is its emphasis on quantitative data, almost to the extent of slighting nonqualitative information, as will be shown below. It is more important, however, that in order to use new tools and to test a hypothesis, Fogel sets up a *testable* hypothesis, regardless of how realistic that hypothesis is. And to disprove the myths, he specifies unrealistic criteria that render his conclusions almost inevitable. For example, to set up a hypothesis that can be tested, Fogel asserts the axiom of indispensability without adequately supporting his assertion. He quotes Sidney Dillon, as a representative of the age and proponent of the axiom, as saying, "The growth of the United States . . . is due not so much to free institutions, or climate, or the fertility of the soil, as to railways." [1] He quotes a second "strong" statement to support the axiom. "By the aid of the railway, the wilderness has been made productive, countless farms brought within reach of the great

[1] Robert W. Fogel, *Railroads and American Economic Growth*, pp. 5–6.

markets, mines opened, mills, factories, and forges built, villages, towns, and cities brought into existence and populous states carried to a higher development than would have been possible in centuries without such aids." [2] Both quotations suggest only the *relative* importance of the railroads; the first suggests only their importance relative to the contribution of free institutions, climate, and soil fertility; the second suggests only the development of certain sectors of the economy to a higher level or a more rapid transition than would have been possible without the railroad. These quotations do not say anything about *indispensability*. Rather, both of them stress relativity or a "more or less" proposition. If, in fact, these statements imply indispensability, Fogel's findings would seem to support the hypothesis, because even a small impact, say a 1 percent social saving, would still be a positive contribution. On the other hand, if relative importance means indispensability, it is incumbent on the investigator to establish whether the railroads contributed more or less than any other sector, and to specify the magnitude of that contribution to *the relevant sectors* of the economy, rather than to the GNP as Fogel has done. Needless to say, both these approaches entail more than can be handled by the methods Fogel uses, and would render his hypothesis irrelevant.[3]

More recently, Albert Fishlow has approached the problem by estimating the relative importance of railroads to the economy. The railroads seem to have been quite important, particularly to agriculture. Contrasting his results with those of Fogel, Fishlow says: "The two books approach the question of the importance of the railroad somewhat differently, and, not surprisingly, yield different answers. Fogel's principal interest is in the necessity of the innovation: could the United States have developed without it? The question I ask, rather, is how much of a stimulus did the railroad afford and by what means? We both may be correct, therefore, when he affirms that the railroad was not 'important' and I that it was." [4]

Another somewhat related question concerns the significance of the estimated social saving to the total economy. It is not clear why the impact of social saving is calculated as a simple percentage of GNP. Saving due to lower transportation costs implies a reallocation of

2 *Ibid.*, p. 7.

3 For a different perspective of this point, see Marc Nerlove, "Railroads and American Economic Growth," *Journal of Economic History* 26 (1966): 112.

4 Albert Fishlow, *American Railroads and the Transformation of the Ante-Bellum Economy*, pp. ix–x.

resources and, hence, indirect effects, or "second round effects . . . namely induced capital formation and expansion in other sectors." [5] Conversely, considering the less efficient alternative, waterways, suggests a second round of decumulation of capital and expansion, which thus increases beyond the estimated sum the total amount of social saving resulting from the use of railroads rather than waterways, unless evidence to the contrary can be found. In other words, the cumulative effect of social saving may be disproportionately larger than suggested by the social saving in any one year. One might in fact question the logic of the concept of social saving. For example, social saving accruing from the differential rates of transportation might not be a social saving at all if these differentials were due to a noncompetitive market structure. On the other hand, there can be no rate differentials and thus no social saving in a perfectly competitive structure. Would the contribution of the railroads be zero? Further, the concept of social saving, as applied, tends to understate the effects of railroads on the economy because the various external economies are hardly taken into consideration. A different way of estimating the effects, also quantitatively, tends to show a much higher marginal social advantage of railroads relative to other means of transportation than Fogel has obtained.[6]

Nowhere in the study does Fogel define *economic growth*. In application, however, it is implicit that *growth* simply means growth of GNP. This tells nothing of the significance of changes in institutional arrangements, banking, population mobility, skills, or the domestic industry of a given region.[7] These effects may or may not have a dollar value reflected in the GNP. Apparently such complications would have made quantitative analysis and testing of the hypothesis impossible. Another conceptual problem associated with both the concept of GNP and social saving is the problem of aggregation. Aggregation hides the impact on regional or local economies. For example, one railroad company might be so inefficient as to add nothing to the social saving, while another might be efficient enough to make a large contribution. Aggregation of

[5] Fogel, *Railroads and American Economic Growth*, p. 30.

[6] Stanley Lebergott, "United States Transport Advance and Externalities," *Journal of Economic History* 26 (1966): 437–461. For a critique of Lebergott's findings see Harry N. Scheiber, "Discussion of papers by Albert Fishlow and Stanley Lebergott," *Journal of Economic History* 26 (1966): 462–465; and Gerald Gunderson, "The Nature of Social Saving," *Economic History Review* 23 (August 1970): 207–219.

[7] On some of these omissions see Nerlove, "Railroads and American Economic Growth," p. 111; also G. R. Taylor's review in *American Economic Review* 55, no. 4 (September 1965): 890–892.

their effects will hide the contribution of the efficient company, even though it might be indispensable to the specific region in the economy. For theoretical purposes, aggregation may be convenient, but for understanding historical change, a more elaborate and disaggregated framework can produce different and more meaningful results.

One final assumption deserves attention. Fogel assumes that the use of hypothetical data in dealing with a historical problem is methodologically sound. He begins his investigation by quoting Morris Cohen that "to say that the thing happened the way it did, is not at all illuminating. We can understand the significance of what did happen only if we contrast it with what might have happened." However, this statement is true only for certain situations. It would be true only if we were certain that what might have happened could in fact have happened, and only if we were interested in comparing the efficiencies of the two *possible* alternatives. But it would not be true if we were interested in the significance of what happened relative to other events that have actually happened. Evaluation of the historical contribution of the railroads would be more meaningful if compared with other historical contributions to the development of the relevant economy than if compared with what might have happened under altogether different circumstances. In choosing techniques, it is legitimate to compare hypothetical cases, assuming all of them are technically and financially feasible; the present context is historical, not hypothetical, and therefore the quotation does not apply. Even though Fogel tries to establish the feasibility of waterways as a substitute, this is far from justifying nonexistent waterways as a historical alternative to the railroads, which are a historical phenomenon. The fact is that the investors chose to invest in the railroads, and not the waterways. In the absence of railroads, capital might have not come into the country, and the entrepreneurs might have turned to other ventures in other countries. Fogel stretches the point a little too far when he poses expansion in the use of motor vehicles as another possible substitute. Motor vehicles were advanced as soon as technology permitted. Even then, railroads continued to render a significant service in spite of decades of highway construction.

As for interpretation of the findings, Fogel is not much more rigorous or less arbitrary than traditional historians. For example, he stipulates the two extremes, one in which social saving is of the magnitude of the GNP and the other in which the social saving approximates zero.

THE NEW ECONOMIC HISTORY

Neither extreme is probable. He adds that little can be said for small social saving, but no critical value is established for interpreting the findings. A social saving of 2.1 percent to 2.4 percent of GNP is dismissed as insignificant. Even an estimated all-commodity transportation social saving of 6.3 percent to 7.1 percent of GNP is dismissed as insignificant. No evaluation of the marginal significance of this social saving is made. Even if we ignore the cumulative magnitude of social saving and the multiplier effect of such a percentage of the GNP, a decline of 6.3 percent in the annual national income would mean a decline of 30 percent in the potential net investment and something like a recession, let alone the concentrated depressive effects of such a decline on the region concerned. A similarly somewhat arbitrary evaluation is applied to the contribution of railroads to the iron industry. Even 17 percent of the total demand for iron does not seem to be impressive. This may well be true, but the judgment is as tenuous as many of the statements criticized by Fogel.

More arbitrary, however, are the heroic and sweeping implications drawn from the study. With little, if any, evidence, Fogel denies that any innovation is vital for growth. Growth is said to be the result of all the knowledge accumulated during all the preceding centuries. Apparently, sooner or later things must happen. Double-entry booking or the steam engine, as well as their effects, would have come anyway. The industrial revolution also would have happened. The paths might have been different, but the sum total of economic change would have been the same. By these implications, Fogel not only challenges the attempt to explain growth through leading sector theories, but he seems to propose putting a lid on all attempts to explain economic growth or the rate at which it proceeds. This approach is reminiscent of deterministic theories of development.

Finally, although Fogel pays some attention to the possible non-economic effects of railroads on growth, he summarily dismisses these effects as lacking supporting evidence and puts the burden of proof on those who attribute credit to them. By the same token, when an economic historian deals with a phenomenon in the magnitude of economic growth, he needs to give more justification for ignoring the social and political factors. The railroads may have been functional in creating an atmosphere congenial for entrepreneurship, risk taking, and growth. The hypothesis posited cannot be meaningfully tested without serious consideration of the relevance of these possible effects.

Fogel, however, is careful in presenting his conclusions. More than once he emphasizes the tentativeness of his findings. More and broader investigations are still needed before conclusive judgment becomes possible. Despite my criticism, there is no doubt that Fogel has made a great contribution by drawing attention to the potentialities of using the new techniques, to the importance of precise measurement, and to the usefulness of deductive method in economic history.

## THE NAVIGATION LAWS IN COLONIAL HISTORY

The second illustration of the new economic history includes two articles by R. P. Thomas.[8] The first article is an attempt to revise the findings on the impact of the Navigation Laws, especially those of Lawrence Harper. The second is a critique of an article by R. B. Sheridan in which he finds that the sugar colony of Jamaica contributed to the growth of the British economy.[9] The two articles are quite similar in approach, assumptions, and even in misconceptions. Both are supposed to be written in the new history tradition, although there is little evidence of extensive use of economic theory or statistical theory, nor are they more precise than the works they criticize. The main tools used are a counterfactual approach and a simple budgeting process comparing costs and benefits in two different situations.

Thomas expends little effort in defining his concepts or in justifying his counterfactual hypotheses. For example, in the essay on the Navigation Laws, he concludes that there was little or no exploitation, but he does not define *exploitation* nor does he specify the criteria that characterize it. He evaluates the benefits Great Britain seems to have derived from the American colonies as a ratio of the per capita income of the whole of Great Britain. He finds these benefits too small to prove exploitation, but would they be as inconsequential if evaluated as a ratio of the income derived from foreign trade, or from the relevant industries in the economy?

Even when Thomas attempts to define a concept, the result seems equally confused. For example, in his second essay, he asserts that "the

[8] R. P. Thomas, "A Quantitative Approach to the Study of the Effects of British Imperial Policy Upon Colonial Welfare," *Journal of Economic History* 25 (1965): 615–638; *idem*, "The Sugar Colonies of the Old Empire," *Economic History Review* 21, no. 1 (April 1968): 30–45.

[9] R. B. Sheridan, "The Wealth of Jamaica in the Eighteenth Century," *Economic History Review*, 2d s. 10, no. 1 (April 1965): 292–311.

contribution of a colony or of any economic activity to the economic growth of the overall economy is precisely the difference (positive or negative) earned by the resources employed there relative to what they would have earned in their next best alternative." According to this definition, if the rates of return of various investments were positive and equal, none of these investments would be a contribution to the overall growth of the economy, since there would be no differential earning by any one of them. He seems to confuse contribution to growth and relative efficiency. An economic activity might contribute less in one situation than in another, but its contribution in the less efficient case might still be positive and strategic. Indeed, if the actual earning is less than it might have been, and if earning is a measure of exploitation, all that can be said is that the activity with less earning is less exploitive, but not that it is nonexploitive, nor that it is a drain on the economy.

Both essays indicate an apparent anxiousness to use counterfactual hypotheses almost to the extent of disregarding the relevance of these hypotheses. For instance, in evaluating the impact of the Navigation Laws on the colonies, Thomas proposes as counterfactual the hypothesis that the colonies were independent. However, if the impact of the Navigation Laws is in question, why not hypothesize only the absence of these laws, holding all other things constant, including the colonial status? To suppose the colonies were independent is to hypothesize a completely different framework, and not only the absence of the Navigation Laws. Probably a more relevant counterfactual hypothesis would be to compare costs and benefits to the colonies with and without Navigation Laws, but in association with the mother country. A similar over-simplification is evident in the essay on the sugar colonies. The counterfactual hypothesis is to suppose the investment elsewhere in the empire of the capital already invested in the sugar colonies, to see which of the two investments gives higher returns. However, there is no logical explanation why investment in Jamaica should be singled out as less productive than investment in any other place in the empire. Why did capital not move elsewhere, as would be natural, assuming full employment and substitutability of capital throughout the Empire? [10]

An equally serious problem common to both essays is one of identifi-

[10] The assumption of full employment is contained in fn. 3, p. 31. Substitutability is implicit in the assumption that capital would be fully employed anywhere else in the Empire. Neither assumption is justified.

cation. What are the components of costs and of benefits? Or what constitutes a burden and an asset? Although Thomas attempts to isolate the economic costs and benefits and assumes externalities to be non-existent, there seems to be a certain degree of confusion and inconsistency in identifying the relevant components. For example, the cost of protecting the colonies is included, but the cost to the colonies of dependence is not. Yet, if the tools used in these essays were applied, it would seem pertinent to assign a value to independence equal to the amount the colonies were willing to expend to gain that independence; and, by the same token, that amount could be a measure of exploitation by the mother country. Similarly, self-protection by the colonies after independence is considered a cost, but no benefit is supposed to accrue from that self-protected independence. There seems little reason for not assuming that the benefit or satisfaction accruing from self-protection is at least equal to the costs the colonists were willing to bear to protect themselves, in which case the cost of protection would be offset by the accruing benefits. Apparently, selectivity and inconsistency were dictated by the fact that one component is directly quantifiable and the other is not.

In both essays Thomas fails to correctly identify other components of cost and benefit by failing to distinguish private from social cost and benefit. For example, a preferential duty or a subsidy might constitute costs or benefits to specific groups within the society, but there is no reason to regard these as *social* costs and benefits. In most cases, they are transfer payments that have little effect on the aggregate. Therefore, unless it is shown or stipulated that these transfer payments were misallocated or were eventually transferred to a foreign economy, it is not obvious they constituted either social costs or social benefits. Thomas stipulates neither, nor does he show evidence for either.

One might even raise a more basic question; namely, whether it is legitimate to select a relatively short period and compare costs and benefits in that period without investigating the background of those costs and benefits. More specifically, to what extent were the initial expenditures in the colonies by the mother country derived from her economy, and to what extent were they derived from the colonies? It may be suggested that a large portion of the stock of capital in Jamaica and of the costs expended in the American colonies originated outside the economy of the mother country. They were accumulated from earnings in the colonies or were made possible by the complementary factors of production offered by these imperial domains. If, in fact, this hypothesis is valid, to that extent all the earnings by the mother country would be pure benefit, and all costs would be discounted as borne by the imperial domains.

Finally, a major question that follows from the use of theory but receives no attention in both essays is this: If the American colonies were not a source of exploitation, and if the sugar colony was a drain on the British economy, why would the British investor and government stay in these places or invest in them? Why did they resist when the colonists sought independence? If we assume a competitive economy with full employment and factor mobility, it would seem rational for the British to have behaved differently from their actual behavior in the colonies. If, however, we recognize the mercantilist tendencies of the period and that the objectives of mercantilist policy included both economic and noneconomic goals (benefits), it would seem futile to ignore these realities. Indeed, to find a more meaningful explanation of the British mercantilist behavior would make it incumbent on the researcher to identify all the relevant components of cost and benefit from a mercantilist perspective. If such a realistic theoretical model were applied, the assumptions of full employment and mobility of capital would be questionable; it would also be difficult to assume away "externalities" or to exclude such benefits as protection of infant industries, highly rewarded employment abroad for the nationals, or the advantages and prestige of ruling a vast empire. Thomas relieves himself of the responsibility by asserting that "there may be other factors . . . that might reverse my conclusions, [and] if so, these must be explored by scholars who feel uncomfortable with my conclusions, and who will then bear the burden of proof."

## NEW VERSUS TRADITIONAL HISTORY: CONCLUDING OBSERVATIONS

For a clearer view of the contrast between the new and the traditional history, Fogel's contribution has been ranked along with the traditional histories in table 4 (p. 105). It will easily be observed that Fogel's contribution is high on relevance and on primary and quantitative data. It is low on secondary, qualitative, and interdisciplinary data, which is consistent with the stated intentions of new economic historians. It is also moderate on the use of historical data in contrast to traditional studies, which invariably rank high on this criterion. Associated with this contrast is another relating to methodological choice; Fogel's contribution is high on deductive analysis, on statistical inference, and on econometrics, whereas none of the traditional contributions rates high on these criteria. Fogel's contribution rates low on both comparison and synthesis in contrast to traditional histories, which very frequently rate moderate or high on these criteria. In other words, certain types of data and methods of analysis go together. A study either rates high on precision, narrowness, deduction, and econometrics, or it rates low on all these features. A middle way does not seem evident. Interest in secondary, qualitative, interdisciplinary, and comprehensive data, for example, may preclude precision, deduction, and the use of econometrics.

The contrast between traditional and new histories is more obvious in the context of the results. Fogel's results are admittedly tentative, but they are highly verifiable because he uses quantitative data and because he explicitly states his method and rules of procedure. However, his generalizations are of the limited and trend types. Although he anticipates these results, apparently he is not satisfied and, like traditional historians, he generalizes to industrialization and growth in general.

In summarizing the work of the new economic historians, a number of observations can be made. First, the new economic historians have already left an impact on the discipline. Whether supporters or critics of the new history, many contributors and researchers have been aroused to reconsider their methods and prospects. Second, the new economic historians have not overcome the problems associated with their proposed methodology. By insisting on a hypothetico-deductive approach, the new historians have had to oversimplify problems and to be quite selective and often arbitrary in their interpretations. They have handled only short periods and relatively small sectors of the economy and have investigated only problems of recent periods for which at least some quantitative data exist. Third, the results they have obtained have not been radically different or more valid than those obtained by traditional historians, nor have they resolved controversies surrounding their research topics. Traditional historians might have been less precise, but their findings are more comprehensive and realistic. Finally, although new blood should be welcomed to maintain vitality in the discipline, caution should be exercised against overrating the potential of the new economic history. By trying to imitate others, we might end up like the crow in the Arabian fable, who, after trying without success to imitate the walk of the pigeon he admired, found he had forgotten his own walk and ended in confusion.

# 10

# Developments in
# Related Social Sciences

The problems of research in economic history and the attempts to deal with them can be considered a part of the social sciences in general. Conversely, the developments in other social sciences are highly relevant to economic history, especially those in sociology, anthropology, psychology, and political science. It is with developments in these four disciplines that we shall be concerned. Economics and history are part and parcel of economic history and therefore will not be treated separately.

These related social sciences have many features in common with economic history. All of them deal with human behavior, even though their individual points of departure may be different. As such, they all face problems that are highly complex, multivariate, and often not directly observable. The motives behind human action are not easily discernible and therefore a certain degree of interpretation is necessary within the framework of the given culture and institutions.

Being concerned with human behavior, these social sciences are largely concerned with observing, measuring, and explaining dynamic behavior. Yet, observation, measurement, and explanation are not easily accessible, especially because controlled experimentation is out of the question in most cases. Reproduction of the data is not possible, unless miniature representation is considered adequately representative of actual behavior.

These disciplines have to cope with two levels of interpretation, with both individual and group behavior. Transference of theory or experience from one to the other is not easily implemented. Therefore, it is often necessary to study behavior on each level independently and to reconcile the experiences and findings of one level with those on the other.

The study of human behavior also has to cope with other complications. First, knowledge of behavior is often derived from common-sense, everyday observation. Therefore these sciences must integrate such

243

knowledge and go beyond it to the more complex study of behavior. Second, any approach to human behavior must be capable of reconciling the observable regularity of behavior, which suggests a certain degree of determinism, with man's alleged free will. Unless this problem is resolved, the researcher will be torn between searching for generalizations and treating each unit of behavior as a unique phenomenon not subject to generalization.

As studies of behavior, these related disciplines may try to isolate their domain of interest from other disciplines, but they cannot overlook the relevance of other disciplines to the subject matter of their study. Therefore, the question looms large as to what extent the study of human behavior should be interdisciplinary.

Being parts of scholarship and intellectual activity, all these disciplines face the challenge of achievements in the natural and physical sciences and try to imitate, innovate, and explore in order to catch up and to proceed on a more scientific basis. Yet, these disciplines cannot adopt ready-made tools from those sciences because of the inherent differences between their subject matter.

These disciplines are also handicapped by the inaccessibility and nonquantifiability of the data. Yet, like economic history, these social sciences have to overcome these problems before they can proceed to systematic and scientific research.

All of the problems of research in sociology, anthropology, psychology, and political science are common to economic history, with two important qualifications. These related sciences face a more serious problem because it is more difficult to deal with social and psychological than with economic variables, especially in the areas of observation, measurement, and control of the data. In other words, the related social sciences deal with questions less subject to objective treatment than are the economic data handled by economic historians. On the other hand, these sciences have an advantage over research in economic history in that they deal mostly with contemporary problems for which data are relatively more extant and more comprehensible than are data relating to the past. With these qualifications in mind, we shall try to find out how the related social sciences have dealt with the common problems, what methodological innovations they have introduced, and what results they have achieved.

At this point a disclaimer is in order. I do not claim expertise in all these various fields, despite my broad interest in the study of human behavior in general and in the unity of the social sciences. Therefore, I shall borrow from the experts in these fields and acknowledge my indebtedness for what they offer. First, I shall explore the recent controversies and pending methodological problems in these fields. Next, I shall explore the recent methodological innovations that seem relevant to economic history, keeping in mind the problem areas discussed above. Finally, I shall gather together the threads and try to find out where we go from here in the study of history and change.

## CONTROVERSIES AND PENDING
## METHODOLOGICAL PROBLEMS

The last two decades have witnessed many changes in the social sciences, both in subject matter and in the methods used. These changes have been associated with certain underlying philosophies and conceptions as to what the social sciences can and should do. The underlying arguments have been reinforced by developments in the physical sciences, in mathematics and statistics, and in computer technology. Although researchers in all the social sciences have attempted new approaches of more precision and better prospects for prediction, both old and new controversies have continued, as has been the case in economic history.

One indication of the controversy is the variety of schools of thought in each of the social sciences. Anthropology, for example, is roughly classified into physical, archaeological, cultural and social, and linguistics anthropology. The social and cultural is broken down into the mechanistic-naturalistic, the structuralist, and the functionalist schools of thought. Political science is classified into the traditional-philosophical, the systematic or theoretic, the analytical, the comparative, the descriptive, and the natural science or behavioristic approaches. Sociology is currently "dominated" by the natural science or experimental neopositivistic approach, which is also described as statistical sociology. Other approaches include the social action, the ideal type, the structural-functional, the historical, and the antinaturalistic. The longest list, however, belongs to psychology with between thirteen to twenty different approaches, all of which are regarded as independent components of psychology. For example, psychology includes associationism; behavior-

246 THE CONFLICT AND ITS RESOLUTION

alism; Gestalt psychology; psychoanalysis; and the structural, functional, hormic, holistic, phenomenological, existentialistic, humanistic, transactional, and biosocial approaches.[1]

It seems that some of the schools of thought in the social sciences developed primarily from an interest in specific methods and tools. In other words, new methods did not evolve in response to the demands of new schools of thought or problems under study, but rather led to those new schools.

The differences among the various schools may be a function of efficiency, or the need for a division of labor, although the division has often had little to do with efficiency or a division of labor. For example, anthropologists argue whether archaeology is a social science or belongs to the humanities, or in fact to the natural sciences, in view of the new tools at its disposal. They also raise questions regarding its affinity to history. The cultural anthropologists debate whether they should use theoretical models, and if so, which models. Should they adopt models from the physical sciences, such as the causal and functional models, or should they use logical, analytical, and symbolic models? Another question that seems to have concerned cultural anthropologists is whether they should search for uniformities among cultures or should study each culture as a functional whole with unique characteristics. Another controversy relating more to substance than to method is concerned with the role of language and the extent to which linguistics can be studied as representative or expressive of a culture.

The controversies in sociology are somewhat similar. It is often asked whether the description and collection of data can be a science. On the other hand, sociologists question whether theory can be formulated before the pertinent facts are collected. Between these two positions fall the proponents of the "middle range" theories who insist that theories should be close to reality and hence derived from the facts. A simple question, which assumes an important place in the debate, is concerned with the priorities that must be observed in research. Should one study major problems even though the appropriate tools of analysis have not been developed, or should the study be limited to those problems for which tools are available and which can be studied scientifically? This question is easily reduced to whether the method or the problem should

[1] For a brief description of each of these, see R. Handy and P. Kurtz, A *Current Appraisal of the Behavioral Sciences*. For a more up-to-date, but a less integrated survey see the UNESCO publication, *The Social Sciences*.

determine the direction and subject matter of research. Another philosophical question is whether one should derive concepts operationally, in such a way that they are observable and experimental, or take a broader view and derive ideal concepts even though they might be unobservable abstractions. An important controversy, common to all the social sciences, is the conflict between holism and reductionism. Should one study the unit as a whole or reduce the problem to partial aspects that can be studied more intensively and in detail. In other words, is it possible to understand the whole through the parts, or must one look at the whole to be able to understand it? All these questions may be connected with the broader and more fundamental question of the objective of sociological study. Should sociologists search for natural laws (nomothetic), or should they concentrate on specific and particular historical events (ideographic)? The first approach leads to generalizations with the hope of discovering laws, whereas the other is analytical and tries to explain the events within their immediate environment.

Most of these same questions have been raised in political science and psychology. In addition, political scientists have been concerned with the role of history in political analysis and with whether it is sufficient to study behavior empirically and scientifically without regard to history. In contrast, it is frequently asked to what extent political science can be scientific, and how important theory is for that purpose. Another question relates to the place of value judgment in political analysis. To what extent should the analyst allow his own views to enter his conclusions? A final question is the relation between political science and the other social sciences, and whether the division between these disciplines is justifiable.

Psychologists also have raised questions of priority in research, but a more serious question has been whether introspection should be encouraged or whether analysis should deal with the facts as they appear. Conflict of opinion has prevailed as to whether psychologists should practice "methodological individualism" or should try to understand group behavior by observing the individual in contrast to social psychologists, who study the impact of the group on the individual. A similar area of conflict is the extent to which molar or molecular explanations should be sought. Molar explanations are based on psychological and observable behavior, whereas molecular explanations deal with the more basic and elementary levels studied in microphysiology.

A third directional conflict is whether the study of behavior should be based on the premise that behavior is instinctive or is subject to conditioning.

The division of labor between and within these disciplines is a fact, and is hardly subject to debate, although the question of cooperation should be raised not as a tactical matter but as a fundamental issue. For instance, is it possible to compartmentalize behavior such that it can be explained adequately by any one or a part of one of these disciplines? This question will be treated within the context of interdisciplinary approaches in social science. Otherwise, there is little room for controversy regarding the division of labor, at least not in the context of methodology. Method can be discussed only after the problem of study has been specified. Therefore, we shall take the subject matter, or the problem of study, as given and concentrate on the methodological controversies within the social sciences, not from a normative standpoint, but as self-image expressions, or as they are seen by members of the disciplines. The controversies and recent developments can be grouped under three headings: (1) the role of history, data collection, and description; (2) recent trends: theory, models, and the degree of scientism in social analysis; and (3) implications of the new trend.

### THE ROLE OF HISTORY, DATA COLLECTION, AND DESCRIPTION

A number of issues must be cleared up before we can explore what the scholars in the various disciplines say about history, or the facts. Much depends on whether *history* means only ordered facts, implies relevance of the past, is regarded as a record of unique events, or is the grounds for inductive generalization and hypothesis formation. It will depend also, when speaking of facts, on the kind of data, their sources and reliability, and their relevance to the purpose of the study. Some scholars have formed an attitude toward these factors in response to certain trends and attitudes or because of uncertainty. For example, it is suggested that because Kroeber was suspicious of regarding anthropology as a social science, he regarded it as history. Thus, under the influence of the American Historical School [2] cultural anthropology "emphasized finding out what happened in the past, especially in preliterate times and non-literate cultures. . . . Anthropologists viewing their work as a kind of history seem to take the concentration on the *past*, the emphasis on specific, 'unique' happenings, and the lack of

[2] Frank Boas, Clark Wissler, A. L. Kroeber.

strict experimentation, as major differentia between history and science." [3] This attitude is based on a conception of science as the source of theory, in contrast to history which aims at the " 'descriptive integration,' the reconstructive effort to preserve reality within its contexts of unique positions in time, space, and quality, and the test of validity by the degree of the fit of the phenomena reported within the totality of conceptual findings." [4] This view is based in part on a sort of correlation found to exist between the material and the study objective; namely, that history relates to the uppermost level matter that shows any degree of constancy. Humanity cannot be reduced to generalized abstractions as required by science. Therefore, it can be treated only by a fully descriptive, integrative historical approach. As will be shown below, this approach has been seriously challenged, even prior to the advent of the more recent behavioralism in the social sciences. The structuralists and the functionalists have viewed anthropology as a generalizing science, while archaeologists and linguists have practiced scientific method in various forms. The physical sciences have had a great impact on the discipline. Yet, the arguments of the historians have not been refuted, except by the anthropologists' practicing a different approach.

The relation between sociology and history is quite confused, although neither sociologists nor historians are ready to admit it. When the subject is debated, one hears the sarcastic expression that "sociology is history with the hard work left out; history is sociology with the brains left out." [5] In a similar vein, it is suggested that "historians and social scientists are separated by the fact that historians know too little social science and social scientists know too little history." [6] The implication is that sociologists often generalize from inadequate data or uncritically accept evidence, while historians often treat unique events and sequences without attempting to compare or conceptualize. In other words, sociologists regard themselves as generalizers in search

[3] Rollo Handy, *Methodology of the Behavioral Sciences* (Springfield, Ill.: Charles C. Thomas, 1964), p. 86.

[4] Robert Redfield, "Relations of Anthropology to the Social Sciences and the Humanities," in *Anthropology Today*, ed. A. L. Kroeber (Chicago: Univ. Chicago Press, 1953), pp. 730–731.

[5] Quoted in *Sociology and History*, ed. W. J. Cahnman and Alvin Boskoff (Glencoe, Ill.: Free Press, 1964), p. 1.

[6] Edward N. Saveth, ed., *American History and the Social Sciences* (Glencoe, Ill.: Free Press, 1964), p. 5.

of laws, whereas historians resort to description which the sociologists eventually use for generalization.

The history of the social sciences tends to belie such a distinction. Many of the classic contributions in both history and sociology have involved the concepts and methodology of the other. Marx, Weber, Pirenne, and Clapham have approached history with a sociological bent. According to Cahnman and Boskoff the difference between the two fields lies "in the kinds of questions asked," not in the methods they use.[7] The questions asked guide the collection and classification of data. The sociologist would be happy to use the historian's facts if these were collected in accordance with sociological concepts; that is, so as to permit comparison of these facts in different times and places.

The relation between sociology and history has, apparently, been muddled by differences that are no longer relevant. For example, it is no longer true that history describes and sociology analyzes. The difference between description and analysis is not genuine, because "these processes necessarily are reciprocal in practice." Another difference that no longer holds is between the ideographic and the nomothetic, or between the unique and the general. Those involved in history are said to distrust scientific approaches and generalization and therefore separate themselves from the generalizing sociologists. In practice, however, this difference is not real. "If historiography is not clearly ideographic, sociology is by no means unequivocally nomothetic."[8] The implication is that the two approaches are not incompatible.

A third area of alleged difference follows from the above; namely, the question of freedom and necessity, or freedom and the determinism implied by the search for laws. This conflict may no longer be relevant, because the concept of probability reduces determinism and increases the area of freedom and thus renders the generalizing and the descriptive disciplines compatible. Even the problem of causation associated with the discovery of laws is no longer significant since the idea of a single cause does not find supporters any more. The majority of sociologists try to formulate theories of causation on the assumption that no single theory could be fully adequate. To do this, they have resorted to comparative method and to historical typologies and thus made use of historical data in an effort to arrive at less than the single causes they once aimed at. Hence, the major differences between the two areas of study have been reduced greatly.

[7] *Ibid.*, p. 3.
[8] Cahnman and Boskoff, *Sociology and History*, pp. 3, 5.

With the major differences cleared away, sociologists can use historical data in one of two main ways. They can apply sociological concepts "for the purpose of describing and analyzing historical situations and problems although, on the whole, on a higher level of generality than ought to be expected of historians." Or, they can use "historical data for the purpose of illustrating and, possibly, testing the validity of sociological concepts, constructs and theories." A supposed variant of this approach is that of Norman Jacobs who, like Marc Bloch and Max Weber, tried to "transform history into a science by ascertaining agreement, disagreement, and concomitant variation through the comparative method, and by selecting and arranging historical data 'for demonstrating a meaningful and coherent sociological argument.' " [9] All these variations suggest that history must be the handmaiden of sociology. But once history becomes scientific, it ceases to be history and becomes sociology. This implication necessarily follows from the conception of history as descriptive and related only to unique events. What of those who insist on the generalizing role of the historian? [10] It is even more disconcerting to hear that cultural anthropologists turned to integrating methodologies such as the structural-functional only because of the lack of data for a historical and detailed description of the cultures they studied. Is it not possible that they were interested in the integrative method, regardless of whether data were available or not? Apparently the historian must remain description-bound, just as the sociologist must remain generality-bound. Even "where American sociology is indeed 'historical'—in the sense of being time-and-space bound in character—the fiction of generality is maintained, either intentionally or by implication." [11]

The conflict between sociology and history should be distinguished from the conflict within sociology between what has been described as the "old-fashioned" and the "modern" diagnosis of social problems. The old-fashioned approach in this context is similar to what has been described as the historical. This approach, in the words of one of its proponents, Barrington Moore, Jr., reflects the "doctrine that all human behavior consists of unique events to be explained by other unique events." The old-fashioned approach, however, rarely goes that far. It holds only that although sociology tends toward the study of general

[9] *Ibid.*, p. 8.
[10] See Louis Gottschalk, ed., *Generalization in the Writing of History*; and E. H. Carr, *What Is History?*
[11] Cahnman and Boskoff, *Sociology and History*, p. 10.

structures and the prediction of future developments, it does not ignore the understanding of unique or single events. Therefore, it is appropriate to look at the difference between the old-fashioned and the modern schools as a division of labor, and hardly as a matter of conflict.[12] The historical approach, however, is indirectly related to the study of broad, or macro, units in sociology. The study of macro units may be justified in part by the fact that the "life-span of most micro-units is short," and therefore significant factors will be overlooked unless the macro unit is considered over a longer life span.[13] In other words, the study of society must reach into the past and cover broad areas.

Recent attempts to reconcile historical and modern sociology are best illustrated by the work of comparative sociologists. Whereas historians should be encouraged to use social science concepts, and sociologists encouraged to use rich historical resources for testing theoretical propositions, historical sociologists might be able to modernize their researches by using behavioral models of comparison by which causal or explanatory relations can be discovered. Thus, historical sociology would proceed from a descriptive, impressionistic to an objective, generalizing methodology without forsaking its historical or realistic character. It is not clear, however, to what extent the variables in such broad comparative historical studies could be measured or formalized, which would be expected of a modern approach. It is only on this basis that reconciliation may be possible.[14]

The conflict within political science is more complicated than it is within sociology, because the discipline is not paralleled by another, as sociology is by anthropology. One might relegate political history to the field of history and leave to political science the treatment of current affairs of government and politics, but there has been little attempt to remove political history from the field of political science. The attack— if it may be called that—on the historical approach seems to be an attack on the unsystematic handling of data and on insufficient theorizing. In a sense, this criticism of the historical approach is an integral part of the critique of traditional methods of political research as being nonscientific. Thus, it seems, by implication at least, that the lack of

[12] Barrington Moore, Jr., "Sociological Theory and Contemporary Politics," *American Journal of Sociology* 61, no. 2 (September 1955): 10, 110

[13] A. Etzioni, *The Active Society*, p. 53.

[14] John F. Flint, "A Handbook for Historical Sociologists," *Comparative Studies in Society and History* 10, no. 4 (July 1968): 492–509.

interest in deduction, as a scientific approach, "usually results in a research report that is essentially historical, descriptive and diagnostic, rather than theoretical in the sense of stating the effects of varying conditions upon the factors specified in the baseline proposition or hypothesis." Furthermore, political analysis, which has been mainly institutional and descriptive, has hardly aspired to the formulation of theory or risen beyond the analysis of norms and procedures of governmental processes. Yet, Avery Leiserson observes that "historical, descriptive and diagnostic studies can be carried on by systematic methods, and their findings can be translated into theoretic propositions." In fact, Leiserson makes it a prerequisite to include a historical section in any good research design and criticizes what would otherwise be a good research design except that proportionally little weight is given to the historical part. Nevertheless, he concludes that a cleavage exists among political scientists in accordance with the apparent conflict between historical, descriptive, and institutional analysis and theory formation. To reduce the conflict, he proposes that in planning their research political scientists try to transform such analysis into "propositions about behavior in political situations." [15]

Leiserson's criticisms can be compared with J. S. Eldersveld's criticisms of voting-behavior research that is neither institutional nor descriptive. The weaknesses he points out include failure to observe rules of scientific method, lack of a *"co-ordinated* assault on the problems of political behavior implicit in the voting process," little planning toward theory construction, insufficient attention to relevant efforts of other disciplines, poor techniques even when the data are amenable to systematic and sophisticated analysis, failure to experiment and control the data, and, finally, insufficient attention to verification.[16] It should be noted that these criticisms were made at a time when attempts to usher in the behavioral approach had just begun, just as the new economic historians did when they tried to introduce the new economic history.

The attack on the traditional approach does not spare the philosophical approach, which deals mostly with the history of ideals. The

15 Avery Leiserson, "Problems of Methodology in Political Research," in *Political Behavior*, ed. Heinz Eulau, Samuel J. Eldersveld, and Morris Janowitz (Glencoe, Ill.: Free Press, 1956), pp. 55, 57, 60.

16 J. S. Eldersveld, "Theory and Method in Voting Behavior Research," in *Political Behavior*, ed. Eulau et al., pp. 272–273.

philosophical approach is analytical, but not in the modern sense of the term. In fact, it has been described as opposed to scientific method in politics and as tending to be qualitative and often descriptive.[17] The attack on the philosophical school is based in part on the normative inclinations of that school, an approach no longer acceptable to social scientists in general.

The traditional school has also been associated with the study of institutions, in contrast to the recent interest in the behavior of individuals, even though it is questionable whether the latter approach should be equated with scientific rigor.[18] An important aspect of the traditional school survives in the form of comparative analysis, which is mainly descriptive. Although unfashionable, this approach still forms the basis of comparative politics.[19] As we shall see, the attitude toward the conflict between the traditional and the modern approach reflects an attack on, or a defense of the modern rather than of the traditional approach, as if the traditional stands or falls on the strength of the modern, and not on its own inherent strength.

The conflict in psychology centers around the relevance of the philosophical and introspective methods, rather than around any historical method. By definition, psychology does not involve history, except in the sense of dealing with the biography or developmental history of an individual. However, the same is not true of description or institutional effects on behavior. In this sense, psychology has dealt with the same problems the other social sciences face by focusing attention on empirical, behavioristic, and experimental methods as steps toward rendering the field more scientific. Certain aspects of psychology, such as the hormic or physiological, are amenable to precise and experimental treatment, and attempts at similar treatment have been made in other areas, including social and clinical psychology. The trend has been toward testing, measurement, and statistical analysis, on the assumption that description and uncontrolled analysis are defective from a scientific standpoint.

The relevance of history to developmental psychology and to clinical psychology should, nevertheless, be noted: developmental psychology is the study of the history of the individual; clinical psychology is the

[17] Handy and Kurtz, *Appraisal of the Behavioral Sciences*, pp. 58–59, 65.

[18] R. Dahrendorf, "Symposia on Political Behavior," *American Sociological Review* 29, no. 5 (October 1964), pp. 734–736.

[19] H. A. Scarrow, "The Scope of Comparative Analysis," *Journal of Politics* 25, no. 3 (August 1963): 565–577.

study of the individual as a unique phenomenon. Both, however, are generalizing schools in the field of psychology, and both are growing rapidly. Developmental psychology deals with "the historical aspects of psychological events," concerns itself with similarities and differences between events, and depends almost completely on the longitudinal method. In particular, developmental psychology emphasizes the role of learning, which is an individualistic process. Nevertheless, it makes a contribution to theory formulation by leading to a "set of concepts of developmental stages." This is similar to the stage approach in history. It is of interest, however, that developmental psychology has been integrated into the modern approaches in psychology. Although it has traditionally yielded "behavioral-descriptive accounts," developmental psychology has more recently made use of experimental and formal methods.[20] In fact, one of the criticisms of Piaget, who has revolutionized the field, is that he has become so mathematical and symbol oriented that many find it difficult to read his contributions.[21]

The attitude toward clinical psychology may be described as a reflection of a growing distinction between "scientists" and "practitioners." The conflict between them may be due in part to the social processes that classify people according to interest and affinity, and to political differences as they are represented by vested interests or by the attempts of each group to secure a larger share in the respective psychology departments. The relevant source of conflict, however, is what has been conveniently described as a schism between scientism and clinicalism. Clinicalism, which is differentiated from clinical psychology, is the attempt to "comprehend every instance in a domain of inquiry in all of its particularity and unique individuality." Clinicalists are suspicious of theory, of statistics, and of probability because all these affect the "uniqueness of the particular case." Clinicalists stress reality and are suspicious of the laboratory environment as being abnormal. Furthermore, they would offer few generalizations about human behavior, although they would welcome improvements in the techniques of studying highly complex behavior.[22] Because of these traditionalist attitudes, clinicalism is attacked as nonscientific. Neverthe-

[20] Sidney W. Bijon, "Ages, Stages, and the Naturalization of Human Development," *American Psychologist* 23, no. 6 (June 1968): 420, 421, 424.

[21] R. D. Tuddenham, "Jean Piaget and the World of the Child," *American Psychologist* 21, no. 3 (March 1966): 215.

[22] Isidor Chein, "Some Sources of Divisiveness Among Psychologists," *American Psychologist* 2, no. 4 (April 1968): 339, 388.

less, clinicalism survives, but for reasons different from those for the survival of developmental psychology. Whereas developmental psychology seems to have adapted itself to the modern techniques, clinicalism derives its power for survival from the demand for its services. Its relevance as an applied discipline sustains it in the face of the new trends in the social sciences.

The attitude toward historical and descriptive analysis has been in direct contrast to a keen interest in facts and data collection. Rather than stressing dependence on documents and secondary sources, as was common in the traditional approach, the recent trend has centered around directly observed facts, field work, surveys, questionnaires, and laboratory experiments. Consequently, interest has shifted from the past to the present. Bernard Berelson suggests that "the behavioral sciences are typically more devoted to the collection of original data reflecting the direct behavior of individuals or small groups as against the more aggregative, indirect, and documentary practices of economists, political scientists, and historians." [23] This statement is not an accurate description of the social sciences, for political scientists and economists have been as concerned with behavioral data as have the other behavioral scientists. The amount of data collected on consumer behavior and on voters testifies to that. Furthermore, the distinction between direct and indirect data is misleading, since even in field work, the data collected usually describe what the individual says he would or did do, but not necessarily what he actually did. In other words, in both cases there is room for interpretation and evaluation of the reliability of the data.

Probably the best indication of the growing interest in data collection is the publication of theoretical arguments for support of data programs and the establishment of data centers. Karl Deutsch argues that data programs actually contribute to the style of thought and to theory formulation. Refinements in data collection help to "pinpoint more sharply the information actually needed," in the same way the microscope did for medicine. He compares data programs with the computer as powerful tools of raising the level of analysis. In a strong statement, Deutsch asserts that "as we make social science data as freely reproducible and as readily available as elementary chemicals are available to chemists, as we get the social science data into the laboratory, and as our data archives and repositories become linked with data labora-

[23] *The Behavioral Sciences Today*, ed. Bernard Berelson, p. 4.

tories, we shall witness, I believe, a renaissance of social science." [24]

Probably few would question this position. The conflict, however, has persisted as to whether emphasis should be on quantitative or qualitative data. The negative attitude toward historical, institutional, and descriptive studies has been equally vehement regarding qualitative data, which are hardly subject to systematic analysis, although this attitude has not remained unchallenged. It has been noted that the nature of data depends on the problem. Political science, for example, cannot ignore qualitative data. Although the usefulness of quantitative data cannot be overestimated, Carl J. Friedrich believes that "the quantitative data may engender a false sense of certainty. . . . Proceeding upon the mistaken belief that such quantitative data are more 'scientific' than other data, some of the protagonists of the use of such [mathematical] methods of inquiry have even advanced the claim that the study of politics will only be truly a science when all of its propositions are cast into such quantitative form. It can confidently be predicted that, if that is true, politics never will be a science." [25]

Friedrich backs his statements with cogent arguments. First, he stresses the importance of quantitative data in dealing with mechanistic processes, which are presupposed by mechanical models. However, non-mechanistic processes can be handled only analytically by qualitative data. Second, quantitative research frequently leaves out counterevidence by analyzing only supporting data. To avoid this, the "quantifier and data gatherer has to go beyond the evidence." Furthermore, the stress on quantification tends to generate hypotheses for which only the relevant data are collected when, in fact, the attempt to explain any given amount of data may generate a number of conflicting hypotheses. To negate the relevance of qualitative analysis is quite restrictive. Friedrich thus sounds a warning that emphasis on either quantitative or qualitative data, or on deduction or induction, could be a misrepresentation of scientific method.[26]

This middle-of-the-road position is common to all the social sciences, but it does not hide the fact that interest in quantitative data has been on the rise. Even when the variables studied are qualitative in nature, attempts have been made to attach quantitative values to the obser-

[24] Karl W. Deutsch, "The Theoretical Basis of Data Programs," in *Comparing Nations*, ed. R. L. Merritt and S. Rokkan, pp. 54–55.

[25] Carl J. Friedrich, *Man and His Government*, pp. 59–60.

[26] *Ibid.*, pp. 60–65.

vations, both for objectivity and for validation. A good example of this inclination is represented by the study of attitude carried out by Robert F. Winche and Douglas M. More.[27] What is of interest here is that quantification was carried out by the observers in interviews. They ranked the subjects' attitudes as they observed them, regardless of how the subjects saw themselves. The values are neither additive nor comparable in an objective manner as quantitative analysis ideally should be. The authors tried to establish the reliability of these rankings by having other analysts repeat them. However, this approach does not take into consideration the possibility that the various groups of analysts who repeated the ranking might have had the same background, which would bias the results in favor of higher reliability. Furthermore, this approach does not overcome the subjective nature of the responses themselves. It is not clear, therefore, to what extent the quantities derived can be used in statistical analysis for the purpose of generalization.

In conclusion, there seems to be a common rebellion in the social sciences against the traditional, historical, descriptive, and qualitative approaches. This rebellion is a way of introducing the modern approach like setting up a strawman and knocking him down to create a vacuum. To understand the significance of the new approach, we should look into the arguments advanced in its behalf.

### THEORY, MODELS, AND THE DEGREE OF SCIENTISM

Social scientists like to think of themselves as objective and scientific. They also set up for themselves aims that include theorizing and predicting. Even when they admit the inevitability of subjective evaluation, they persist in the view that theory and generalization are within the scope of their endeavor. Being scientific in this context "follows the general pattern of any Western knowledge, . . . careful observation of data, explanation of the data by induced theory, and then indirect verification of the theory by examining if the facts are in accord with the deductive consequences of the theory."[28] Thus, the first stage results in a theory (induction), and the second stage verifies the theory

[27] "Quantitative Analysis of Qualitative Data in the Assessment of Motivation: Reliability, Congruence, and Validity," *American Journal of Sociology* 61, no. 5 (March 1965): 445–452.

[28] Jacques J. Macquet, "Objectivity in Anthropology," *Current Anthropology* 5, no. 1 (February 1964): 47–55, 53, 155.

(deduction). That theory is an integral part of scientific research is an accepted fact in the social sciences. The relevant questions are how to derive a theory, what the function of the theory is, and how to validate it. As McEwen put it, "social anthropology as a science strives for theoretical understanding. . . . Such understanding requires the creation of a formal system of terms with specified properties and rules for relating the terms, which system can be shown to fit some field of experience." [29] A central problem in science building is to fit experience to theoretical ideas or to validate them empirically. From this it appears that a basic requirement in science building is formalism, and another is validation.

The trend in sociology has been described as the natural-science approach, which emphasizes symbolism, observation, and measurement. Although it is denied that quantification is essential, it is held that everything observable is measurable. This behaviorist approach is said to be the dominant in American sociology.[30] It regards symbolism or abstraction and precision as prerequisites for scientific sociology. In elaboration of these views, Moore suggests that "science advances in so far as it can find adequate procedures for simplifying and ordering its factual raw materials" free from common sense and the facts as observed in nature and based on creative imagination as exemplified in the work of the natural and physical scientists. To use creative imagination, it is necessary to construct " 'ideal types' and mathematical models of portions of social reality." Hence, the scientific approach stresses strict laboratory and experimental conditions. Understanding current problems can be stressed only as a "mere by-product." Yet, two pages later, the same author suggests that a theory that reduces vast experiences into general principles is only a "set of tools whose usefulness is tested in their ability to solve concrete problems." [31]

This brings out three more features of scientism in the social sciences: abstraction from current problems as in the laboratory; the necessity to construct models for research; and acceptance of the limited scope of individual understanding.

The place of theory in psychology is well established. Theories of personality, child development, and learning have a long history. The

[29] William McEwen, "Forms and Problems of Validation in Social Anthropology," *Current Anthropology* 4, no. 2 (April 1963): 155.

[30] George A. Lundberg, "The Natural Science Trend in Sociology," *American Journal of Sociology* 61, no. 3 (November 1955): 191–202.

[31] Moore, "Sociological Theory and Contemporary Politics," pp. 108, 110.

complaint about the lack of theory, when it prevails, refers more to specific areas than to a general lack. For example, psychologists have debated among themselves the extent to which they have contributed to the study and improvement of international relations. They observe that their contribution has been limited because they have failed to develop theories of international behavior.[32] Or they may wonder why no major theories to explain and predict behavior relatively accurately have been developed, as has been the case in the physical sciences. In all these cases, there is no questioning of the feasibility or legitimacy of formulating theories. The trend, however, has extended beyond the philosophical justification of theorizing, and into associating theory with specific methods of research. For instance, the new trend in psychology has been characterized as experimental, quantitative, predictive, and hypothetico-deductive. It is also reductionist in adopting concepts and propositions, often arbitrarily, in order to fulfill the requirements of scientific method, as long as the propositions are testable.[33]

The attitude toward theory in psychology has been well expressed in the debate between Skinner and his critics, a debate that has lasted for almost two decades. Skinner questions the imminence of a positive role for theory and suggests that negative effects are probable. Theory may be useful if one studies an inner system that cannot be observed, but it adds little to the study of empirical behavior. Theory tends to channel observations into its own narrow confines and thus to overlook many relevant aspects of the subject matter. Rather, Skinner would look at all the facts and try to generalize from them. In other words, his objections seem to be aimed at deductive analysis, rather than at theorizing in general. In essence, Skinner recommends experimentation, depth, and a search for explanations which take the purpose of behavior into consideration. His approach does not need theory, sophisticated statistics, or a large number of cases for observation.[34]

Skinner's views have been criticized severely as "antitheoretical," "ultraempirical," "nontheoretical," and "radical."[35] Scriven insists that

[32] James T. Tedeschi and E. F. Malagodi, "Psychology and International Relations," *The American Behavioral Scientist* 8, no. 2 (October 1964): 10–13.

[33] Chein, "Sources of Divisiveness Among Psychologists," pp. 337, 341.

[34] B. F. Skinner, "Are Theories of Learning Necessary?" *The Psychological Review* 57, no. 4 July 1950): 193–216; also *idem*, "Operant Behavior," *American Psychologist* 18, no. 8 (August 1963): 503–515.

[35] For a detailed critique see M. Scriven, "A Study of Radical Behaviorism," *Minnesota Studies in the Philosophy of Science* 1, ed. H. Feigl and M. Scriven (Minneapolis: Minnesota Univ. Press, 1956), pp. 330–339.

theories are necessary to explain why a particular law should apply in a given situation. This, however, is not in conflict with Skinner's position; whether we proceed or end with a theory should make no difference for the explanation. Scriven also suggests that theory is helpful in explaining individual behavior or raises the "level of probability in explaining an individual response." It appears that much of the debate centers on the degree of emphasis on theory, and on the procedure by which a theory is derived.[36] The significance of this debate may be reflected in the observation that commitment to scientific method has continued to rise, and has rendered research in psychology almost sterile and irrelevant to human problems. The methods have tended to guide research away from human problems into the narrow channels determined by the theory, the hypotheses, or the statistical tools available to the researcher, as Skinner predicted.[37] The trend seems to have continued.

A little over a decade ago it was possible to say that "most political scientists, although perhaps a diminishing majority, are skeptical of both the possibility and importance of systematic theory." [38] The movement toward scientific politics begun by Merriam, Munro, and Catlin in the 1920s had reached its peak and had started to decline. Antagonism toward theory and scientism was carried on by people like Elliott, Corwin, Gulick, Hart, Beard and others throughout the following decade. Their objections were aimed as much against a value-free study of politics as against impractical theorizing and scientism. They regarded political scientists duty bound to lead the way to better statehood and better societies.[39] However, a revival of interest in theory has been noted during the last two decades. This revival has been associated with an apparent interest in convergence within political science toward a unified discipline.[40] Since then, an increasing number of political scientists have turned to theorizing and to systematic rather than pragmatic or problem-oriented research. This is what has been known as behavioralism; behaviorists concentrate on behavior rather than on political phi-

[36] For a comparison of Skinner and Scriven see R. J. Johnson, "A Commentary on 'Radical Behaviorism,' " *Philosophy of Science* 30, no. 3 (July 1963): 274–285.

[37] Nevitt Sanford, "Will Psychologists Study Human Problems?" *American Psychologist* 20, no. 3 (March 1965): 192–202.

[38] Leiserson, "Problems of Methodology," p. 57.

[39] Albert Somit, *The Development of American Political Science*, chap. 9.

[40] David B. Truman, "Disillusion and Regeneration," *American Political Science Review* 59, no. 4 (December 1965): 870. For a survey of political science at the beginning of the revival see David Easton, *The Political System*, chap. 2.

losophy or institutions. The objectives of behavioralism, according to Leiserson, include "the development of a systematic body of theoretical propositions; . . . the acquisition of analytical skills and data collecting procedures for relating empirical uniformities and deviations to our theoretical concepts and categories" on the basis of "relatively microscopic studies which have undertaken the tedious task of identifying and validating the conceptual variables." Although both induction and deduction are considered legitimate, he proposes that "a problem becomes scientific when it can be formulated in such a way as to test the main proposition asserted" about the given behavior in the given framework. This becomes possible when the research follows a "theory-hypothesis-data" pattern, in which the theory is the main proposition and the hypothesis is derived from it. The data are collected accordingly to test the hypothesis.[41] It is not clear whether the pretheory stage should necessarily be considered unscientific; nor is it specified how the theory can be derived if it is to precede the empirical research and analysis.

In addition, behavioralists postulate that the "truth or falsity of values (democracy, equality, freedom, etc.) cannot be established scientifically." Therefore, political science should pursue pure research, abandon "great issues," and remain value free. At the same time, there should be more scrutiny of method and more interaction with other disciplines in search of better techniques, theories, and concepts.[42]

However, as in the previous period of theoretical and scientific upsurge, counterarguments have been numerous, and quite similar. They touch upon the nature of data, the difficulty of measurement, the relevance of public policy, and the need to maintain the integrity and identity of the discipline.[43] The arguments of one recent critic, Christian Bay, closely resemble some of those presented during the 1930s, during the period of reaction against early scientism. In a serious indictment of modern political science, Bay notes the lack of theory, or the lack of theory of a given type. He charges that the recent trend has been away from politics toward what he calls pseudopolitics. His main argument is that the new politics has removed itself from the normative and the real in politics, and into research that glorifies the status quo and thus distorts the real objectives of political science.[44] Despite all the critics,

[41] Leiserson, "Problems of Methodology," pp. 57–58, 60, 61.
[42] Somit, Development of American Political Science, pp. 178–179.
[43] Ibid., pp. 180–182.
[44] Christian Bay, "Politics and Pseudopolitics," American Political Science Review 59, no. 1 (March 1965): 39–51.

the trend toward more theoretical and behavioral research has continued, especially among the younger generation of political scientists.[45]

Most of the arguments and counterarguments discussed above have been repeated in anthropology. In a recent symposium anthropologists listened to a plea for modernizing their methods and increasing the validity of their findings, as would be expected in a science. The reactions to this plea were as varied as the number of speakers. A summary of the various reactions indicates the types of arguments against the modern approach.[46] To begin with, while agreeing that abstraction and theory building are helpful, Irving Goldman questioned whether deviation from reality, which is inevitable in that case, is useful. A realist's approach, or a middle-range theory, would be the proper scientific approach in anthropology. C. W. Hart compared modern anthropology with botany and biology of the nineteenth century in that anthropology is still in the stage of "orderly qualitative progress" during which history and facts play an important role. The implication is that anthropology is still premature for more advanced methods. Harry B. Hawthorn and E. R. Leach tried to relate the method and language of science to the specific topic under study, suggesting that description and analysis would be economical in treating cultural data, whereas theoretical analysis would be more appropriate for other data. John J. Honigmann asked why anthropologists should not use a variety of models or approaches, including a historical model. "If too intensely committed to the model of science as reflected in some physical sciences and psychology or sociology, cultural anthropology may head at breakneck speed down a dead-end track, or else become very well equipped to solve limited but largely inconsequential exercises." A. J. F. Kobben warned that "what one gains in precision one loses in applicability," thus questioning the value of reductionism and quantification. Marion J. Levy, Jr. went farther by noting that some social scientists are in the habit of choosing their study problems according to the measurability of the data, thus allowing the means to determine the ends, and asked if there is any reason why there should not be a division of labor between those concerned with description and those with analysis. Each approach should have its place in the process of scholarly endeavor. Horace M. Miner

[45] For a bibliographic and approach survey of the new trend see Somit, *Development of American Political Science*, pp. 183–194.

[46] William McEwen, "Problems of Validation in Social Anthropology," pp. 155–183.

raised questions regarding the meaning of *scientific method* and *validation*. For example, in dealing with folk-urban ideal types "there is a nonquantitative method of validation which provides as good confirmation as any statistical test of measure"; this is the method of validation by repetitive observation. Furthermore, without the mass of qualitative and historical information already accumulated, it would not be possible to apply the modern techniques of analysis and testing. In essence, then, the debate relates only to the feasibility of theory and scientific method under certain conditions that characterize anthropology and other social sciences.

Looking at these various fields, we find that certain characteristics are common to the recent developments in all these sciences. There is common stress on the importance of theory, the need for systematic and formal presentation of data and conclusions, and the necessity of validation. Social scientists also urge the use of symbolism or abstraction, measurement, and reductionism as indispensable. In addition, experimentation and prediction are considered essential features of scientific method and therefore necessary in modern research. Finally, whether inductive or deductive, research must follow a pattern, preferably the pattern of theory–hypothesis–data, so that the hypothesis, and the theory from which it is derived, can be tested by empirical data.

Although these characteristics have been accepted by large numbers of scholars in the social sciences, two fundamental questions, dealing with the legitimacy of generalization or theorizing on complex behavior, still persist. To what extent, for example, is it legitimate to predict human behavior without getting involved in the problems of causality? And, how does one reconcile theory building and prediction, both of which imply determinism, with individuality and volition of behavior? These are the same questions with which we have dealt in the context of causation and generalization in history. The contrasting views of Popper and Carr have been treated above. Therefore, only a brief discussion will be given here to represent some of the views in the related social sciences and to determine how social scientists have coped with these questions.

Anthropologists agree that theories of social change are integral parts of their research objectives, but a conflict arises as to whether they should search for "developmental" or for "causal" theories. Developmental theories are usually associated with evolution and are based on the premise that laws of social development are possible. Such laws would be deterministic in the sense that they would establish the conditions that are both sufficient and necessary for certain development phenomena to appear. The pattern of development would be sequential in the sense that a given stage must follow a given preceding stage. The pattern of development would determine the direction and sequence of change, but the timing or the rate of change would remain indeterminate. In practice, studies in the tradition of the development school have tended to be holistic or totalistic in the sense of taking a whole culture or a complex institution as the unit of study such that the behavior of the individual in society or the particular in culture remains unexplained. In fact, change will, in this approach, tie one complex situation to another but without associating any single event with any given cause or factor of change. By this means, the question of free will, which relates to individuals, is no longer an issue. At the same time, the problem of causation is altogether avoided.

The developmental approach has been criticized by the proponents of causal theories, who suggest that no law of development is possible. The boundaries of the unit of study in the developmental tradition cannot be defined and, therefore, no such law can be used for prediction. It is also suggested that causal theories are indispensable because each event can thus be explained in terms of the initial conditions and a more general covering law. Time is important here, not as a sequence, but in terms of contiguity between initial conditions and events. Explanation states only *sufficient* conditions, thus involving neither determinism nor a singularity of causation. Accordingly, no conflict prevails between causal theories of this type and individual freedom. Explanations are based on the hypothetico-deductive method, according to which, given certain initial conditions, there is reason to expect certain results. This approach also avoids the problem of ambiguity, the difficulty of validation, and the problematic question of laws of behavior.

Although the representatives of these two approaches do not agree with the evaluations of their own approach by proponents of the other, they all seem to agree that causal explanation in broad terms is a legitimate enterprise for anthropologists. They also seem to agree that the problems of freedom and volition can be avoided. The question, however, is which of these approaches is more relevant to the study of social change in a scientific manner. Neither group will concede to the other on these issues.[47]

[47] Leon J. Goldstein, "Theory in Anthropology: Developmental or Causal?" in *Sociological Theory: Inquiries and Paradigms*, ed. Llewellyn Gross (New York: Harper & Row, 1967), pp. 153–180.

Traditionally, the sociologist deals with contemporary society, and developmental theory therefore has no relevance to sociology. Sociologists have generally accepted the premise that causation in the absolute sense is not possible. To explain behavior they have resorted to either strict empiricism or functionalism.[48] As seen by the empiricists, their approach needs no causal theory nor any abstraction. Instead, they carefully seek to "uncover the interrelationships of the real world" in terms of dependent and independent variables. This approach, apparently, would explain individual events without trying to tie the fragments into a unified whole or into a theory of behavior. A second alternative, which is a version of functionalism, is the search for the contribution of a given factor to a certain event. Broadly speaking, this approach avoids singular causality and searches for contributing factors in a fashion somewhat similar to the causal approach of anthropology.

Proponents of both alternatives have been under attack among sociologists because, according to the critics, they apply causal theory without admitting it and leave implicit what should be stated explicitly. They also tend to confuse the meaning of cause with that of function, and thus do, in fact, use function as cause. How, otherwise, would they assume a necessary integration or equilibrium of the social system? Having noted the weaknesses of these alternatives, many sociologists have revived the idea of causation, and have attempted to reconcile it with individual freedom, as was the case in anthropology. On one hand, they have committed themselves to the idea that a conceptual framework is necessary and that causation in the modern sense might be that framework. However, causation and empiricism can be combined in such a way that the causal framework is explicitly stated.[49] On the other hand, to avoid the problem of causality in the classical sense, they propose that multiple causation can be substituted and thus there will be room for volition and freedom of behavior. Although multiple causation does not solve the problem of the single cause, it avoids the issue by allowing for alternatives as well as combinations of causal factors. Here again we find the search to be directed toward sufficient rather than necessary conditions. A third approach to causation has been borrowed from classical physics by sociologists who assume the constancy

[48] George A. Theodorson, "The Uses of Causation in Sociology," in Gross, *Sociological Theory*, pp. 131–152.

[49] R. P. Dore, "Function and Cause," *American Sociological Review* 26, no. 6 (December 1961): 843–853.

of energy and view behavior in a macroscopic (holistic) world, thus avoiding the microscopic events that require individual explanation, and who consider macroscopic behavior deterministic. This approach has been criticized as having been abandoned by the physicists themselves in view of Heisenberg's "uncertainty principle," which renders precise prediction or determinism impractical: to establish precisely the position of a particle or its momentum, one has to concentrate on one or the other; hence the area of uncertainty.[50]

These alternative approaches to the problem of causation and determinism have not withstood the sustained impact of modern scientific approaches. The tendency has been toward limited causal explanations, derived from specific theories and given initial conditions. Such theoretical premises would permit formulation of hypotheses that can be tested, but only within the limited framework postulated. Thus, the views expounded in the other social sciences have found their way into sociology. However, to a limited degree, causation and generalization are again in vogue.

The problems of causation and determinism have been equally common in psychology, and the controversy between the clinical and the experimental psychologists continues. To what extent, it is asked, can one formulate laws that render behavior deterministic, and how does one reconcile such determinism with volition and free will? The scientifically oriented assume away the issue and regard the discovery of trends and laws as an integral part of their work. Others are suspicious of this approach and call for a return to traditional and volitional psychology. Some psychologists, however, question the relevance of vitalism or volition and insist on the inevitability of modern scientific method. They insist that determinism is more the rule than the exception.[51] They argue that Heisenberg's "uncertainty principle" does not mean indeterminate, but only uncertain, results. Furthermore, Heisenberg's principle applies only to the physical world and need not apply to human behavior. They suggest that freedom is actually an illusion— probably a necessary one, but an illusion just the same. Behavior is free only within given constraints. Even the attempt to resolve the problem of causality and determinism by probability theory is an illusion, be-

[50] For a recent discussion of the relevance of Heisenberg's principle to human behavior, see Ludwig Immergluck, "Determinism-Freedom in Contemporary Psychology," *American Psychologist* 19, no. 4 (April 1964): 272–273.
[51] For a survey of the debate see *ibid.*, pp. 270–280.

cause probability implies only a certain degree of certainty or uncertainty, but does not preclude determinism or certainty as impossible. It only means that certain factors have not been taken into consideration, and that the findings are therefore less than perfect.

This position has been attacked because of its potential consequences and because it reflects a misunderstanding of what *freedom* means. Freedom, according to one critic, means "that there are volitions (desires, motivations, etc.), that volitions have behavioral consequences, and that they are not reducible to variables of the physical environment or to variables of physiological process." [52] These premises of freedom are held to be compatible with determinism in the sense that their expression need not be irregular or fail to follow a discoverable pattern. Immergluck's position has been further criticized because of internal contradictions since he "exhorts us to cling to a philosophical position of determinism in matters psychological, just as though we had some freedom of choice in what we believe about free will versus determinism." [53]

As has been implied, the trend in psychology has been toward the discovery of laws and causes of behavior, at least in a limited sense, in a probabilistic framework, and within the restricted environment of the subject. The problem of universality of causation or of determinism seems to have become irrelevant. The findings are determinate only to a certain degree (probabilistic) and only as they relate to initial conditions.

The behavioral trend in political science has already been noted. The decline of traditional approaches has been accompanied by a redefinition of the concepts and relations. Interest in theory has been associated with the development of testable, causal propositions. Causation, in this context, has little similarity to the classical conception of causation. In its present form, causation implies correlations or associational relations between what can be identified as dependent or independent variables. To take an example, Donald J. McCrone and Charles F. Cnudde explain democratic political development causally as proceeding sequentially from urbanization to education, to communication, and then to

[52] Isidor Chein, "On Freedom and Determinism," *American Psychologist* 20, no. 10 (October 1965): 839–840.

[53] John Nolte, "On Freedom and Determinism," *American Psychologist* 20, no. 10 (October 1965): 840.

democracy.[54] One might consider this sort of explanation as a stage theory that identifies the stages without explaining the process of development from one stage to another or the nature of causal interdependence. It is noteworthy that all the models discussed in McCrone and Cnudde's article allow for a multiplicity of causal explanations, and for deviation from the propositions in accordance with observation. Thus the propositions lead to probabilistic results rather than to deterministic predictions. Finally, the propositions derived from these models are broad enough to permit the derivation of more limited hypotheses that can be tested by measurable data. For example, "mass communication occurs when literacy and educational levels rise in society." This proposition can be narrowed down to make it testable in an environment in which literacy and education as well as communication can be operationally defined and measured.

In summary, it is evident that a new trend has been introduced in all the related social sciences, although the intensity of the trend varies from one field to another. The trend has been accompanied by serious challenges to the traditional approaches, a certain degree of commitment to generalization and causal interpretation, an interest in scientific method including formalization and validation of hypotheses, and by an increasing interest in precision and measurement. The nature of causality in the new trend has been modified such that multiple causation is sought and probabilistic conclusions are the ideal. As a result, there has been an inclination toward behavioral research and a recognition of the interrelation of the various social sciences. The new trend will be explored under the headings of measurement, and formalization.

## Measurement

Although caution has been voiced frequently against any blind commitment to quantitative measurement in the social sciences, the trend has unmistakably been in that direction. In fact, arguments about measurement have in general been arguments about quantification. Social scientists are aware of the difficulty of attaching quantitative values to many of the variables they deal with, but they have nevertheless made

[54] Political science examples can be found in Donald J. McCrone and Charles F. Cnudde, "Toward a Communications Theory of Democratic Political Development: A Causal Model," *American Political Science Review* 61, no. 1 (March 1967): 72–79, 78.

serious attempts to quantify and often to limit their research to the quantifiable. To render quantification and measurement possible, social scientists have compromised on several criteria of classical measurement.

First, they have accepted as impossible the application of cardinal or ratio scales to the variables they deal with. At best, they are content with ordinal and interval scales, although exceptions may be noted. Second, they have redefined many concepts "operationally" to make quantitative measurement possible. Third, they have frequently depended on derived measurement to avoid the problem of observing what may not be observable. Finally, they have usually described their findings as tentative, depending in part on the reliability of the measures they have obtained.

Measurement in political science has depended greatly on the operational definition of concepts. For example, the concept of liberalism, for purposes of measurement, might be defined according to the distribution of votes on a variety of issues classified on a standard or scale; the more frequently one votes yes on certain classes of issues, the more liberal he is considered. The issues might be classified by fixed intervals on a continuum so that the more liberal issues tend to one end and the less liberal to the other. This is known as the Guttman Scale.[55] The issues are classified in an ordinal fashion, but the scale is an interval scale so that the more or less on the scale can be defined in terms of fixed intervals.

Another attempt to measure political values is to derive these values from related criteria. For example, political power or influence might be measured in terms of the distribution of income, wealth, or property. Such an attempt has been applied to land tenure and political stability. The measure is an application of the Lorenz curve, which relates the cumulative percentage of population to the cumulative percentage of wealth, income, or land they own. The same approach has been applied in the study of the distribution of power among social groups.[56] Unfortunately, such attempts inherently oversimplify the issues to make them measurable. As viewed by one critic in his study of inequality, Russett's quantitative tests of de Tocqueville's propositions, "while highly interesting, led him to 'conclusions' which are more uncertain and tentative than the original proposition which was to be tested by them. In that

[55] H. R. Alker, Jr., *Mathematics and Politics*, pp. 23–24.

[56] *Ibid.*, pp. 30ff; also B. M. Russett, "Inequality and Instability: The Relation of Land Tenure to Politics," *World Politics* 16, no. 3 (April 1964): 442–454.

sense, they serve as a striking illustration of the limited value of such 'tests.' " [57]

It is obvious that such derived measures have many limitations. The indicator itself is not always easily measurable. How, for instance, does one measure income, wealth, or land ownership? Even assuming that these indicators are measurable, it is not obvious that they reflect power on a one-to-one ratio, or that the marginal power value of land is constant. Furthermore, the significance of land tenure varies according to the value system of each environment under consideration; the American value system is different from that of India, Egypt, or Scandinavia, regardless of the income derived from the land.

These problems are illustrated in more detail by the attempts to measure social power. Conceptually, there should be no difficulty in measuring the power of an individual or a group, given an operational definition of power. The difficulty arises when it becomes necessary to assign precise values to the components of power or to its indirect indicators. For example, Dahl defines the power of A over B to be the extent to which "A can get B to do something that B would not otherwise do." The constituents of power in this framework are:

(a) the *base* of power, i.e., the resources (economic assets, constitutional prerogatives, military forces, popular prestige, etc.) that A can use to influence B's behavior.
(b) the *means* of power, i.e., the specific actions (promises, threats, public appeals, etc.) by which A can make actual use of these resources to influence B's behavior.
(c) the *scope* of power, i.e., the set of specific actions that A, by using his means of power, can get B to perform.
(d) the *amount* of power, i.e., the net increase in the probability of B's actually performing some specific action X, due to A's using his means of power against B. . . .
(e) the set of individuals over whom A has power—this we shall call the *extension* of A's power.[58]

Harsanyi suggests two additional variables as necessary for a quantitative characterization of power:

(f) the opportunity costs to A of attempting to influence B's behavior, i.e., the opportunity costs of using his power over B (and of acquiring this

[57] Friedrich, *Man and His Government*, p. 60.

[58] Quoted in John Harsanyi, "Measurement of Social Power," in *Game Theory and Related Approaches to Social Behavior*, ed. M. Shubik, p. 184.

power over B in the first place if A does not yet possess the required power), which we shall call the costs of A's power over B; and

(g) the opportunity costs to B of refusing to do what A wants him to do, i.e., of refusing to yield to A's attempt to influence his behavior. As these opportunity costs measure the strength of B's incentives for yielding to A's influence, we shall call them the *strength* of A's power of B.[59]

According to this approach the amount of power is the "difference of two probabilities, and therefore is directly given as a *real number*" for each action X. The total power of A over B for all actions is then a vector rather than a single number, unless aggregation is possible.

We shall not enter into the details of these conceptual dimensions of power. Within the present context, it is sufficient to note that the resulting measurements are subjective in the sense that the probabilities must be assigned by the investigator. Although these values are numerical, aggregation would have little significance as far as total power is concerned. For example, if A has a certain amount of power $P_i$ for each of three actions $X_j$, is it possible to aggregate all $P_i$ to arrive at P? Or, suppose three individuals are able to have action X performed, can we say that they are three times as powerful as any one of them separately? In fact, it is conceivable that cooperation between these three individuals might lead to a mobilization of the opposition such that the combined power of the three individuals would be disproportionately less than if they acted separately.

Aggregation is complicated also by the fact that the amount of power of A over B may vary not only in terms of the dimensions enumerated by Dahl and Harsanyi, but also in terms of the sequence of actions performed by B under the influence of A. It is to be expected that the more successes A obtains over B, the higher becomes the relative power value of his resources and the easier it becomes for him to influence B. Thus, the probabilities assigned will also vary according to the number of successes and failures and the relative significance of the individual actions performed in the given environment. The above approach is quite useful in a game-theoretic framework, but it is doubtful it can be used empirically.

An easier approach to measuring power in an empirical situation may be to compare the probabilities of individuals A and B independently, having action X performed in a given period of time and with a given

[59] *Ibid.*, p. 185.

amount of resources. In essence this would be a comparison of efficiencies, the efficiency of performing in lieu of the power to have the action performed. This approach would also permit comparison and measurement of power within a context larger than two persons. Furthermore, by means of this approach it would be possible to assign empirically derived probabilities by investigating the political history of the actor under consideration. Nevertheless, it can be concluded that political scientists have been measurement conscious and have attempted seriously to overcome the problems by operationalizing the concepts with which they deal.

The trend toward more precise measurement in psychology has been a little more advanced than in the other social sciences, partly because of the experimental nature of the field. Under controlled conditions behavioral data can be measured on predetermined scales. This is obviously difficult in social psychology and in the psychology of personality, the fields most relevant to our discourse. When arguments against precise measurement have been raised, they usually have been concerned with quantification and its feasibility, rather than with its usefulness or desirability.[60] Nevertheless, serious attempts toward the quantitative measurement of qualitative values have continued. Winch and More summarize the steps "from the conceptualization of the problem in not-very-researchable Freudian categories to the production of quantitatively analyzable ratings."

1. Conceptualization of the problem in Freudian categories.
2. Recasting the problem in terms of conceptually 'cleaner,' i.e., unidimensional variables.
3. Use of several data-gathering procedures of varying degrees of directness: need interview, case history, TAT [Thematic Apperception Tests].
4. Use of two kinds of analysis:
    a) The more direct: content analysis—on need interview ($NI_1$).
    b) The less direct: holistic analysis—on need interview ($NI_2$), case history (CH), and TAT.
5. Producing plural sets of ratings on each of these instruments (NI, $NI_2$, CH, and TAT) for the purpose of estimating inter-rater reliabilities.
6. Final conference considering all three reports prepared in 4b and concluding with:
    a) A single consistent report based on the three reports.

[60] For relevant arguments and counterarguments see R. Perloff, "A Note on Brower's 'The Problem of Quantification in Psychological Science,'" *Psychological Review* 57, no. 4 (July 1950): 188–192, 452.

b) A consensual set of ratings.

7. Calculation of estimates of congruence of ratings from the different instruments: $NI_1$, $NI_2$, CH, and TAT.

8. With final conference ratings (FC) regarded as our 'best' data, and hence as criterion score, calculation of estimates of the validities of $NI_1$, $NI_2$, CH, and TAT.[61]

It is interesting to observe that the measure of validity of each instrument is the correlation coefficient between the ratings on that instrument and the final conference rating. In other words, validity is reflected in the majority opinion of the final conference.[62] Thus, although quantitative measurements have been conducted, the ratings are largely subjective. Furthermore, this procedure may be applicable only to a limited number of observations in which several ratings can be conducted within a relatively short period of time. This procedure would hardly be relevant to a relatively large number of case studies or to a period during which motives and attitudes may have changed. It is not clear either that the ratings serve more than as rank orderings in which no addition can be applied.

This approach, however, is significant in that it illustrates psychologists' awareness of the limited usefulness of order scales or intensive measures, and of the virtual impossibility of securing ratio scales or extensive measures. Therefore, there have been arguments for interval scales or a measure somewhere between the ordinal and the cardinal as the best possible compromise. Interest has also shifted from measurements that are consistent with classical criteria to operational and productive measurements, regardless of whether the resulting scores are additive or not. As Comrey put it, "the true criterion by which a scientific procedure is to be judged is productivity. A theory, method, or system will remain or be discarded depending upon its contribution to the description, explanation, or control of the world about us." [63] This criterion is applied to psychological measurement such that it is necessary only to establish an equal unit or interval scale and have fixed meanings that are operationally defined. Obviously, such scales would have numerical descrip-

[61] Winch & More, "Quantitative Analysis of Qualitative Data," *American Journal of Sociology* 61, no. 5 (March 1956): 452.

[62] *Ibid.*, p. 450.

[63] Andrew L. Comrey, "An Operational Approach to Some Problems in Psychological Measurement," *Psychological Review* 57, no. 3 (May 1950): 217–228, 221–222.

tions that are not additive, but higher than the rank-order scales. An example of the operationally equal unit is the "equal-sense-distance" scale. The subject was exposed to two widely separated sound frequencies and was given control of three keys on a pitch scale, which he could adjust to intermediate frequencies. He was instructed to vary the frequencies of these three keys until the five frequencies were separated by psychologically equal intervals. Thus an equal unit could be derived and calculated.[64] Such a scale, however, is limited in usefulness to the specific operation for which it was devised and must be understood as a subjective or psychological scale.

A similar example is the centile scale which ranks the performers on a centile scale, but in which the numerical differences on the scale have a rank significance in interpreting the performance. This is an equal-unit scale with an arbitrary zero point. Actually Comrey suggests that there are methods for devising ratio scales for psychological research. He mentions one example in which length ratios between a number of lines were computed by having subjects assign a number of points, out of a possible hundred, to each line according to its length relative to another line. The average number of points assigned to each line was used to compute a ratio, the denominator being the average given to each other line. The total number of ratios for each pair of lines was N–1, since one ratio was made available by direct comparison.[65] In other words, one ratio was used as a standard or numeraire, and all other ratios were computed relative to the numeraire. The standard, however, was not arbitrarily assigned, but was derived from the responses of the subjects who assigned the points as they perceived the length of each line. It is interesting that the ratios obtained did not deviate in any case by more than .08 from the ratios obtained by actual measurement. Although the ratios were obtainable, it is not certain that they were of much usefulness for fundamental measurement. The viability of the method becomes even more tenuous when subjects are requested to deal with less tangible and less constant variables than lines drawn on a cardboard, as were the lines in the experiment. How would one apply the method to expressions of interest, anger, or devotion? Comrey is aware of these complications and admits that these scales might not

[64] The measure was devised by Stevens and Volkmen (Comrey, "Operational Approach to Some Problems," pp. 225).

[65] *Ibid.*, pp. 227–228.

be adequate in the application of many statistical methods and operational analyses.[66]

The problem of measurement in sociological research has received wide attention. Attempts have been made to approximate cardinal measurement, but the results have been limited. The reasons are those of the social sciences in general, but the experts have persisted, and quantitative research has continued to accumulate. One of the most common approaches to measurement has been the survey approach, which depends primarily on counting and which results in a description of distributions. For example, surveys have been conducted to determine the occupational status in a given environment by ranking occupations according to the size of the "vote" in favor of each. These results are mainly ordinal and subjective. They are also limited to the society or culture in which the experiment has been conducted. Furthermore, these results do not explain the values of different occupations because the rankings are judgments and not values inherent in the occupations themselves.[67]

Counting, however, is inadequate for the measurement of qualitative variables such as attitudes or values, which may vary in direction with greater or lesser intensity. The same is true of sociological concepts such as anomie, cohesion, prestige, or social status. In these cases, attempts have been made to attach numerical values to the manifestations associated with these concepts. For example, group cohesion has been measured by finding the ratio of the number of times *we* was used to the number of times *I* was used in various groups. Such an index is not a fundamental measurement. It may, however, be operational, but at a cost. For example, indexing reduces the amount of information that can be analyzed and therefore allows for a certain degree of ambiguity. Although the ambiguity can be removed, or at least reduced, by specifying the dimensions included in the index, to do so becomes more difficult as the number of dimensions that are theoretically relevant increases. Nevertheless, in the absence of cardinal or interval measurements, index numbers used uniformly may lead to generalizations that go beyond the specific community for which the index was originally devised.[68]

[66] For a critique of similar scales in psychology see J. Coleman, *Introduction to Mathematical Sociology*, p. 63.

[67] *Ibid.*, pp. 63, 73.

[68] *Ibid.*, pp. 73ff.

Some indexing operations have managed to avoid dimensions that are not subject to counting and observation, such as the ambitious attempt by Allen and Bentz to measure sociocultural change.[69] The authors specify thirty-two indicators of change and measure the percentage change in each of them during the period 1940 to 1960 for forty-eight of the fifty United States. These indicators cover population, government and politics, communications, transportation, education, agriculture, health, welfare, crime, and the family. In all cases, however, the data are obtained by counting—the authors seem to leave out all dimensions that cannot be counted—such indicators as attitudes, class relations, and political views and values. To take an example, change in government and politics is measured only by the percentage changes in per capita state expenditure and the number of state government employees. Having measured the percentage changes in these indicators, the authors compute intercorrelations between them, apply factor analysis, and end up with four main factors of change: a rising standard of living, population growth, industrial-technological-urban development, and increasing education. Each of these factors represents a complex of indicators from among the original thirty-two indicators. Finally, the authors search for an overall index like that used by economists, and like the I.Q. used by psychologists. An arithmetic average of the relevant indicators is such an index in which the indicators are given equal weight. A variant of this is a weighted score index which, however, is found to be highly correlated with the unweighted index. Thus, the authors find it appropriate to rank the individual states according to the index to determine their relative position in sociocultural change.

Although the authors may have succeeded in computing a general index, it is not certain they resolved the problems of measurement of sociocultural phenomena. Not only have they left out the nonquantitative dimensions of change, but they seem to have defined change in a tautological manner. Social change implies a change in the standard of living, among other criteria, and a change in the standard of living implies social change. Measuring one means measuring the other. There is also a high degree of oversimplification. What significance does an increase in the size of government mean? Quantitatively it is a change, but how does it imply social and cultural change? To ignore these questions renders the whole procedure of measurement insignificant. In

---

[69] Francis R. Allen and W. Kenneth Bentz, "Toward the Measurement of Sociocultural Change," *Social Forces* 43, no. 4 (May 1965): 522–532.

other words, by leaving out information and by operationally defining change, quantitative measurement can be made feasible, but will be sterile.

Despite these problems, index measurement has been widely used in recent years, and in different versions, in a search for improvements. According to a survey of the years 1959 to 1963, 986 different indices and scales were used in the measurement of 46 conceptual areas of sociology. It is interesting that 17.4 percent of these measurements dealt with socioeconomic status. However, only 217 measures, or 22 percent of the total, were used more than once, thus implying the lack of agreement on the value of these measurements. At the same time, this suggests the intensive activity among sociologists to improve their tools and increase the precision of measurement.[70]

The deficiency of counting is especially conspicuous in attempts to generalize from individual to group behavior. This is essentially a problem of aggregation. Except in dichotomous behavior, such as voting or suicide, aggregation by adding observations of individual behavior overlooks the impact of interaction between individuals. The physical scientist can ignore this problem because of the homogeneity between members of the group and the invariant behavior of its members, but the sociologist cannot do so. Social structure is not homogeneous, and the members vary their behavior by developing attachments, establishing institutions, and rebelling against rules. Aggregation in such social situations would ignore the basic problems the sociologist deals with. Yet, this procedure has been common. Social cohesion has been measured by adding the "number of sociometric choices made to persons within the group, [dividing] this by the total number of sociometric choices, and consider[ing] this ratio as a measure of 'group cohesion.' " Such measurement of a group has no corresponding social phenomenon to justify it, nor does it as a group concept "allow the reproduction of the individual-level relationships" as would be possible in the physical sciences.[71] Sociologists have attempted to allow for the variance in social structure or the lack of homogeneity, but the problems have not been overcome.

By their own admission, anthropologists have made less use of quantitative data and measurement tools. Although the material they work

---

[70] Charles M. Bonjean, Richard J. Hill, and S. Dale McLemore, "Continuities in Measurement, 1959–1963," *Social Forces* 43, no. 4 (May 1965): 532–535.

[71] Coleman, *Introduction to Mathematical Sociology*, p. 87.

with is similar to what the sociologist and psychologist work with, they lag behind for two reasons. First, anthropologists handle a relatively wider range of subject matter, both in terms of space and of content. Second, they study people who think less quantitatively than do the people studied by sociologists and psychologists. Therefore, quantitative data tend to be less accessible. Nevertheless, many attempts, beginning in the early years of this century, have been made to introduce quantitative analysis in social and cultural anthropology.[72]

The problems of measurement in anthropology are similar to those of the other social sciences and there is therefore no need to go into these problems in detail. However, a few differences may be noted. Anthropologists tend to use a different unit of study. They deal with tribes, clans, or families and kinship groups instead of individuals. It is more difficult to observe and record behavioral events of tribes than of individuals. Anthropologists also deal with cultural units, such as folklore, which can hardly be manifested in directly observable behavior. As a result, measurement in anthropology seems to have been reduced to a matter of counting the observed frequency of behavioral events. Studies of folklore are reduced to the classification and inventory of relevant stories. Social and political traits are tabulated and classified to establish stage patterns of development. The purpose of most of these studies seems to be the application of statistical analysis to the data. In search of validation of the findings, anthropologists have resorted to correlation and factor analysis and to probability theory, all of which require numbers. This objective has been pursued actively, although frequently at the cost of oversimplification, and counting has usually ended in merely establishing the existence or nonexistence of a trait, regardless of the intensity of its manifestation. The desire to quantify has reached unrealistic proportions in the attempts to quantify personality tests. Tests such as the Rorschach Ink Blot, TAT, or Goodenough's Draw-A-Man have been applied by the Indian Administration Research, and attempts have been made to quantify the results at a time when personality psychologists have become suspicious of their own efforts in this area.[73]

Despite the potential difficulties and dangers of these approaches, anthropologists have proceeded in these efforts. Some of them have even

---

[72] Harold E. Driver, "Statistics in Anthropology," *American Anthropologist* 55, no.1 (January–March 1953): 42.

[73] *Ibid.*, pp. 49–54.

regarded quantification and statistical analysis as legitimate substitutes for comparative studies.[74] This has been noted as a trend in the search for validation. Being aware of the limitations of case study illustrations and typological (comparative) analyses as validation tools, anthropologists have resorted to statistical analysis.[75] The results, however, have remained limited both in scope and degree of validation.

In conclusion, social scientists in all the related fields have become measurement conscious. While accepting the fact that cardinal measurement is beyond their reach, they have persisted in quantification even when dealing with unobservable, qualitative concepts. To do so, they have resorted to operationalization of the concepts, to devising special scales, and to the construction of indices, even though frequently at the cost of oversimplification and the loss of information.

*Formalization*

The use of numbers and statistical tools has been the main approach of social scientists to precision and the verification of their findings. However, even where numbers are not accessible, formalization has been advocated as a substitute for vague and diffuse description of the relations observed and the phenomena analyzed. This has been one of the justifications for introducing mathematics into the social sciences. And to compensate for the difficulty of experimentation and comprehensive or exhaustive empirical observation, and as a source of hypotheses, social scientists have resorted to pseudoexperimentation in the form of gaming and simulation.

The use of mathematics has been advocated, for formalizing relations and for abstracting from observed data, both as a source of economy of words and as a powerful tool of transformation by which logical conclusions can be deduced beyond the observed relation. Mathematics is a language with certain properties that render it more useful in research than the language of words. Mathematics has the advantage of being neutral, so that once a system of relations has been perfected, it can be applied to any situation in which similar relations might exist. And, once the objects have been represented by mathematical symbols, these objects can be manipulated experimentally by proxy to predict their behavior, which may not be feasible in the case of the objects themselves.

---

[74] For example, Albert C. Spaulding, "Statistical Techniques for the Discovery of Artifact Types," *American Antiquity* 18, no. 4 (April 1953): 305.

[75] McEwen, "Problems of Validation in Social Anthropology," pp. 156ff.

It is in this area that game theory and simulation are useful. The main precondition for such manipulation is that the initial conditions of the system containing these objects be well known.[76]

A good example of the contribution of mathematics is Durkheim's study of suicide. Durkheim tried to locate the relevant variables affecting the probability of suicide, but the coefficients of determination, or the degree to which each variable affected that probability, could be determined only by the use of mathematical tools. Thus, mathematics helps to determine the significance of each variable, and not only its relevance.[77]

The use of mathematics as an abstraction of observable behavior and as a tool of analysis is no longer a point of debate. The main arguments and counterarguments center around the feasibility of its application, given the oftentimes inadequate knowledge of initial conditions and relations on which the analysis is based. As theory and data become more accessible, mathematics and statistics seem to acquire additional significance. One area that needs elaboration, however, is the use of mathematics for prediction by hypothetical models that can neither be verified nor are complex enough to approximate reality. This is the case of game theory and simulation models which have become fairly common in social science research. These approaches may be considered substitutes for comprehensive observation and for experimental techniques, which are inapplicable to the social sciences.

Game theory is essentially the building of mathematical models of behavior from which theories can be deduced. The model must be precise, and all its elements well specified. It is usually based on reality, but not a reproduction of reality, for the simple reason that reproduction of reality is not possible. If reproduction were possible, the need for the model would no longer prevail. Therefore, the model builder tries to take into consideration the essential features of reality. However, he finds it necessary to make assumptions regarding those aspects of reality that are unknown or are too complex to represent in the model. Game theory, therefore, is an approach by which behavior under certain conditions can be studied and predicted, but only under certain conditions. Generally, game theory deals with conflict situations in which each party to the game must make a decision within the framework of the established rules of the game, which are known to all the

[76] Coleman, *Introduction to Mathematical Sociology*, p. 3.
[77] *Ibid.*, pp. 4–7.

players. The players are assumed to be rational in the sense that they are self-interested, and they try to maximize their gains or minimize their losses. Because their decisions depend on the decisions or moves of other players, which are not known in advance, the game would specify the various alternatives that may be anticipated. The players then choose those decisions that best serve their objectives. And to the extent that the game approximates reality, the predicted behavior forms a basis on which a theory of such behavior can be formulated and policy recommendations made. Unfortunately, the game itself is usually carried out in an unrealistic or simulated environment, which renders the results less useful than they may seem at face value. The usefulness of game theory depends to a large degree on the relevance and comprehensiveness of the assumptions. For example, to what extent are all the players rational? To what extent do they know all the rules? To what extent is it possible to expect that the game will be completed within the given context, without change in the environment? In an idealized, or hypothetical, situation all these assumptions might be satisfied, but are they meaningful in a complex situation in which change is the rule rather than the exception?

On the positive side, game theory offers an important opportunity to formalize behavioral relations, to deduce additional relations, and to formulate hypotheses that can be subjected to testing in empirical situations. In other words, gaming serves a heuristic function related to reality at least in essential features. For example, diplomats in international relations, military commanders in the field, labor unions engaged in bargaining with industry, or players of poker all behave in a manner that can be represented in games. Even though certain elements of the situation remain absent, the theory of behavior derived from such gaming might eventually be modified to approximate reality. And in the absence of sufficient grounds for induction, and to avoid pure intuition, gaming offers a good source of hypotheses of behavior in somewhat similar situations. Economists and political scientists have recognized these positive aspects and have taken advantage of them.[78]

The same evaluation can be applied to simulation, which is the construction of an operable representation of a real situation in which the

[78] For more detail, Handy and Kurtz, *Appraisal of the Behavioral Sciences*, chap. 13; Shubik, *Game Theory*, esp. chap. 1; also Samuel Klausner, *The Study of Total Societies*, pp. 30–44.

actors behave as if they were in a real situation. The observations made
of their behavior become the source of hypotheses or theories of behavior in real situations. Essentially, this is experimentation under conditions that approximate reality. Simulation models offer an advantage
in that the researcher can manipulate the construction by varying one
variable at a time to allow for change, and can thus observe behavior
under changing conditions. Another advantage of simulation is that it
allows the researcher to gain insight into problems on which there is
little past experience. For example, urban problems under fast-changing
technology are recent phenomena on which history provides little information. Simulation serves as a substitute, if only to suggest possible
alternative decisions in such situations. Even when historical parallels
exist, simulation serves the purpose of evaluating problems relatively
rapidly prior to historical analysis, which may require more time than
is available. In other words, simulation in the social sciences may be a
short-cut method to policy recommendations. This is particularly true
in international and political matters which require fast decisions.[79]

Simulation may be based on human decision making, as in game
theory, or it may be computer simulation. In human simulation, the
decision rule specifies who chooses a given outcome, whereas in computer simulation it specifies what the outcome will be. One of the best
examples of human simulation is the model of the United Nations in
which students play the roles of the representatives of the various nations, carry on debates, and reach conclusions they consider to be consistent with the objectives of their hypothetical home countries.[80]

In contrast to human simulation, computer simulation requires the
writing of a rigorous program that specifies all the relevant choices and
variables with only one degree of freedom left.[81] It also requires "a fairly
strong theoretical grasp of the process" one is trying to simulate, or "at
least a body of tentative preconceptions" one is willing to put to test.[82]

[79] For these and other uses see R. C. Snyder, "Some Perspectives on the Use of
Experimental Techniques in the Study of International Relations," in *Simulation in
International Relations*, Guetskow et al., pp. 1–11.

[80] R. A. Brody, "Varieties of Simulation in International Relations Research,"
in *Simulation in International Relations*, Guetskow et al., pp. 190–220.

[81] Ithiel de Sola Pool, "Computer Simulations of Total Societies," in *Study of
Total Societies*, Klausner, pp. 48–49.

[82] Robert A. Abelson, "Lectures on Computer Simulation," in *Mathematics and
Social Sciences*, vol. 1, comp. S. Sternberg et al. (Holland: Mouton & Co., 1965),
p. 446.

Such simulation has been carried out in psychology, sociology, economics, and political science. An impressive example is the simulation model constructed by Bernstein and Abelson which deals with political controversies and local communities. The model specifies the general assumptions on which behavior is analyzed—how voting on an issue might be influenced. The model also allows for resistance to the possible influence on the voting decision, for varying influences and types of exposure, for the lapse of time between the beginning of the campaign and the voting date, and for variation in the characteristics of the voters. The model was tested in a limited way by surveying the effect of influences on the vote in a mock fluoridation campaign. The authors call this kind of simulation "prognastic simulation," in contrast to process simulation, because it carries "present statistics into anticipated future statistics in one leap without concern for the details of the intervening process." [83]

The significance of such models is obviously limited, since frequently neither the theory nor the data are available. The influences and factors that are relevant are oftentimes not easily identifiable. Therefore, the results can hardly be indicative of the real behavior in similar situations. Yet, such results can be invaluable as heuristic sources of hypotheses and theories. The question is whether such processes are worth the costs they incur. The variability of behavior and the volitionistic nature of social relations are such that the simulation of complex social situations is highly imperfect, in contrast to simulation in the physical sciences in which the environment and the elements can be controlled. Nevertheless, in the absence of more useful techniques, simulation serves an important function, which explains the expansion of its application in the social sciences. As Brody put it, simulators "share a common commitment to the proposition that social realities can be understood *via* the study of scaled-down versions of these realities. . . . Whether programmed for high-speed computers or set into motion by human decision-makers enacting roles, a simulational model requires attention to operational theory that is unusual in social research. In the end, this development of operational theory may be simulation's most significant contribution." [84]

[83] *Ibid.*, p. 479.

[84] Brody, "Varieties of Simulation," p. 220; also, Guetskow et al., *Simulation in International Relations*, pp. 33–36; Pool, "Computer Simulations of Total Societies," pp. 45–65.

## IMPLICATIONS OF THE NEW TREND

The emphasis on precision and the use of mathematical tools have had direct and indirect effects on the social sciences. The direct effects include increased specification, the search for validation, and emphasis on quantification and measurement, all of which are manifestations of the movement toward a more scientific methodology. The indirect effects, which are equally important, include a revival of the holistic approach, at a time when reductionism has been in vogue, and an increased interest in interdisciplinary methods and the unity of the sciences. These two tendencies are intertwined and will be treated jointly.

The scientific trend has emphasized the need for limiting analysis to manageable proportions and hypotheses that are narrow and specific enough to be subject to testing. Thus, instead of concentrating on total communities or organizations as units of study, research has been geared toward partial aspects of these units. This is what can be called reductionism in scope, which implies dealing with specific and partial aspects while holding all other aspects constant. However, reductionism also means concentrating on fewer variables by subsuming, or ignoring, most of the others to make scientific investigation technically possible. Such reductionism is justified for the sake of manageability, and is best illustrated by the artificial division between disciplines. Reductionism in terms of variables has also been encouraged by the emphasis on abstraction associated with scientism and as a step away from the comprehensive, descriptive, traditional approach. This tendency can be noted especially in anthropology, which has been the stronghold of traditional and holistic methodology. In the attempt to advance their discipline, anthropologists have been converging with other disciplines. They have borrowed concepts from economics and from psychology, especially in the area of personality theory. Convergence with sociology has gone farthest in that anthropologists have been tending toward the study of social organization, although their domain used to be social change. In the study of social movements and political institutions anthropology has converged extensively with sociology and psychology by assimilating concepts and methods from these other fields.[85] The same tendency can be noted in political science. Political scientists, anxious to convert their field into a science, have tried to demonstrate the simi-

[85] Morris Janowitz, "Anthropology and the Social Sciences," *Current Anthropology* 4, no. 2 (April 1963): 150–154.

larity between political and economic data and the relevance of economic theory to political analysis. Concepts of choice or preference, equilibrium, and maximization are among the concepts relevant to both, at least for pure theory. Political scientists have actually used the competitive model of economics to analyze political democracy. The common factors that render such convergence possible include the attitude toward scientism and the neutral language of science that seems to be appropriate for this purpose.[86]

The trend, however, seems to be undergoing modification, in response to advances in gaming and simulation, and also because the general systems approach has become common in recent years. General systems theory takes into consideration all the inputs, outputs, and the processes that constitute the system, thus avoiding reductionism in scope. Conceptual reductionism, however, is possible, but it must be defended as helpful for understanding the functioning of the system. Nevertheless, there has been a move away from reductionism as a logical result of the new trend in social science. The combined advances in mathematical tools and in computer use have rendered reductionism in scope unnecessary. It has become possible, at least in principle, to cope with many more variables and with a larger unit of study, and to pursue a holistic approach and still fulfill the precision requirements of scientific method. It is now possible to simulate a total economy or polity and to set up a game with $N$ players and non-zero-sum payoffs, as would be the situation in a relatively large unit of study.[87]

Given this relaxation of reductionism as unnecessary, it has become possible and necessary to take into consideration variables that have traditionally been relegated to various other disciplines. The necessary specification of the context and of the rules governing behavior in gaming and simulation goes beyond any one discipline. This is necessarily so because any attempt to represent reality cannot remain within the economic or sociological context and ignore all the others. In fact, the mere admission that the outcome of a game or a simulated situation is uncertain, and not a mechanical result of the process, implies that all possible influences must be taken into consideration. The new tools have made this possible. To take an example, in a study of the relation

[86] Duncan Black, "The Unity of Political and Economic Science," in *Game Theory*, ed. Shubik, pp. 110–119; for an example of application see Anthony Downs, *An Economic Theory of Democracy* (New York: Harper & Row, 1957).

[87] Rapoport, "Mathematical, Evolutionary, and Psychological Approaches to the Study of Total Societies," in *Study of Total Societies*, ed. Klausner, pp. 114–143.

between ownership and production, Shapley and Shubik have found it necessary and feasible in a game-theoretic approach to include questions of distribution, power, bargaining, and coalition between owners and nonowners or workers in various structural contexts.[88] Previously, such a study would have concentrated on the economic aspects only and held all other factors constant.

Revival of the interdisciplinary approach has been augmented also by the tendency to operationalize concepts to permit measurement. To operationalize a concept frequently implies dissecting it into component manifestations of behavior that go beyond the confines of any one discipline, as has been the case with the concepts of social change, power, and rationality. Furthermore, operationalizing a concept requires knowledge of what other disciplines offer for a better understanding of the concept. The sociologist deals with social change, but to measure it he borrows from the psychologist and the economist, statistician, and methodologist.[89] Borrowing from other disciplines, however, should be differentiated from adapting or assimilating concepts from these other disciplines. Once concepts have been developed in one discipline, they become accessible to other disciplines, as do tools and methods. This, however, does not mean interdisciplinary analysis, even though it may promote unity between the sciences. But if assimilation of the concepts has been advanced such that the borrowing discipline undergoes some modification, an interdisciplinary approach can be said to have developed. Borrowing concepts and using them as such leads to what can be called intradisciplinary, whereas borrowing with assimilation can be called interdisciplinary convergence. In the first case, one would study the economics of the family and the psychology of the family as if they were separate categories. In the second case, the researcher would investigate the interaction between the economic and the psychological forces that impinge on the behavior of the family.[90]

Intradisciplinary borrowing can be encouraged by the desire for scientism, whereas interdisciplinary integration can be facilitated by more sophistication in theory, mathematical tools, and computer science. A

[88] L. S. Shapley and Martin Shubik, "Ownership and the Production Function," *Quarterly Journal of Economics* 81, no. 1 (February 1967): 88–111.

[89] Recall the study by Allen and Bentz, "Toward the Measurement of Sociocultural Change."

[90] For a more detailed discussion of the two types of borrowing see Klausner, ed., "Links and Missing Links Between the Sciences of Man," in *Study of Total Societies,* pp. 3–29.

good example of interdisciplinary attempts is provided by Russell Ack-off's study of systems and operations research.[91] The manager of a large office building wanted to reduce the complaints against poor elevator service in his building. Various engineering and economic proposals seemed impractical or too expensive to implement. Bringing in the psychologist proved to be the solution. The psychologist proposed reducing the impact of waiting for the elevators, rather than increasing the service, which was not feasible, by installing large mirrors on the walls of the lobbies, which would keep the waiting users busy watching themselves. The complaints stopped immediately.

Finally, one additional factor may aid in promoting interdisciplinary research in the social sciences, namely, the recurrent self-consciousness of social scientists regarding their responsibility in policy and applied matters. We have seen the complaints of anthropologists, psychologists, and political scientists concerning the apparent indifference of these disciplines to the affairs of the real world. However, such concern is usually accompanied by a revival of interest in policy, in which case it becomes necessary to deal with reality, which defies segregation into separate disciplines. The best example of the concern and involvement of social scientists in everyday affairs comes from economics. Harry G. Johnson asserts that economics is not indifferent to social problems, and applies economics to the explanation of restlessness and demonstrations at universities.[92] Another example is the widespread movement for the study of ecology and the environment by interdisciplinary methods.

In conclusion, it is apparent that a revival of holistic and interdisciplinary research has been underway. This trend derives support from the advances in methodological designs and tools of analysis and from increasing awareness of policy matters and the totality of the environment. However, many problems are still pending, and much of what has been achieved has been possible only through oversimplification and abstraction from reality. It is even possible that attempts to deal with real situations would meet with less success than has been implied by this discussion.[93]

[91] Russell L. Ackoff, "Systems, Organizations, and Interdisciplinary Research," *General Systems* 5 (1960): 6.

[92] Harry G. Johnson, "The Economic Approach to Social Questions," *Economica* 35, no. 137 (February 1968): 1–21.

[93] For an evaluation of the trend towards holism and interdisciplinary research see Klausner, ed., "Prospects for the Study of Total Societies," in *Study of Total Societies*, pp. 193–206.

## THE IMPACT ON THE STUDY OF HISTORY AND CHANGE

The last two decades have witnessed various attempts to raise the level of scientism in social-science research. Both the new economic historians and other social scientists have tried to steer away from traditional approaches by drawing attention to the need for specification and explicitness in stating the problem and method of research. They have also aroused interest in measurement, validation, abstraction, and limited hypotheses. The degree of success in each of these areas has varied according to the field and the period under study, but there have been many failures that may be as important as the successes. And if the history of the other sciences has any relevance to economic history, we should expect a trend similar to what has been witnessed in these sciences. The apparent trend reversal in the other social sciences may be paralleled by a similar reversal in economic history. In fact, the reversal in economic history, if it should come at all, might be expected to be more intensive than in the other fields because of the historian's interest in the past, in trends, and in relatively large units of study.

The trend in the social sciences, as in economic history, has included a division between those who lean toward a scientific approach and those who are content with a less precise, and more introspective, approach. Both groups, however, have shown interest in some kind of theory, either to guide the analysis or to be derived from it. Both have accepted the possibility of innovation in method. It is these innovations that should be of interest to us, including the degree of relevance they have to economic history.

Formalism has become an integral part of modern research. The building of models and the use of mathematics have become central in the training of professionals, often to the extent of making the procedure more important than the subject matter. We have seen why this emphasis is impractical in economic history. Therefore, although the emphasis on form may be relevant as an idea, it has little to offer in terms of facilitating the use of the same methods in economic history. Mathematics and other formal models can be useful in economic history only after full knowledge of the subject matter has been attained, which is itself the domain of economic history. The same observations can be applied to the restriction of research to limited hypotheses. To test the validity of hypotheses "scientifically," the tendency has been to formulate limited and testable hypotheses. Although this may be helpful in history, the topics history deals with are usually too broad to limit temporally, spacially, and culturally. That is why reductionism cannot be recommended for economic history. So far there has been a slight reversal away from reductionism because of the difficulty of comprehending the relevant situation when it is reduced to a limited framework; hence the apparent trend back to holism and interdisciplinary approaches. Economic history, and history in general, have more reason to abide by holistic and interdisciplinary approaches than do the social sciences that deal with single events or with much more limited frameworks. It is true that economic historians can reduce their data to the economic variables only, as most of them do, but such an approach breaks down as soon as the historian begins to handle periods long enough for the noneconomic parameters to change. In other words, a simplification that might be possible in other social sciences is not possible in economic history. The same applies to the use of interdisciplinary approaches. As we have seen, social scientists have found it necessary to concern themselves with policy matters, which can be treated only if interdisciplinary relevances are considered. Although economic history is not concerned directly with policy, its implications for economic development and growth are such that all the relevant variables must be integrated in the analysis.

A significant difference between economic history and the other social sciences relates to subject matter. The social sciences have adopted a behavioralist approach for treating observable behavior. Past behavior that is neither observable nor comprehensively recorded cannot be studied in the same fashion. Consequently, history must depend greatly on indirect indicators and on analytical and interpretative devices. Behavioralism as practiced in political science, sociology, and psychology cannot be applied to historical analysis. Gaming and simulation are useless as tools of economic history. These tools have been used for heuristic purposes in policy contexts. Furthermore, these tools require complete knowledge or specification of the rules of behavior and of the initial conditions to predict what decisions will be made. Economic history might be concerned with decisions made in the past, but if the rules of behavior and the initial conditions were fully known, there would be no need for gaming or simulation of the past. And even if gaming and simulation were applied, there would be no way of testing the models constructed. Therefore, it would be presumptuous to imitate these innovations, unless economic history is reduced to a study of economic growth in the contemporary world.

Economic history can learn from the other social sciences in the area of measurement. These sciences have generally settled on interval and ordinal scales, and have rendered their concepts measurable by operationalizing them. Although counting has remained the main objective of measurement, special indices and scales have been devised for more limited objectives. Economic historians can apply similar approaches by operationalizing their concepts. Operationalizing a concept by decomposing it might be inelegant, but it is useful for rendering the concept measurable. This would be true with concepts such as utility, economic change, development, and welfare.

A recurrent problem has been the question of causation. Probabilistic explanations have become the rule in the social sciences. Probability, however, is applicable when a given event can be associated with certain initial conditions and given causal factors. This may not be as easy to pinpoint when dealing with developmental trends in history. No precise probability estimate can be assigned for developments such as capitalism or feudalism, each of which must be related to a whole complex of factors and conditions. Although the interpretation would still be probabilistic in the sense of being tentative, precision may be out of the question. In fact, precision can be acquired only at the cost of reductionism and oversimplification. To the extent that such precision is not essential in analyzing directional developments, economic history cannot imitate the other social sciences in that respect. The generalization of a broad coverage can be more useful and relevant for the historian than the treatment of single events and limited periods, even if precision were to be lost in the process, especially when qualitative data are the basis of the analysis.

The impact on economic history of these trends in the related social sciences can be significant primarily as a warning to economic historians against unwarranted optimism about achieving more precision and more highly predictive results. These trends suggest that the problems the new economic historians blame on their predecessors are essentially inherent in the study of human behavior. The new economic historians, like their counterparts in the other social sciences, cannot solve these problems by wishful thinking nor by blaming them on the weaknesses of the more traditional scholars. They must show the viability of the new approaches and their capability of better explaining human behavior. The new economic historians must go beyond the reconsideration of past conclusions toward breaking new ground and discovering new theories or laws of behavior. They also must reach for generalizations broader than ones they have reached so far in order to explain total behavior. Until this is done, it is doubtful that the traditional and the new economic history can be reconciled. It is also doubtful that the new economic history can be more successful than the other social sciences in developing sophisticated and useful techniques, or in being less superficial and imitative than they have been. And until then, insights, challenging hunches, and general theoretical formulations will continue to flow from the so-called traditional approaches to history and the social sciences.

Indeed, economic historians already seem to be reconsidering their tendencies of the past few years. At the last meeting of the Economic History Association a growth economist applied personality psychology to economic analysis, a sociologist discussed Weber and his models as applicable to noncapitalist countries, and new economic historians analyzed institutional change in a broad and traditional fashion. Even a stage theorist was invited to survey the recent past.[94] Could it be that economic historians are already reviving the broad-topic, interdisciplinary, and traditional approaches? Whatever their reasons and expectations, it is clear that social scientists and economic historians are still searching for better ways of understanding human behavior.

[94] E. E. Hagen, "The Internal Functioning of Capitalist Organizations"; W. Stephen Warner, "The Role of Religious Ideas and the Use of Models in Max Weber's Comparative Studies of Non-Capitalist Societies"; Lance Davis and Douglas North, "Institutional Change and American Economic Growth: A First Step Towards a Theory of Institutional Innovation"; and W. W. Rostow, "The Past Quarter-Century as Economic History and the Tasks of International Economic Organization," in *Journal of Economic History* 30, no. 1 (March 1970). See also Douglass C. North and Robert Paul Thomas, "An Economic Theory of the Growth of the Western World," *The Economic History Review*, 2d s. 23, no. 1 (1970): 1–17.

# SELECTED BIBLIOGRAPHY

It would be difficult to include in this bibliography all the references consulted and recommended. Hence, only selected items are included as a point of departure. The selections are offered in three parts: (1) a general bibliography relating mainly to chapters 1 through 3; (2) the representative case studies, and critiques of the studies or their authors offered to give the reader a chance to look at other evaluations of these contributions; and (3) a brief bibliography of sources in the related social sciences.

(1)

Albert, Ethel M. "Causality in the Social Sciences." *Journal of Philosophy* 51 (1954): 695–706.

Aitken, Hugh G. J. "On the Present State of Economic History." Canadian Journal of Economics and Political Science 26 (February 1960): 87–95.

———, ed. *The Social Sciences in Historical Study.* Social Science Research Bulletin no. 64. New York, 1954.

Aron, Raymond. *The Dawn of Universal History.* Translated by Dorothy Pickels. New York: Praeger, 1961.

———. "Evidence and Inference in History." In *Evidence and Inference,* edited by Daniel Lerner. Glencoe, Ill.: Free Press, 1959.

Ashley, W. J. "On the Study of Economic History." *Quarterly Journal of Economics* 7 (January 1893): 115–136.

Ashton, T. S. "The Relation of Economic History to Economic Theory." *Economica,* n.s. 13 (May 1946): 81–96.

Ayres, C. E. "The Co-ordinates of Institutionalism." *American Economic Association, Papers and Proceedings* 41 (May 1951): 47–55.

———. "Moral Confusion in Economics." *International Journal of Ethics* 45 (January 1935): 170–199.

——— et al. "New Look at Institutionalism: Discussion." *American Economic Association, Papers and Proceedings* 47 (May 1957): 13–27.

Barker, Sir Ernest. *Change and Continuity.* Oxford: Oxford University Press, 1949.

Barnes, H. E. "Economic Science and Dynamic History." *Journal of Social Forces* 3 (November 1924): 37–56.

Basmann, R. L. "The Role of the Economic Historian in Predictive Testing of Proffered 'Economic Law.'" *Explorations in Entrepreneurial History,* 2d s. 2 (1965).

294 SELECTED BIBLIOGRAPHY

Becker, Carl L. *Everyman His Own Historian: Essays on History and Politics.* Chicago: Quadrangle Books, 1966.

———. "What Are Historical Facts?" *Western Political Quarterly* 8 (1955): 327–340. Reprinted in *The Philosophy of History in Our Time,* edited by Hans Meyerhoff. Garden City, N.Y.: Doubleday, 1959.

Berlin, Isaiah. *Historical Inevitability.* New York: Oxford University Press, 1954.

———. "History and Theory: The Concept of Scientific History." *History and Theory* 1 (1960): 1–31.

Bloch, Marc. *The Historian's Craft.* Manchester: Manchester University Press, 1954.

Bock, Kenneth E. *The Acceptance of Histories.* University of California Publications in Sociology and Social Institutions, vol. 3. Berkeley and Los Angeles: University of California Press, 1956.

Boulding, K. E. "A New Look at Institutionalism." *American Economic Review* 47 (May 1957): 1–12.

Brinton, Crane. "The New History: Twenty-five Years After." *Journal of Social Philosophy* 1 (1936): 134–147.

———. "The 'New History' and Past Everything." *American Scholar* 8 (1939): 144–157.

Brown, Murray. *On the Theory of Measurement of Technological Change.* Cambridge: Cambridge University Press, 1966.

Bunge, Mario. *Causality: The Place of the Causal Principle in Modern Science.* Cambridge, Mass.: Harvard University Press, 1959.

Burns, Arthur L. "Ascertainment, Probability and Evidence in History," *Historical Studies: Australia and New Zealand* 4 (1951): 327–339.

———. "International Theory and Historical Explanation." *History and Theory* 1 (1960): 55–75.

Burns, E. M. "Does Institutionalism Complement or Compete with Orthodox Economics?" *American Economic Review* 21 (March 1931): 80–87. Correction: June 31: 278.

Bury, John B. "The Science of History" and "Darwinism and History." *Selected Essays.* Cambridge: Cambridge University Press, 1930.

Butterfield, Herbert. "The History of Science and the Study of History." *Harvard Library Bulletin* 13 (1959): 329–47.

Cairns, J. F. "Some Problems in the Use of Theory in History," *Economic Record* 26 (December 1950): 239–253.

Carr, E. H. *What Is History?* New York: A. A. Knopf, 1962.

Cassirer, Ernst. *The Problem of Knowledge; Philosophy, Science, and History since Hegel.* New Haven: Yale University Press, 1950.

Childe, V. Gordon. *History.* London: Corbett Press, 1947.

———. *What Is History?* New York, H. Schuman, 1953.

Cohen, Morris R. *The Meaning of Human History.* La Salle, Ill.: Open Court, 1947.

———. "Reason in Social Science." In *Readings in the Philosophy of Science,* edited by H. Feigl and May Brodbeck. New York, APC, 1953.

Cole, Arthur H. *The Historical Development of Economic and Business Literature*. Boston: Baker Library, Harvard Graduate School of Business Administration, 1957.

Collingwood, R. G. "Economics as a Philosophical Science." *International Journal of Ethics* 36 (January 1926): 162–185.

———. *An Essay in Philosophical Method*. Oxford: Clarendon, 1934.

———. "On the So-called Idea of Causation." In *Proceedings of the Aristotelian Society* 38 (1937–1938): 85–112.

Danto, Arthur C. "On Explanations in History." *Philosophy of Science* 23 (1956): 15–30.

———. *Analytical Philosophy of History*. Cambridge: Cambridge University Press, 1965.

———. "On Historical Questioning." *Journal of Philosophy* 51 (1954): 89–99.

Davis, L. E., J. R. T. Hughes, and S. Reiter. "Aspects of Quantitative Research in Economic History." *Journal of Economic History* 20 (December 1960): 539–547.

Deguchi, Y. "On Historical Research in Social Sciences." *Kyoto University Economic Review* 2 (October 1953): 22–36.

Dorfman, J. "The Role of the German Historical School in American Economic Thought." *American Economic Association, Papers and Proceedings* 45 (May 1955): 17–28.

Dovring, Folke. *History as a Social Science: An Essay on the Nature and Purpose of Historical Studies*. The Hague: Martinus Nijhoff, 1960.

Dray, William H. "Historical Understanding as Rethinking," *Toronto Quarterly* 27 (1958): 200–215.

———. *Laws and Explanation in History*. New York: Oxford University Press, 1957.

Easterlin, Richard A. "Is There Need for Historical Research on Underdevelopment?" *American Economic Review* 55 (November 1965): 104–108.

Engel-Janosi, Friedrich. *The Growth of German Historicism*. Johns Hopkins University Studies in History and Political Science, vol. 62, no. 2. Baltimore: Johns Hopkins Press, 1944.

Eucken, Walter. *The Foundations of Economics: History and Theory in the Analysis of Economic Reality*. Translated by T. W. Hutchinson. London: Hodge, 1950.

Feuer, Lewis S. "Dialectic and Economic Laws." *Science and Society* 5 (1941): 336–361.

———. "The Economic Factor in History." *Science and Society* 4 (1940): 168–192.

———. "Ethical Theories and Historical Materialism." *Science and Society* 6 (1942): 42–272.

———. "What Is Philosophy of History?" *Journal of Philosophy*, 49 (1952): 329–340.

Finberg H. P. R., ed. *Approaches to History: A Symposium.* Toronto: University of Toronto Press, 1962.
Fischer, David Hackett. *Historians' Fallacies: Toward a Logic of Historical Thought.* New York: Harper & Row, 1970.
Fischer, Franklin. "On the Analysis of History and the Interdependence of the Social Sciences." *Philosophy of Science* 5 (April 1960): 147–158.
Fitzsimons, Mathew, Alfred B. Pundt, and Charles E. Nowell, eds. *The Development of Historiography.* Harrisburg, Pa.: Stackpole, 1954.
Fogel, R. W. "The Reunification of Economic History and Economic Theory." *American Economic Review* 55 (May 1965): 92–97.
Fores, M. J. "No More General Theories," *Economic Journal,* March 1969.
Frankle, Charles. "Explanation and Interpretation in History." *Philosophy of Science* 24 (1957): 137–155.
Frisch, Ragnar A. K. *Knut Wicksell: A Cornerstone in Modern Economic Theory.* Oslo: Universitetets Socialøkonomiske Institutt, 1951.
Gardiner, Patrick. *The Nature of Historical Explanation.* New York, Oxford University Press, 1952.
Gardiner, Patrick, ed. *Theories of History: Readings from Classical and Contemporary Sources.* Glencoe, Ill.: Free Press, 1959.
Gasking, D. "The Historian's Craft and Scientific History." *Historical Studies: Australia & New Zealand* 4 (1950): 112–124.
Gay, E. F. "Tasks of Economic History." *Economic History Association: The Tasks of Economic History* 1 (December 1941): 9–16.
Gerschenkron, A. *Continuity in History and Other Essays.* Cambridge, Mass.: Harvard University Press, 1968.
Geyl, Pieter. *From Ranke to Toynbee.* Northampton, Mass.: Smith College, 1952.
Giddings, Franklin H. "A Theory of Social Causation." In *Papers and Proceedings of the Sixteenth Annual Meeting.* New York: American Economic Association, 1904.
Gibson, Quentin. *The Logic of Social Enquiry.* London: Routledge, 1960.
Glassburner, B. "Alfred Marshall on Economic History and Historical Development." *Quarterly Journal of Economics* 69 (November 1955): 577–595.
Goodhue, E. W. "Economics as a Social Philosophy." *International Journal of Ethics* 36 (October 1925): 54–70.
Goodrich, C. "Economic History: One Field or Two?" *Journal of Economic History* 20 (December 1960): 531–538.
Gottschalk, Louis, ed. *Generalization in the Writing of History.* A report of the Committee on Historical Analysis of the Social Science Research Council. Chicago: University of Chicago Press, 1963.
Gould, J. D. "Hypothetical History." *Economic History Review* 22 (August 1969): 195–207.
Gras, N. S. B. "The Present Condition of Economic History," *Quarterly Journal of Economics,* Vol. 34, pp. 209–224, Feb. 1920.
———. "The Rise and Development of Economic History." *Economic History Review* 1 (January 1927): 12–34.

———. "Stages in Economic History." *Journal of Economic and Business History* 2 (May 1930): 395–418.

Hamilton, E. J. "Use and Misuse of Price History." *Economic History Association: Tasks of Economic History* 4 (December 1944): 47–60.

Handman, M. S. "Scientific Trends in Economics." *International Journal of Ethics* 39 (October 1928): 41–49.

Handy, Rollo and Paul Kurtz. *A Current Appraisal of the Behavioral Sciences*. Great Burrington, Mass.: Behavioral Research Council, 1964.

Hanson, Norwood R. *Patterns of Scientific Discovery: An Inquiry into the Conceptual Foundations of Science*. Cambridge: Cambridge University Press, 1958.

Hayek, F. A. von. "Scientism and the Study of Society." *Economica*, n.s. 10 (February 1943): 27–39.

Heinemann, F. H. "Reply to Historicism." *Philosophy* 21 (1946): 245–257.

Hempel, Carl G. "The Function of General Laws in History." *Journal of Philosophy* 34 (1942): 35–48.

Hempel, Carl G. and P. Oppenheim. "Studies in the Logic of Explanation." *Philosophy of Science* 15 (1948): 135–175.

Hockett, Homer C. *The Critical Method in Historical Research and Writing*. New York: Macmillan, 1955.

Homan, Paul T. "The Institutional School." In *Encyclopedia of the Social Sciences*, edited by E. R. A. Seligman. 5th ed. New York: MacMillan Co., 1957. Pp. 387–392.

———. "Why Systematic Economy Theory?" *Social Forces* 8 (September 1929): 29–36.

Hoxie, R. F. "Historical Method vs. Historical Narrative." *Journal of Political Economy* 14 (November 1906): 568–572.

Hull, L. W. H. *History and Philosophy of Science*. London: Longmans, 1959.

———. "Integration of Economic Theory and Economic History." *Journal of Economic History* 17 (December 1957): 509–602.

Jeffreys, Harold. *Scientific Inference*. 2nd ed. Cambridge: Cambridge University Press, 1957.

Joynt, C. B. and Nicholas Rescher. "The Problem of Uniqueness in History." *History and Theory* 1 (1961): 150–163.

Kaplan, Abraham. *The Conduct of Inquiry*. San Francisco: Chandler, 1964.

Keirstead, B. S. "Cause and Economic Change." *Canadian Historical Review* 27 (September 1946): 249–257.

———. *The Theory of Economic Change*. Toronto: Macmillan, 1948.

Klappholz, K. and J. Agassi "Methodological Prescriptions in Economics [review article]." *Economica* 26 (February 1959): 60–74.

Klipansky, Raymond and H. J. Paton, eds. *Philosophy and History: Essays Presented to Ernst Cassirer*. London: Oxford University Press, 1936.

Knight, Frank H. "Confusion on Morals and Economics." *International Journal of Ethics* 45 (1934–1935): 200–215.

————. "Institutionalism and Empiricism in Economics." *American Economic Review* 42 (May 1952): 45–55.

————. "Some Notes on the Economic Interpretation of History," *Studies in the History of Culture*. Menasha, Wisconsin, 1942.

Komatsu, Y. "The Study of Economic History in Japan." *Economic History Review* 2 (August 1961): 115–121.

Kuznets, Simon. *Economic Change*. New York: Norton, 1953.

Laski, Harold J. *Faith, Reason and Civilisation: An Essay in Historical Analysis*. New York: The Viking Press, 1944.

Lee, Dwight E. and Robert N. Beck. "The Meaning of 'Historicism.'" *American Historical Review* 59 (1954): 568–578.

Lee, Harold. "The Hypothetical Nature of Historical Knowledge." *Journal of Philosophy* 51 (1954): 213–220.

Lerner, Daniel, ed. *Evidence and Inference*. Glencoe, Ill.: Free Press, 1959.

Levy, Marion. "Some Basic Methodological Difficulties in the Social Sciences." *Philosophy of Science* 17 (1950): 287–301.

Loos, I. A. "Historical Approach to Economics." *American Economic Review* 8 (September 1918): 549–63.

MacIver, R. M., W. H. Walsh, and M. Ginsberg. "Explanation in History and Philosophy." Supplement to *Proceedings of the Aristotelian Society*, 21 (1947).

MacIver, R. M. "Historical Explanation." In *Logic and Language*, edited by Anthony Flew. 2d ed. New York: Philosophical Library, 1953.

MacKinnon, D. M. *On the Notion of a Philosophy of History*. London: Oxford University Press, 1954.

Malin, James C. *Essays on Historiography*. Lawrence, Kansas: James C. Malin, 1946.

Mandelbaum, M. "Historical Explanation: The Problem of Covering Laws." *History and Theory* 1 (1961): 229–242.

Marrou, Henri-Irenee. "La methodologie historique: orientations actuelles a propos d'oubrages recents." *Revue Historique* 209 (1935): 256–270.

Masnda, S. "The Study of Western Social and Economic History as It Now Stands in Japan." *Japan Science Review* 1 (1953): 62–65.

Meehan, Eugene J. *Explanation in Social Science: A System Paradigm*. Homewood, Ill.: Richard D. Irwin, Dorsey Press, 1968.

Meyer, J. R. and A. H. Conrad. "Economic Theory, Statistical Inference, and Economic History." *Journal of Economic History* 17 (December 1957): 524–544.

Mill, John S. *A System of Logic*. London: Longmans, Green and Co., 1919.

Mises, Ludwig Von. *The Ultimate Foundation of Economic Science*. Princeton: D. Van Nostrand Co., 1962.

Murphy, George G. S. "The 'New' History." *Explorations in Entrepreneurial History*, n.s. 2 (1965), no. 2.

————. "On Counterfactual Propositions." Supplement to *History and Theory* 9 (1969): 14–38.

Nagel, Ernest. "Determinism in History." *Philosophy and Phenomenological Research* 20 (1960): 291–317.

———. "The Logic of Historical Analysis." *Scientific Monthly* 74 (1952): 162–169.

Nagel, Ernest and Carl Hempel. "Symposium: Problems of Concept and Theory Formation in the Social Sciences." In *Science, Language and Human Rights*. Philadelphia: University of Pennsylvania for the American Philosophical Assn., 1952.

Nef, J. U. "The Responsibility of Economic Historians." *Economic History Society, The Tasks of Economic History* 4 (December 1944): 1–19.

Nichols, Roy F. "Confusions in Historical Thinking." *Journal of Social Philosophy* 7 (1942): 334–343.

North, Douglass C. "The State of Economic History." *American Economic Review* 55 (May 1965): 86–91.

———. "Quantitative Research in American Economic History," *American Economic Review* 53 (March 1963): 128–130.

Ortega y Gasset, José. *History as a System, and Other Essays toward a Philosophy of History*. New York: Norton, 1961.

Pirenne, Henri. "De la methode comparative en Histoire." *Compte Rendu du Ve. Congres International des Sciences Historiques*, Brussels, 1923, pp. 19–32.

———. "What Are Historians Trying to Do?" In *Method in Social Science*, edited by S. A. Rice, pp. 435–445. Chicago: University of Chicago Press, 1931.

Pitt, J. "Generalizations in Historical Explanation." *Journal of Philosophy*, 61 (1959): 225–247.

Polanyi, Michael. *Personal Knowledge*. Chicago: University of Chicago Press, 1958.

Popper, Karl R. *The Poverty of Historicism*. Boston: Harper & Row, 1961.

———. "The Poverty of Historicism," pts. 1–2. *Economica*, n.s. 11 (May 1944): 86–103; 11 (August 1944): 119–137; 12 (May 1945): 69–89.

———. *The Logic of Scientific Discovery*. New York: Basic Books, 1959.

Postan, M. M. "Function and Dialectic in Economic History." *Economic History Review*, 2d ser. 14 (April 1962): 397–407.

———. *The Historical Method in Social Science: An Inaugural Lecture*. Cambridge: Cambridge University Press, 1939.

Renier, Gustaf J. *History: Its Purpose and Method*. Boston: Beacon, 1950.

Rice, Stuart A., ed. *Methods in Social Science: A Case Book*. Chicago: University of Chicago Press, 1931.

Ritter, Gerhard. "Scientific History, Contemporary History, and Political Science." *History and Theory* 1 (1960): 261–279.

Robinson, James H. "The Newer Ways of Historians." *American Historical Review* 35 (1930): 245–255.

———. *The New History*. Glencoe, Ill.: Free Press, 1937.

Rogin, Leo. *The Meaning and Validity of Economic Theory: A Historical Approach*. New York: Harpers, 1956.

Rostow, W. W. "A Historian's Perspective on Modern Economic Theory." *American Economic Association, Papers and Proceedings* 42 (May 1952): 16–291.

————. "The Interrelation of Theory and Economic History." *Journal of Economic History* 17 (1957): 509–523.

Sanders, Jennings B. *Historical Interpretations and American Historianship.* Yellow Springs, Ohio: Antioch Press, 1966.

Schumpeter, J. A. "The Analysis of Economic Change." *Review of Economics and Statistics* 17 (May 1935): pt. 2, pp. 2–10.

————. "Science and Ideology." *American Economic Review* 39 (March 1949): 345–359.

Schweitzer, Arthur. "Spiethoff's Theory of the Business Cycle." *University of Wyoming Publications* 8: 1–30. Laramie: University of Wyoming, 1940.

Slater, G. "Psychological Basis of Economic Theory." *Sociological Review* 15 (July–October 1923): 215.

Social Science Research Council. *Theory and Practice in Historical Study.* Bulletin No. 54. New York, 1946.

Spengler, Joseph J. "Quantification in Economics: Its History." In *Quantity and Quality*, edited by Daniel Lerner, pp. 129–211. New York: Free Press, 1959.

Strong, E. W. "How Is Practice of History Tied to Theory?" *Journal of Philosophy* 46 (1949): 637–644.

————. "Criteria of Explanation in History." *Journal of Philosophy* 49 (1952): 57–67.

Supple, B. E. "Economic History and Economic Growth." *Journal of Economic History* 20 (December 1960): 548–556.

Takashima, Z. "A New Methodological Approach to the History of Economic Thought: An Attempt at Unification of the Historical and Theoretical Approaches." *Hitotsubashi Academy*, Tokyo, 9 (October 1958): 1–13.

Teggart, F. J. *Theory and Processes of History.* Berkeley and Los Angeles: University of California Press, 1960.

Thrupp, Sylvia. "The Role of Comparison in the Development of Economic Theory." *Journal of Economic History* 17 (December 1957).

Tinbergen, J. "Schumpeter and Quantitative Research in Economics." *Review of Economics and Statistics* 33 (May 1951): 109–111.

Veblen, Thorstein. "Economic Theory in the Calculable Future." *Supplement to American Economic Review* 15 (March 1925): 48–55.

————. "The Evolution of the Scientific Point of View." *University of California Chronical,* October 1908, pp. 395–416.

————. "Gustav Schmoller's Economics." *Quarterly Journal of Economics* 16 (November 1901): 69–93.

————. "The Preconceptions of Economic Science." *Quarterly Journal of Economics*, January 1899, pp. 121–150; July 1899, pp. 396–426; January 1900, pp. 240–269.

————. "Why Is Economics Not an Evolutionary Science?" *Quarterly Journal of Economics*, July 1898, pp. 373–397.

Watkins, J. W. N. "Historical Explanation in the Social Sciences." *British Journal for the Philosophy of Science* 8 (1957): 104–117.

Weber, Max. *Max Weber on the Methodology of the Social Sciences.* Translated and edited by Edward Shils and Henry Finch. Glencoe, Ill.: Free Press, 1949.

———. *The Theory of Social and Economic Organization.* Translated by Talcott Parsons. New York: Oxford University Press, 1947.

White, Morton. *The Foundations of Historical Knowledge.* New York: Harper & Row, 1965.

———. "Attack on the Historical Method." *Journal of Philosophy* 42 (June 1945): 314–331.

———. "Towards an Analytic Philosophy of History." In *Philosophic Thought in France and the United States,* edited by M. Farber. University of Buffalo Publications in Philosophy. New York, 1950.

Whitehead, A. N. *Adventures of Ideas.* New York: Penguin Books, 1948.

Wiener, A. P. "On Methodology in the Philosophy of History." *Journal of Philosophy* 38 (1941): 309–324.

Wiener, Norbert. *Cybernetics.* New York: John Wiley & Sons, 1948.

Wilkins, Burleigh Taylor. "Pragmatism as a Theory of Historical Knowledge: John Dewey on the Nature of Historical Inquiry." *American Historical Review* 64 (1959): 878–890.

Winkler, Robert L. "The Quantification of Judgement—Some Methodological Suggestions." *Journal of the American Statistical Association* 62, no. 320 (December 1967).

Zilsel, E. "Physics and the Problem of Historico-Sociological Laws." *Philosophy of Science* 8 (1941): 567–579.


(2)

Andersen, Per Sveas. *Westward Is the Course of the Empire: A Study in the Shaping of an American Idea: Turner's Frontier.* Oslo: Oslo University Press, 1956.

Ashley, Wm. "The Economic Development of France and Germany," *Economic Journal* 31 (September 1921): 353–356.

Beckman, Allan C. "Hidden Themes in the Frontier Thesis: An Application of Psychoanalysis to Historiography." *Comparative Studies in Society and History* 8, no. 3 (April 1966): 361–382.

Bendix, Reinhard. *Max Weber: An Intellectual Portrait.* New York: Doubleday, 1960.

Benson, Lee. "The Historical Background of Turner's Frontier Essay." *Agricultural History* 25 (April 1951): 59–82.

———. *Turner and Beard: American Historical Writing Reconsidered.* Glencoe, Ill.: Free Press, 1960.

Bergstrasser, Arnold. "Wilhelm Dilthy and Max Weber: An Historical Approach to Historical Synthesis." *Ethics* 57 (1947): 92–110.

Bloom, S. F. "Man of His Century: A Reconsideration of Historical Significance of Karl Marx." *Journal of Political Economy* 51 (December 1943): 494–505.

Bober, M. M. *Karl Marx's Interpretation of History.* New York: W. W. Norton, 1965.

————. "Marx and Economic Calculation." *American Economic Review* 36 (June 1946): 344–357.

Boyce, Gray C. "The Legacy of Henri Pirenne." *Byzantion* 15 (1940/1941): 449–464.

Cameron, Rondo et al. *Banking in the Early Stages of Industrialization.* London: Oxford University Press, 1967.

Careless, J. M. S. "Frontierism, Metropolitanism, and Canadian History." *Canadian Historical Review* 35 (1954): 1–21.

Clapham, John. *The Economic Development of France and Germany, 1815–1914.* Cambridge: Cambridge University Press, 1961.

Clay, Clive. "Mercantilism." *American Historical Review* 41 (April 1936): 534–536.

Colville, A. (Review of Pirenne's *Mohammed and Charlemagne.*) *Journal des Savants* (1938): 97–104.

Cornforth, M. *Historical Materialism.* London: Lawrence, 1953.

Curti, M. E. "The Section and the Frontier in American History: The Methodological Concepts of Frederick Jackson Turner." In *Methods in Social Science,* edited by Stuart A. Rice. Chicago: Chicago University Press, 1931.

Dalton, J. H. "Colony and Metropolis: Some Aspects of British Rule in Gold Coast and Their Implications for an Understanding of Ghana Today." *Journal of Economic History* 21 (December 1961): 552–565.

Danhof, Clarence H. "Economic Validity of the Safety-Valve Doctrine." *The Tasks of Economic History,* supplement to *Journal of Economic History* 1 (1941): 96–106.

Deguchi, Y. "The Economic Theory Conceived by Max Weber." *Kyoto University Economic Review* 27, no. 1 (April 1957): 1–13.

Del Vecchio, Giorgio. "Historical Materialism and Psychologism." *Scienza Nuova,* 1955, no. 2, pp. 5–14.

Dennett, Daniel C., Jr. "Pirenne and Muhammad." *Speculum* 23 (April 1948): 165–190.

Dibblee, G. B. "The Economic Development of France and Germany." *English History Review* 36 (October 1921): 605–608.

Elkins, Stanley and Eric McKitrick. "A Meaning for Turner's Frontier." *Political Science Quarterly* 69 (1954): 321.

Fischoff, E. "The Protestant Ethic and the Spirit of Capitalism: The History of a Controversy." *Social Research* 11 (February 1944): 53–77.

Fishlow, A. *American Railroads and the Transformation of the Ante-Bellum Economy.* Cambridge, Mass.: Harvard University Press, 1965.

Fogel, Robert W. *Railroads and American Economic Growth: Essays in Econometric History.* Baltimore: Johns Hopkins University Press, 1964.

Freund, R. "Turner's Theory of Social Evolution." *Agricultural History* 19 (April 1945): 78–87.

Ganshof, F. L. "Henri Pirenne and Economic History." *Economic History Review* 6 (April 1936): 179–185.

Green, Robert W., ed. *Protestantism and Capitalism: The Weber Thesis and Its Critics.* Boston, Heath, 1959.

Gressley, G. M. "The Turner Thesis: A Problem in Historiography." *Agricultural History* 32 (October 1958): 227–249.

Grushin, B. A. "Karl Marx und die modernen Methoden der Geschichtsforschung," *Sowjetwissenschaft, Gesellschaftwissenschaftliche Beitrage,* no. 10 (1958), pp. 1155–1172.

Gunderson, Gerald. "The Nature of Social Saving." *Economic History Review* 23 (August 1970): 207–219.

Gurley, J. G. "Banking in the Early Stages of Industrialization." *American Economic Review* 57 (September 1967): 950–953.

Haley, B. F. "Heckscher's Mercantilism." *Journal of Political Economy* 45 (June 1937): 370–393.

Halphen, L. (Review of Pirenne's *Mohammed and Charlemagne.*) *Revue Historique* 85 (1939): 149–151.

Hanigscheim, P. "Max Weber as Historian of Agriculture and Rural Life." *Agricultural History* 23 (July 1949): 179–213.

Hansen, A. H. "The Technological Interpretation of History." *Quarterly Journal of Economics* 36 (November 1921): 72–83.

Havighurst, Alfred F., ed. *The Pirenne Thesis: Analysis, Criticism and Revision.* Boston: Heath, 1958.

Hayek, Friedrich von, ed. *Capitalism and the Historians.* Chicago: University of Chicago Press, 1954.

Heaton, Herbert. "Heckscher on Mercantilism." *Journal of Political Economy* 45 (June 1937): 370–393.

———. "Other Wests than Ours." *Journal of Economic History,* supplement 6 (1946): 50–62.

Heckscher, Eli F. "Revisions in Economic History." *Economic History Review* 7 (November 1936): 44–45.

———. *Mercantilism.* Vol. 1. 2d ed. rev. London: Allen & Unwin, 1934.

Heimann, E. "What Marx Means Today." *Social Research* 4 (February 1937): 33–51.

*History & Theory,* supplement 9, 1969 [devoted to recent trends].

Hofstadter, Richard. "Turner and the Frontier Myth." *American Scholar* 28 (1949): 433–443.

Jacobs, Wilbur R., John W. Caughey, and Joe B. Frantz. *Turner, Bolton and Webb: Three Histories of the American Frontier.* Seattle: University of Washington Press, 1965.

Johnson, E. A. J. "Mercantilism." *American Economic Review* 36 (1936): 306–307.

Joranson, E. (Review of Pirenne's *Mohammed and Charlemagne.*) *American Historical Review* 44 (1939): 324–325.

Kocka, H. F. "Karl Marx and Max Weber Ein Methodologischer Vergleich." *Zeitschrift fur die Gesamte Staatswissenschaft* 122, no. 2 (April 1966). English summary in *Economic Abstracts,* December 1966.

Kolko, Gabriel. "A Critique of Max Weber's Philosophy of History." *Ethics* 70 (1959): 21–36.

Krieger, Leonard. "Marx and Engels as Historians." *Journal of the History of Ideas* 14 (1953): 381–403.

————. "The Uses of Marx for History." *Political Science Quarterly* 75 (1960): 355–378.

Lambrechts, Pierre. "Les Theses de Henri Pirenne dur la fin du monde antique et les debut du moyen age." *Byzantion* 14 (1939): 513–516.

Laurent, H. "Les travaux de M. Henri Pirenne sur la fin du monde antique et les dubuts du moyen age." *Byzantion* 7 (1932): 495–509.

Law, A. "The Economic Development of France and Germany." *Scottish History Review* 18 (July 1921): 297.

Lebergott, S. "United States Transport Advance and Externalities." *Journal of Economic History* 26 (December 1966): 437–461.

Leontief, W. L. "The Significance of Marxian Economics for Present-day Economic Theory." *American Economic Association Papers and Proceedings* 28 (March 1938): 1–9.

Levy-Leboyer, Maurice. "Le role historique de la monnaie de banque." *Annales, economies, societes, civilisations* 23, no. 168, pp. 1–8.

Lipson, E. "The Industrial Revolution in the 18th Century," *Economic History Review*, 2d s. 2 (January 1929): 183.

Lopez, R. S. "Mohammed and Charlemagne." *Speculum* 18 (1943): 14–38.

Mantoux, Paul. *The Industrial Revolution in the Eighteenth Century.* New York: Harper & Row, 1961.

Marx, Karl. *Capital.* Vol. 1. New York: International Publisher, 1947.

Mayo, H. B. "Marxism as a Philosophy of History." *Canadian Historical Review* 34 (1953): 1–17.

Meek, R. L. "Marx's 'Doctrine of Increasing Misery.'" *Science and Society* 26 (February 1960): 422–441.

Nerlove, Marc. "Railroads and American Economic Growth." *Journal of Economic History* 26 (March 1966): 107–115.

Ostrander, G. M. "Turner and the Germ Theory." *Agricultural History* 32 (October 1958): 258–261.

Pierson, George Wilson. "The Frontier and Frontiersmen of Turner's Essays," *The Pennsylvania Magazine of History and Biography* 64 (October 1940): 449–478.

Pirenne, Henri. *Mohammed and Charlemagne.* New York: World Publishing Co., 1964.

Pressnell, L. S. "Money Finance and Industrialization." *Business History* 11 (July 1969): 128–133.

Price, Jacob M. "Money and Credit in Early Industrialization: Some Methodological Problems in Comparative Analysis" [Review of Cameron et al.]. *Comparative Studies in Society and History* 12 (April 1970): 229–233.

Price, L. L. "The Industrial Revolution in the 18th Century," *English Historical Review* 21 (July 1906): 594.

Rees, J. R. "The Industrial Revolution in the 18th Century." *Economic Journal* 5 (1929): 133–134.

Riemersma, J. C. "Max Weber's 'Protestant Ethic': An Example of Historical Conceptualization." *Explorations in Entrepreneurial History* 1, no. 6 (June 1949): 11–19.

Riising, Anne. "The Fate of Henri Pirenne's Thesis." *Classica et Mediaevalia* 13 (1952): 87–130.

Roover, Raymond de. "Banking in the Early Stages of Industrialization." *Journal of Economic History* 28 (1968): 650–652.

Salomon, Albert. "Max Weber's Methodology." *Social Research* 1 (May 1934): 147–168.

Samuelsson, Kurt. *Religion and Economic Action: A Critique of Max Weber.* Translated by E. A. French. New York: Harper & Row, 1961.

Scheiber, Harry N. "On the New Economic History—and Its Limitations." *Agricultural History* 41, no. 4 (1967): 383–395.

———. "Discussion." *Journal of Economic History* 26 (December 1966): 462–465.

Sheridan, R. B. "The Wealth of Jamaica in the Eighteenth Century." *Economic History Review*, 2d s. 1 (April 1965): 292–311.

Somerville, John M. "Methodology in Social Sciences: A Critique of Marx and Engels," Ph.D. diss., Columbia University, 1938.

Taylor, G. R., ed. *The Turner Thesis.* Boston: Heath, 1949.

———. "Comment" [on Fogel]. *American Economic Review*, September 1965, pp. 890–892.

Thomas, R. P. "A Quantitative Approach to the Study of the Effects of British Imperial Policy upon Colonial Welfare: Some Preliminary Findings." *Journal of Economic History* 25 (December 1965): 615–638.

———. "The Sugar Colonies of the Old Empire: Profit and Loss for Great Britain." *Economic History Review* 21 (April 1968): 30–45.

Treadgold, Donald W. "Russian Expansion in Light of Turner's Study of American Frontier." *Agricultural History* 26 (1952): 147–152.

Tucker, R. S. "Frontier as an Outlet for Surplus Labor: Did the City Dweller Settle the Agricultural Frontier?" *Southern Economic Journal* 7 (October 1940): 158–186.

Tunzelmann, G. N. von. "The New Economic History: An Econometric Appraisal." *Explorations in Entrepreneurial History*, 2d s. 5, no. 2 (1968): 175–200.

Turner, Frederick J. *The Frontier in American History.* New York: Henry Holt & Co., 1921.

Usher, A. P. "The Economic Development of France and Germany." *American Political Science Review* 15 (November 1921): 599–600.

———. "Mercantilism." *Political Science Quarterly* 60 (1936): 448–451.

Warner, R. Stephen. "The Role of Religious Ideas and the Use of Models in Max Weber's Comparative Studies of Non-Capitalistic Societies." *Journal of Economic History* 30 (March 1970): 74–99.

Webb, Walter P. *The Great Frontier.* Boston: Houghton Mifflin, 1952.

———. "The Frontier and the 400 Year Boom." *Harper's Magazine*, October 1951, pp. 26–33.

Weber, Max. *The Protestant Ethic and the Spirit of Capitalism.* Translated by Talcott Parsons. New York: Charles Scribner's Sons, 1958.

Wyman, Walker D. and Clifton B. Kroeber, eds. *The Frontier in Perspective.* Madison: University of Wisconsin Press, 1957.

(3)

Alker, Hayward R., Jr. *Mathematics and Politics.* New York: Macmillan, 1965.

Alker, Hayward R., Jr. and Bruce M. Russett. "On Measuring Inequality." *Behavioral Science* 9 (1964).

Bay, Christian. "Politics and Pseudopolitics: A Critical Evaluation of Some Behavioral Literature." *American Political Science Review* 59, no. 1 (March 1965): 39–51.

Bentley, Arthur. *The Process of Government: A Study of Social Pressures.* Evanston, Ill.: Principia Press, 1949.

Berelson, Bernard, ed. *The Behavioral Sciences Today.* New York: Basic Books, 1963.

Berelson, Bernard and Gary A. Steiver. *Human Behavior: An Inventory of Scientific Findings.* New York: Harcourt, Brace and World, 1964.

Berger, Bennett M. "It's more than a matter of Insiders vs. Outsiders." *New York Times Book Review,* 20 September 1964.

Bixenstine, V. Edwin. "Empiricism in Latter-day Behavioral Science." *Science* 145 (1964): 464–467.

Black, C. E. *The Dynamics of Modernization: A Study in Comparative History.* New York: Harper & Row, 1966.

Blalock, Hubert M., Jr. *Causal Inferences in Non-experimental Research.* Chapel Hill: University of North Carolina Press, 1964.

———. *Methodology in Social Research.* New York, McGraw-Hill, 1968.

Blankenship, L. V. "Community Power and Decision-Making: A Comparative Evaluation of Measurement Techniques." *Social Forces* 43, no. 2 (December 1964): 207–216.

Blumer, Herbert. "Sociological Analysis and the 'Variable,' " *American Sociological Review* 21 (December 1956): 683–690.

Borko, Harold, ed. *Computer Applications in the Behavioral Sciences.* Englewood Cliffs: Prentice-Hall, 1962.

Boyle, Richard. "Causal Theory and Statistical Measures of Effect: A Convergence." *American Sociological Review* 31 (December 1966): 843–851.

Buckley, Walter. *Modern Systems Approach for the Behaviorist Scientist.* Chicago, Aldine Publishing Co., 1968.

———. *Sociology and Modern Systems Theory.* Englewood Cliffs: Prentice-Hall, 1967.

Butler, David. *The Study of Political Behavior.* London: Hutchinson, 1958.

Carber, L. J. "Social Sciences: Where Do They Fit in the Politics of Science?" *Science* 154 (1966): 488.

Catlin, George. *Systematic Politics: Elementa Politica and Sociologica.* Toronto: University of Toronto Press, 1962.

Charlesworth, J. C., ed. *The Limits of Behavioralism in Political Science.* Philadelphia: American Academy of Social and Political Science, 1962.

Cicourel, Aaron V. *Method and Measurement in Sociology.* New York: Free Press, 1964.

Coleman, James S. *Introduction to Mathematical Sociology.* New York: Free Press, 1964.

Crick, Bernard. *The American Science of Politics.* Berkeley and Los Angeles: University of California Press, 1959.

Dahl, Robert A. *Modern Political Analysis,* Englewood Cliffs: Prentice-Hall, 1964.

————. "The Behavioral Approach in Political Science: Epitaph for a Monument to a Successful Project." *American Political Science Review* 55 (1961).

Duncan, Otis D., A. Cuzzart and B. Duncan. *Statistical Geography.* Glencoe, Ill.: Free Press, 1961.

Easton, David. *The Political System: An Inquiry into the State of Political Science.* New York: A. A. Knopf, 1953.

Ehrlich, H. J. and J. W. Rinehart. "A Brief Report on the Methodology of Stereotype Research." *Social Forces* 43, no. 4 (May 1965): 564–574.

Eldersveld, Samuel. *Political Parties: A Behavioral Analysis.* Chicago: Rand McNally, 1964.

Etzioni, Amitai. *The Active Society: A Theory of Societal and Political Processes.* New York: Free Press, 1968.

Eulau, Heinz. *The Behavioral Persuasion in Politics.* New York: Random House, 1963.

————. *Recent Developments in the Behavioral Study of Politics.* Stanford: Stanford University Press, 1961.

Feuer, Lewis S. "Causality in the Social Sciences." *Journal of Philosophy* 51 (1954): 681–695.

Francis, Roy G. "On the Relations of Data to Theory." *Rural Sociology,* 22 (1957): 258–266.

Friedrich, Carl J. *Man and His Government: An Empirical Theory of Politics.* New York: McGraw-Hill, 1963.

Garvey, William D. and Belver C. Griffith. "Scientific Information Exchange in Psychology." *Science* 146 (1964): 1655–1659.

Gruenbaum, Adolph. "Historical Determinism, Social Activism and Predictions in the Social Sciences." *British Journal of Philosophical Science* 7 (1956).

Guetskow, Harold et al. *Simulation in International Relations.* Englewood Cliffs: Prentice-Hall, 1963.

Halman, S. F. and D. F. Duns. "Validations in Communicative Behavior of Attitude—Scale Measures of Dogmatism." *Journal of Social Psychology* 70, no. 4 (January 1965): 403–415.

Handy, Rollo and Paul Kurtz. *A Current Appraisal of the Behavioral Sciences.* Great Burrington, Mass.: Behavioral Research Council, 1964.

Harman, Harry. *Modern Factor Analysis*. Chicago: University of Chicago Press, 1960.

Immergluck, Ludwig. "Determinism—Freedom in Contemporary Psychology: An Ancient Problem Revisited." *American Psychologist* 19, no. 4 (April 1964): 270–281.

Kagan, J. "American Longitudinal Research in Psychological Development." *Child Development* 35 (1964): 1–32.

Klausner, Samuel Z., ed. *The Study of Total Societies*. Garden City, N.Y.: Doubleday, 1967.

Krause, J. T. "Some Implications of Recent Research in Demographic History." *Comparative Studies in Society and History* 1 (1958/1959).

Lasswell, Harold. *The Analysis of Political Behavior: An Empirical Approach*. London: Kegan Paul, 1947.

————. *The Future of Political Science*. New York: Atherton Press, 1963 [esp. pp. 1–42].

Lazarsfeld, Paul F. "Observations on Organized Social Research in the United States." *Information*, December 1961, pp. 3–37.

Lerner, Daniel and Harold D. Lasswell, eds. *The Policy Sciences: Recent Development in Scope and Method*. Stanford: Stanford University Press, 1951.

Lundberg, G. A. "The Natural Science Trend in Sociology." *American Journal of Sociology* 61 (November 1955): 191–202.

Macridis, Roy C. *The Study of Comparative Government*. Garden City, N.Y.: Doubleday, 1955.

Marsh, James G. and Herbert A. Simon. *Organizations*. New York: John Wiley, 1958.

Marsh, Robert M. "Comparative Sociology 1950–1963." *Current Sociology* 14 (1966): 1–40.

Marvick, D., ed. *Political Decision-Makers: Recruitment and Performance*. Glencoe, Ill.: Free Press, 1961.

Mayer, K. "Developments in the Study of Population." *Social Research* 29 (October 1962): 293–320.

McEwen, W. J. "Forms and Problems of Validation in Social Anthropology." *Current Anthropology* 4 (1963): 155–183.

Merritt, R. L. and Stein Rokkan, eds. *Comparing Nations: The Use of Quantitative Data in Cross-National Research*. New Haven: Yale University Press, 1966.

Meyerhoff, Hans, ed. *The Philosophy of History in Our Time*. Garden City, N.Y.: Doubleday, 1951.

Michotte, A. *The Perception of Causality*. Translated by T. R. and Elaine Miles. New York: Basic Books, 1963.

Naylor et al. "Computer Simulation Experiments with Economic Systems: The Problem of Experimental Design." *Journal of American Statistics Association* 62 (December 1967): 320.

Ranney, A., ed. *Essays on the Behavioral Study of Politics*. Urbana: University of Illinois Press, 1962.

Ray, Donald P., ed. *Trends in Social Science.* New York: Philosophical Library, 1961.

Riker, William H. *The Theory of Political Coalitions.* New Haven: Yale University Press, 1962.

Rosebom, W. and A. Kaplan. *The Conduct of Inquiry: Methodology for Behavioral Science.* San Francisco: Chandler Publishing Co., 1964.

Rudner, Richard. *Philosophy of Social Science.* Englewood Cliffs, N.J.: Prentice-Hall, 1966.

Russett, Bruce M., Hayward R. Alker, Jr., Karl Deutsch, and Harold Lasswell. *World Handbook of Political and Social Indicators.* New Haven: Yale University Press, 1964.

Scrinivas, M. N., ed. *Method in Social Anthropology: Selected Essays.* Chicago: Chicago University Press, 1958.

Senn, Peter R. "What Is 'Behavioral Science'?—Notes Toward a History." *Journal of the Behavioral Sciences* 2 (1966): 107–122.

Shubik, Martin, ed. *Game Theory and Related Approaches to Social Behavior.* New York: Wiley, 1964.

Sibley, Elbridge. *The Education of Sociologists in the United States.* New York: Russell Sage Foundation, 1963.

Simon, Herbert A. *Models of Man, Social and Rational: Mathematical Essays on Rational Human Behavior in a Social Setting.* New York: Wiley, 1961.

Somit, Albert. *The Development of American Political Science: From Burgess to Behavioralism.* Boston: Allyn & Bacon, 1967.

Somit, Albert and Joseph Tanenhaus. *American Political Science: A Profile of a Discipline.* New York: Atherton Press, 1961.

———. "Trends in American Political Science: Some Analytical Notes." *American Political Science Review* 57, (1963): 933–947.

Spengler, Joseph J. and Otis D. Duncan, eds. *Demographic Analysis: Selected Readings.* Glencoe, Ill.: Free Press, 1956.

Storing, Herbert H., ed. *Essays on the Scientific Study of Politics.* New York: Holt, Rinehart & Winston, 1962.

Truman, David. "The Implications of Political Behavior Research." *Items* 5 (1951): 39.

———. "Disillusion and Regeneration: The Quest for a Discipline." *American Political Science Review* 59, no. 4 (December 1965): 865–873.

Tyron, R. C. "Psychology in Flux: The Academic-Professional Bipolarity." *American Psychologist* 18 (1963): 134–143.

UNESCO *The Social Sciences: Problems and Orientations.* Paris, The Hague: Mouton-Unesco, 1968.

Varma, B. N., ed. *A New Survey of the Social Sciences.* London: Asia Publishing House, 1962.

Winch, P. *The Idea of a Social Science and Its Relation to Philosophy.* London: Kegan Paul, 1958.

# INDEX

Abelson, Robert A., 283, 284
Ackoff, Russell L., 288
Adelman, Irma, 31
Aitken, H. G. J., 10
Allen, Francis R., 277–278
American frontier, 120, 137, 144, 197, 214–215; vital forces in evolution of, 165–166; as a system, 171–172
American Historical School, 248
Anthropology: classification of approaches, 245; controversies, 246; as history, 248–249; modern theoretical trends, 263–265; developmental vs. causal approach, 264–265; quantitative measurement in, 278–280, trend toward interdisciplinary approach, 285. *See also* Social sciences
Ashley, Sir William, 10
Aydelotte, William O., 43–44

Banking, early: data on, 120–121, 144, 151, 215–216; amount of banking in England, 125–126; amount of banking in France, 126; rise of banks, 137-138; in Russia, 138, 156; *anonymes* and *commandites* in France, 138–139; in Scotland, 156, 187–188; functions in economic development and industrialization, 166–168; systems approach to, 172–173; short-term credit in England, 186–187; official system vs. provate sector, in England, 187; French economy, 188–189; and free competition, 198–199
*Banking in the Early Stages of Industrialization* (Cameron et al.), 93. *See also* Banking, early; Cameron, Rondo, et al.
Barker, S. F., 61
Bay, Christian, 262
Behavioralism, in political science, 261–263
Bentley, Arthur F., 51

Bentz, W. Kenneth, 277–278
Berelson, Bernard, 256
Bloch, Marc, 4, 251
Boskoff, Alvin, 249, 250, 251
Boulding, K.E., 56
British economy, contribution of Jamaica to, 238–241
Brody, R. A., 284

Cahnman, W. J., 249, 250, 251
Cairns, J. F., 30–32
Calvinism, *See* Protestant ethic and capitalism
Cameron, Rondo, et al.: methodology and philosophy of history, 93, 102–104; unit of study and data relevance, 113–114; use of primary and secondary data, 120–121; use of historical-hypothetical data, 125–126; use of quantitative and qualitative data, 137–139; use of interdisciplinary data, 139, 144; selectivity of data, 151; use of descriptive analysis and synthesis, 156; use of conceptual scheme, 166–168; use of systems analysis, 172; use of deduction and induction, 186–189; statistical inference and econometrics, 189, 190; use of comparison, 197–199; generalizations and conclusions reached, 215–216
*Capital* (Marx), 93, 94–96. *See also* Capitalism in England; Marx, Karl
Capitalism in England, 108–109, 115–116, 145–146, 157–158, 173–176, 201–204; working conditions of workers, 115–116, 129–130, 134–136; quantitative economic data, 127–129, 145–146, 157–158; data on weaving industry, 134; interdisciplinary approach of Marx, 139–141; the cotton industry, 153–154; bourgeois society, 174–175; laws of value and exchange, 175–176; comparison with other so-

311